Forgotten Voices

Forgotten Voices

The Hidden History of a New England Meetinghouse

Carolyn Wakeman

Wesleyan University Press
Middletown, Connecticut

Wesleyan University Press
Middletown CT 06459
www.wesleyan.edu/wespress

Manufactured in the United States of America
Designed by David Wolfram
Typeset in Adobe Garamond Pro, ITC Franklin Gothic

Library of Congress Control Number: 2019949472
Paperback ISBN: 978-0-8195-7923-2
Ebook ISBN: 978-0-8195-7924-9

5 4 3 2 1

Contents

Preface
New Light on Old Stories

For last year's words belong to last year's language
And next year's words await another voice.

T. S. Eliot, *Little Gidding*

Lost segments of New England's past await discovery in the scattered records of its meetinghouses. The first public buildings in early colonial settlements witnessed Sabbath lessons and prayers, town meetings and court hearings, militia drills and punishments. Today documents tucked away in libraries, archives, and attics help piece together the events, controversies, and personalities that shaped developing towns and their churches. Forgotten voices survive in sermons, in town and parish records, in wills, deeds, and court testimonies, in newspapers, diaries, and family letters. They speak of scripture and salvation, liberty and taxes, controversy and scandal, patriotism and privilege, enslavement and exclusion. Despite the passage of time, these primary accounts of religious duty, moral behavior, and civic responsibility retain a startling familiarity.

This book tells the story of four consecutive meetinghouses, no longer standing, that defined the religious and secular life of a prominent Connecticut town over 250 years. Established by the colony's General Court in 1665/6, the town called Lyme (later Old Lyme), initially covered more than eighty square miles of forest, meadow, and salt marsh at the mouth of the Connecticut River. By then local Pequots had been pushed east, then massacred when Captain John Mason in 1637 led a colonial force that torched their village near the Mystic River, incinerating elders, women, and children.

Three decades later settler colonists had negotiated with Mohegan chief Uncas for lands stretching north along the Connecticut River and east along Long Island Sound and chose a hilltop location for their first public gathering place. Until a fire caused by a lightning strike destroyed the third meetinghouse on that site, Lyme's colonial inhabitants prayed, sang, argued, voted, judged, and disciplined in a combined church, community hall, and justice court. A stately fourth meetinghouse with pillared façade and soaring spire, built in 1817 a mile west at the junction of the town's two "highways," excluded secular gatherings. Funded by prospering parishioners with increasingly cultivated tastes, the new edifice was designed as a house of God.

As tourism developed after the Civil War and a railroad bridge across the Connecticut River improved access to the coastal town, metropolitan artists discovered the beauty of Old Lyme's landscape and the charm of its historic homes. At a time of growing industrialization and immigration, the scenic town became a summer destination and an art colony. Childe Hassam, regarded as the dean of American impressionism, captured the rural meetinghouse, described as "a perfect piece of colonial architecture" and the "ideal New England church," bathed in autumn light and color in 1905. "Nothing more American on all the continent," sculptor Lorado Taft remarked about Hassam's *Church at Old Lyme.*

Over the centuries, what transpired within the town's meetinghouse walls slipped from view. To explore a forgotten past, I searched for voices that reached across the decades to reveal what people thought, why they acted, and how they responded to changing circumstances, values, and opportunities. My search began when Lyme's first church, now the First Congregational Church of Old Lyme, celebrated its 350-year history in 2015. Existing accounts left me uncertain about church beginnings, curious about what had unfolded inside early meetinghouses, and intrigued by the role of public memory in the prevailing narrative. Booklets and family memoirs offered summary information and flattering anecdotes about acclaimed ministers and prominent residents. More probing local histories added documentation and depth, but gaps waited to be filled, emphases reconsidered, and assumptions challenged. To shed new light on old stories, I searched for details, connections, and contexts.

Forgotten Voices gathers short passages from period texts to reexamine, expand, and personalize the local past. Whether a memorial to the colonial legislature about Christianizing Indian families, a Revolutionary-era sermon posing the alternatives of independence or slavery, a faded notebook detailing the formation of a Female Reading Society, or a brief notation about erasing church records to obscure anti-abolition views, the selected passages convey decisions and beliefs that resonate beyond the confines of one Connecticut town. Ties of marriage, commerce, education, and faith connected local families to New England's centers of influence and power, to the cotton-rich South and the developing West, to New York and Barbados, London and Canton. Words that echo from Lyme's pulpits, pews, parlors, and taverns detail events that shaped a particular community but also sketch the regional contours of the evolving American experience.

Accompanying images make distant lives and times visible. The mark of an enslaved woman consenting to her deed of sale, a hand-drawn map of the town's parishes, a wooden box that transported tea from Canton, the pocket Bible carried by a Civil War recruit, a nostalgic cover illustration for the *Ladies' Home Journal*, all pull a forgotten past into present focus. The surviving documents, objects, photographs, and paintings also prompt reflection on what remnants and representations of the past survive and what is missing from the visual record.

Silences spoke loudly as I searched for meetinghouse voices. Ministers, judges, and merchants, the dominant landowners whose public influence defined the town's religious and secular affairs, spoke clearly and authoritatively in sermons, church records, town meeting reports, and court decisions. Women's reflections, while publicly muted, filled family letters and lingered in journals, albums, and scrapbooks. The voices of those marginalized and enslaved echoed faintly from birth records, baptismal lists, property transactions, runaway notices, and grave markers in the town where three branches of my family had settled in the 1660s.

I remembered a fourth-grade class trip to Meetinghouse Hill, where no trace of the town's first gathering place remained and a country club offered scenic views of the Connecticut River. We children peered through the underbrush at a mile marker left by Benjamin Franklin's postal route surveyors measuring the distance to New London. We examined lichen-crusted inscriptions on crumbling gravestones in an early cemetery. We learned that the hilltop location had provided protection from Indian attack. We did not learn about the systematic elimination of Native American presence or that the town's ministers and prominent families owned enslaved servants for a century and a half. We had no idea that in the third meetinghouse on that site, seats for "the black people" in the corners of the rear gallery had been raised only in 1814 so they "could see the minister." Even today, when scholars articulate the consequences of settler colonialism and document the persistence of chattel slavery in Connecticut, it's local impact has largely disappeared from public memory.

As my search for the meetinghouse past brought startling discoveries about privilege and power, about the intersection of private lives and public actions, about habits of memory and forgetting, its history continued to evolve. When a Pakistani couple in New Britain, the taxpaying owners of a successful pizza restaurant, received notice of impending deportation for an alleged visa violation, the town's fifth meetinghouse became literally a sanctuary. Church members in 2018 invited Sahida Altaf and Malik bin Rehman to set up housekeeping in a former Sunday school classroom. Their five-year-old daughter Roniya, an American citizen, joined them on weekends while the immigration appeals process worked its way through the courts. For seven months, until the deportation order was temporarily lifted, the threatened South Asian immigrant family remained sequestered. An ankle bracelet assured that Malik would not step outside. When award-winning author and journalist Dave Eggers reported the story in the *New Yorker* in August 2018, national attention focused again on Old Lyme's meetinghouse, where new voices spoke from inside its walls.

Author's Note

The sections that follow focus closely on local events and personalities between 1664 and 1910, and detailed endnotes provide historical and scholarly context. To make distant voices more accessible, I modernize spelling, capitalization, and punctuation in early texts. As a reminder of the calendar change in 1752, when Britain and its colonies adopted the Gregorian calendar that shifted the start of the new year from March 25 to January 1, I retain the use of a slash for dates between those months. Because early births and deaths were inconsistently recorded, life dates provided are sometimes approximate. Also, I refer to the town as Lyme until 1857, when the original first parish became the separate town of Old Lyme. Portions of this book appeared earlier in articles posted online for the Florence Griswold Museum's history blog *From the Archives*.

Forgotten Voices is being published at a time when churches, communities, colleges, and families are recovering long-buried histories, probing past actions, engaging in truth and reconciliation projects, and acknowledging their roles in slavery and the subjugation of Indigenous peoples. My own reconstruction of the history of a Connecticut meetinghouse reflects that wider effort. This book recovering lost segments of the New England past may serve as a resource for others who seek to cast new light on old stories.

Acknowledgments

Many friends and colleagues helped make this book possible. I am most grateful for generous support from Rev. Steven Jungkeit and the First Congregational Church at Old Lyme; from Rebekah Beaulieu and the Florence Griswold Museum; and from the Old Lyme Ladies Benevolent Society. I especially thank Amy Kurtz Lansing, Mell Scalzi, and my expert assistant Amber Pero for their multiple contributions. My thanks also to Linda Alexander, Carolyn Bacdayan, Richard Buel, Emily Fisher, Elizabeth Kuchta, Jim Lampos, Jane Ludington, Townsend Ludington, Marilyn Nelson, Elizabeth Normen, Michaella Pearson, John Pfeiffer, Bruce P. Stark, Leslie Starr, Celine Sullivan, Nadine Tang, Nicholas Westbrook, Douglas Winiarski, Linda Winzer, Rodi York, and Caroline Zinsser for advice and assistance at various stages of this project. For reading and commenting, more than once, on the manuscript, I thank my wise colleagues John E. Noyes and George Willauer. For caring guidance and encouragement from the outset, I thank my friend and fellow church historian Elizabeth Webster. I am especially grateful to Suzanna Tamminen, editor-in-chief at Wesleyan University Press, for essential recommendations and for guiding this project to fruition. I also thank Glenn E. Novak for his skilled copyediting, David Wolfram for his elegant design, and Ann Brash, Stephanie Elliott Prieto, and Jaclyn Wilson at Wesleyan University Press for their patient and expert assistance. My deepest gratitude goes to my cousin Janet York Littlefield, my children Frederic Wakeman, Matthew Wakeman, and Sarah Wakeman, and my husband Robert B. Tierney, who shared the journey.

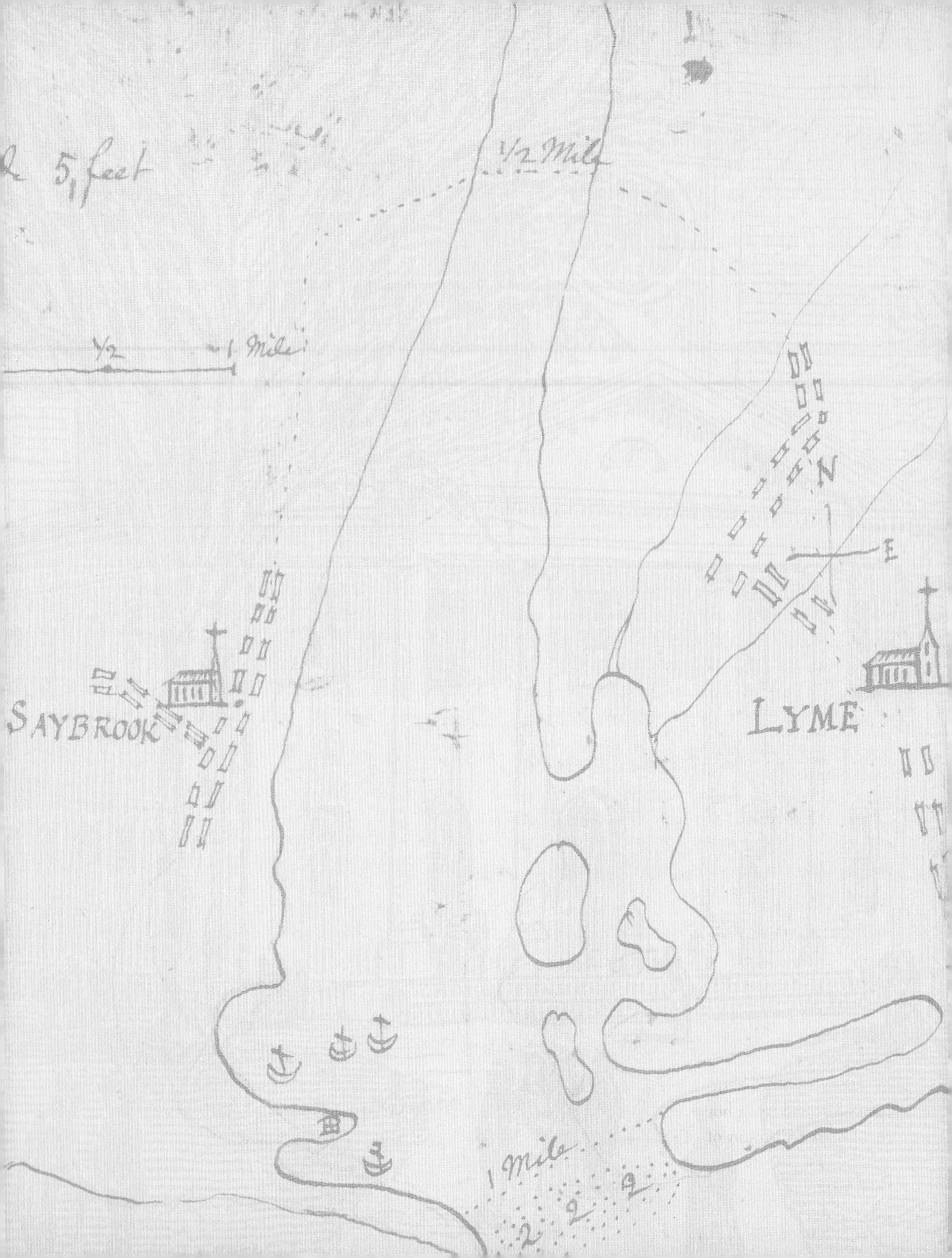

5 feet

1/2 Mile

1/2 1 Mile

N

E

SAYBROOK

LYME

1 Mile

2 2 2 2

Chapter one

Meeting Together

Instructions from a New London court offer the earliest indication of colonial religious practice in the coastal Connecticut settlement that would later be named Lyme.

This Court, apprehending a necessity of government on the east side of the river of Saybrook, do order . . . that the people at such times and seasons as they cannot go to the public ordinance in the town on the other side, that they agree to meet together at one place every Lord's day at the house agreed upon by them for the sanctification of the Sabbath in a public way according to God.

Soon after Connecticut's General Court granted permission in 1663 for the town of Saybrook to separate into two plantations, a lower court in New London issued instructions for governing the new colonial settlement on the east side of the Great River. It ordered inhabitants to designate a constable, provide religious instruction to children and servants, and "agree to meet together at one place every Lords day."

The court acknowledged that during certain "times and seasons," those living on the east side of the Connecticut River could not go to "the public ordinance in the town on the other side." Releasing them from the obligation to attend meetings on the Lord's day in Saybrook, it required the east side's recent inhabitants to gather instead in "a house agreed upon by them for the sanctification of the Sabbath in a public way." Surviving records do not reveal whether they mutually chose a dwelling house in which to worship, but other interactions led to controversy and required court intervention.

English colonists seeking a "more comfortable subsistence" had first crossed the river to clear and cultivate tribal land after a committee surveyed Saybrook's "outlands" in 1648/9. Intent upon acquiring property and developing trade, settlers in the east quarter contested the ownership of horses, argued about the "miscarriage" of goods, disputed boundary lines, and charged neighbors with slander. In 1659 the General Court dispatched representatives to investigate "suspicions about witchery."

Two years later the Particular Court in Hartford heard testimony that Nicholas Jennings (1612–1673), who had property in Saybrook's east quarter, had, together with his wife Margaret, "entertained familiarity with Satan." By then eight persons accused of witchcraft, a capital crime in

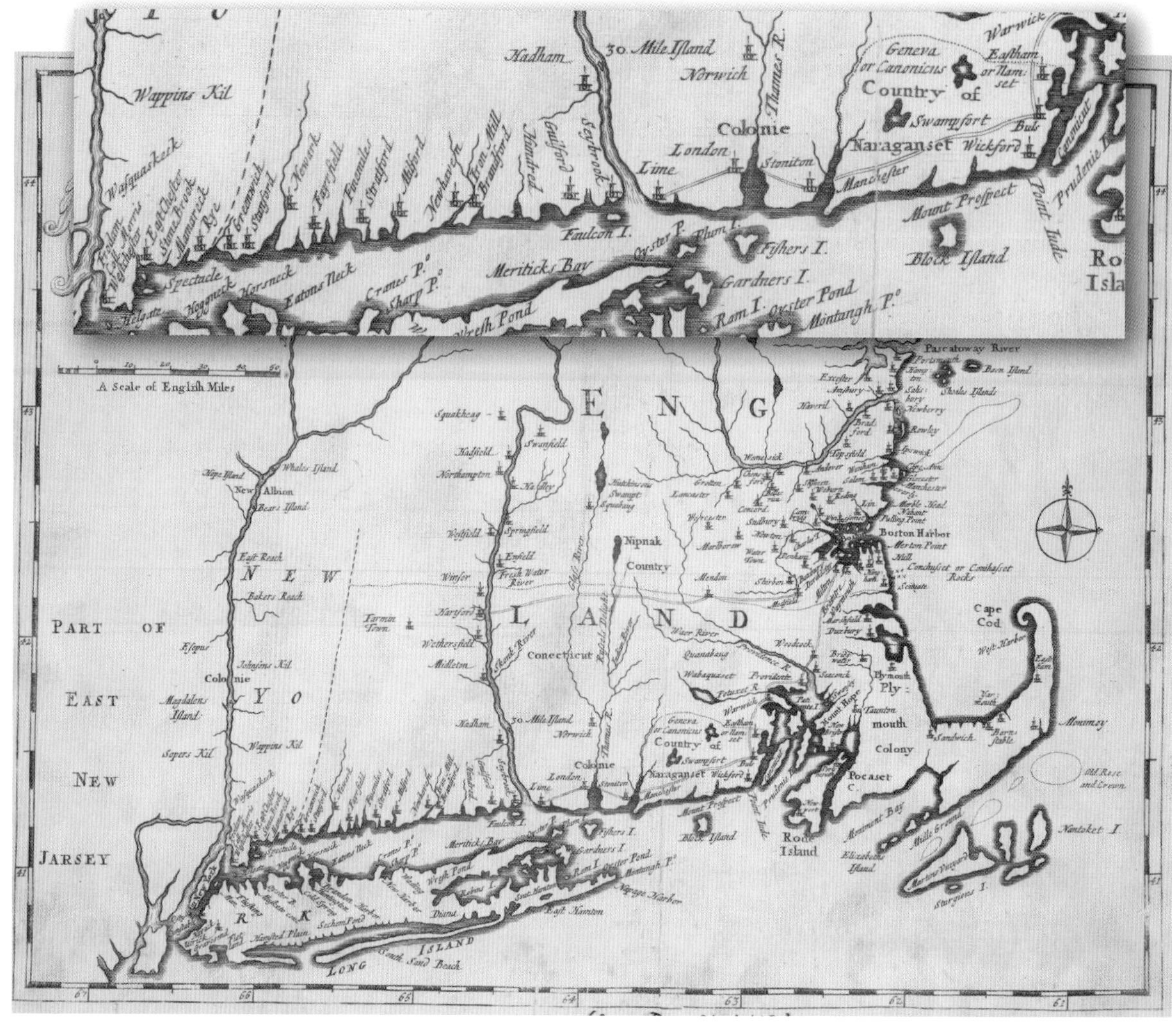

The Exact Map of New England and New York, which appeared as a fold-out insert in Cotton Mather's multivolume ecclesiastical history *Magnalia Christi Americana*, focused attention on the spread of towns and churches across what colonists considered wilderness areas. The map, which shows churches scattered sparsely along the coastline of New London County in 1702, see inset, erases native presence.

the Connecticut colony since 1642, had already been executed. The first to be hanged was Alyse Youngs (1600–1647), executed at Hartford for a witch in the yard of the meetinghouse in 1647. Allegedly Mr. Jennings and his wife Margaret, with Satan's help, had "done works above the course of nature . . . with other sorceries." Because the sorceries were said to have caused at least two deaths, the indictment stated that "according to the law of God and the established laws of this Commonwealth," Mr. Jennings "deservest to die." A majority of jurors found the suspects guilty, but without a unanimous verdict the court acquitted the accused couple. It later questioned the evidence, refused to pay costs for those who had traveled to Hartford to testify, and declined to pay for "any other upon such accounts for the future."

In that contentious environment, the "committees chosen" to implement Saybrook's division into two plantations sought an amicable separation. "Several propositions" had already been initiated when representatives from both sides of the river drafted Articles of Agreement in February 1665/6 to assure a "loving parting." The articles specified financial obligations, clarified claims to tribal land, and required mutual concessions. One article required east side inhabitants to resign "all their rights, titles, & claim" to Hammonasset land. Another confirmed "that the Indians at the Niantic have the lands agreed upon by the covenants made betwixt the inhabitants of Saybrook and them." A third article obligated the thirty families on the east side to continue supporting Saybrook's minister for three months,

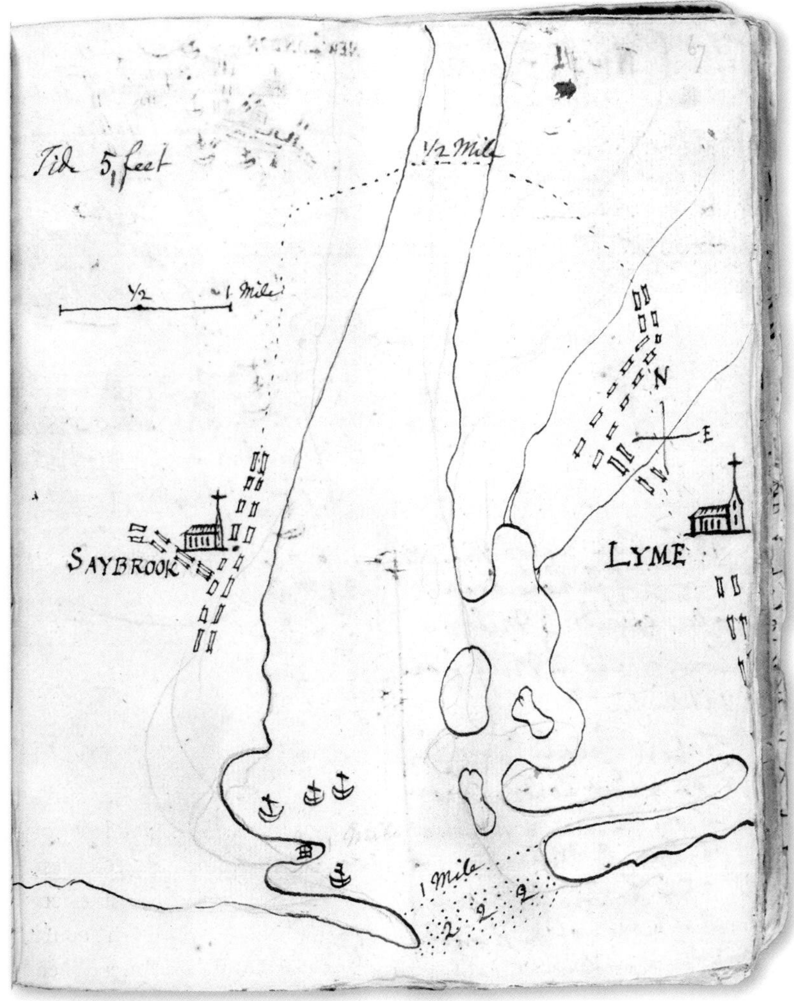

When Rev. Ezra Stiles sketched the mouth of the Connecticut River in 1768, he located the meetinghouses in Saybrook and Lyme and also marked the ferry crossing.

VIEW OF THE GREAT MEADOWS, AND SIX MILE ISLAND. RICHARD ELY'S PLANTATION
LYME, CONNECTICUT, TAKEN FROM PROSPECT HILL, LOOKING WESTWARD

An etching made in 1878 when the Ely family held a festive reunion in Lyme shows the site of Richard Ely's Six Mile Island Farm. Light streams through the clouds as visitors enjoy the view across the Connecticut River.

until May 1, 1666, after which they would receive an eight-month exemption. If they failed to settle their own minister by the end of the following January, they would resume paying rates for the minister on the west side.

Well within that interval, the General Court in October 1666 established a committee "for entertaining and approving such as are received inhabitants on the east side of the river at Saybrook." The next day a town meeting approved the "intendment" of Moses Noyes (1643–1729), a twenty-two-year-old Harvard graduate from Newbury, Massachusetts, to take up a parcel of salt meadow on the east side's Great Island. His older brother James Noyes (1640–1719) already served as minister in nearby Stonington, twenty-five miles to the east along the Long Island Sound shoreline. By then coastal Connecticut, with its available land, navigable rivers, and opportunities for trade with West Indies planters, had attracted a flow of Massachusetts migrants. Among them was Nicholas Noyes (1647–1717), age twenty-one and also a Harvard graduate, who followed his cousins from Newbury and settled in 1668 as minister across Lyme's northern boundary in East Haddam.

Witchcraft rumors circulated again on the east side soon after Moses Noyes's arrival when the Particular Court heard a complaint from the settlement's most influential inhabitant. Matthew Griswold (1620–1698) had acquired a large tract of land along the shoreline called Black Hall and

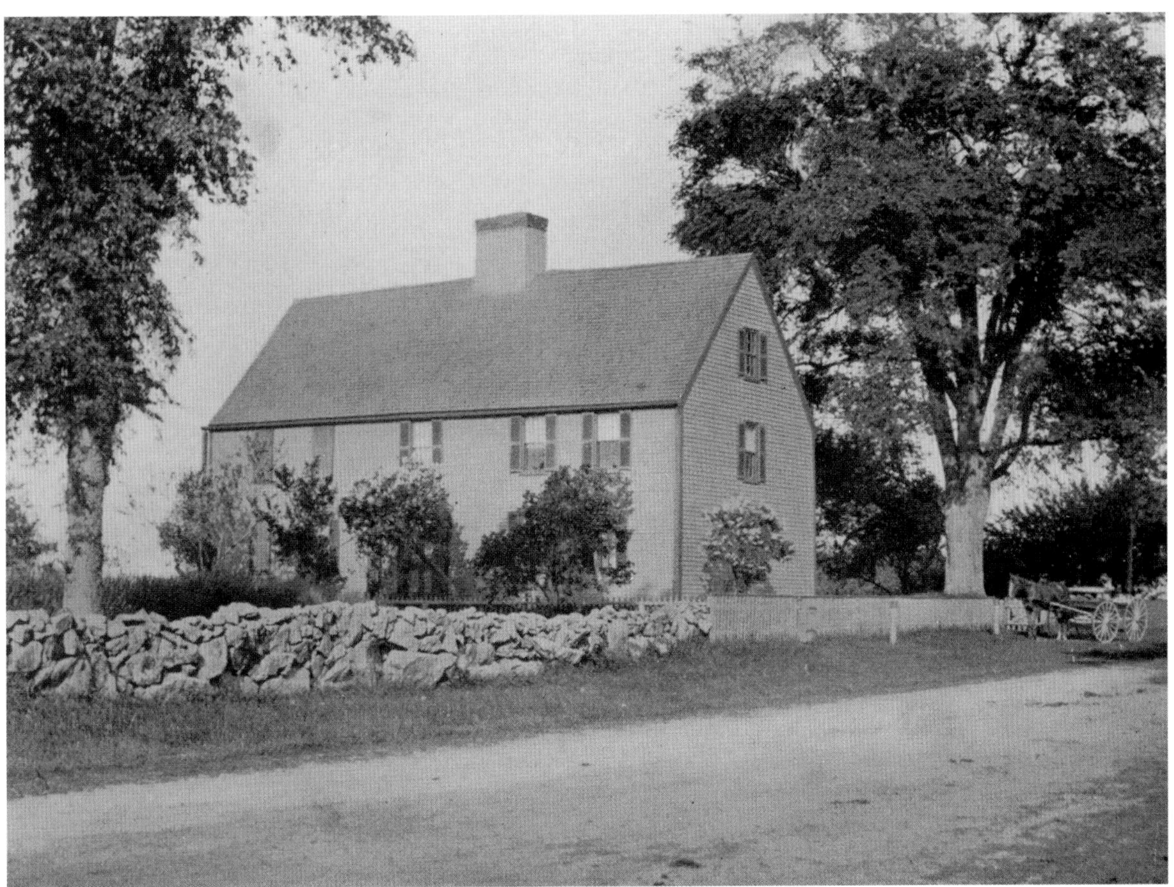

At age twenty-two Moses Noyes left his comfortable family home in Newbury, Massachusetts, shown here in a photograph taken in 1891, to pursue land and opportunity in a new settlement along the Connecticut coastline.

had served multiple times after 1647 as a deputy to the General Court. In May 1667 he alleged that his neighbor John Tillerson (1618–1685) had used expressions "tending to lay the said Matthew Griswold's wife under suspicion of witchcraft or words to such effect." Tillerson the previous year had purchased a forty-acre parcel of upland and meadow at Bride Brook bounded on two sides "by the lands of Matthew Griswold." The court judged that Tillerson had greatly sinned to be jealous of Mrs. [Anna] Griswold (1621–1704), who had been "a loving helpful neighbor to him in affording him what help she could." The court did not see "how the said Tillerson [could] sufficiently recompense the said Mrs. Griswold by reason of his poverty" and imposed only a small fine, but it also ordered the constables on both sides of the river to announce the decision at public meetings to clear Mrs. Griswold's name.

That same month the General Court formally established the east side plantation as a separate town that would "for the future be named Lyme." Moses Noyes likely began regular preaching two

Henry Ward Ranger's *Meetinghouse Hill,* ca. 1902, offers a sun-drenched view of the rock-strewn landscape that surrounded Lyme's first meetinghouse.

months later, in August, when a town meeting appointed two inhabitants to compile a list of property owners "to meet the minister's rate for the year ensuing." Support for Mr. Noyes increased in 1669 when the town approved for his use a parsonage lot with one hundred acres of upland stretching east along the shoreline and inland along Mile Creek. The General Court approved his status as a freeman the next year, allowing him to vote in colonial elections, and in 1672 he received an additional allocation of sixty acres adjoining the parsonage farm. Two years later the minister's younger brothers Thomas Noyes (1648–1730) and William Noyes (1653–1743) had also acquired land in Lyme.

To assure Sabbath observance in the Connecticut colony, the General Court required in 1668 that constables in every town "make search after all offenders." The ruling specified that anyone who "shall keep out of the meeting house during the public worship unnecessarily, there being convenient room in the house," would pay five shillings for each offense or sit in the stocks one hour. Not everyone in Lyme complied. Two years later the county court in New London heard "the complaint of the constable of Lyme concerning Mr. and Mrs. Ely, their profanation of the Sabbath and also contempt of authority." The clerk summoned Richard Ely (1610–1684) together with his wife and "ye Negro servant

Moses" to appear at the next court session in June 1670 to answer the charges.

Richard Ely was Lyme's wealthiest inhabitant. After prospering in Boston as a merchant in the West Indies trade, he had acquired a vast tract of land on the east side of the Connecticut River through his marriage in 1664 to Elizabeth Cullick (1624–1683), sister of the former Saybrook Colony's governor George Fenwick (1603–1657). Mr. Ely served as Lyme's townsman, or selectman, in 1668, and his extensive property, called Six Mile Island Farm, included "housing, fencing, cattle, horses, household goods, and two negroes."

A meetinghouse almost certainly stood on the brow of a hill between two small rivers when Richard Ely failed to observe the Sabbath in 1670, but surviving records do not date its construction. The first town meeting reference appears in 1673/4 when inhabitants voted to "remake the highway from the meeting house to John Comstock's [1624–1689] as it shall be most for the town's good and the neighbors there a better connection." At the same town meeting they decided to offer Moses Noyes "the sum of 60 pounds upon the consideration of settlement."

Fresh Water River

L A N

Russels Delight

Indian River

Skonk River

Conecticut

30. Mile Island

Hadham

Norwich

Thames R.

Colonie

Guilford

Seybrook

Hundred

London

Lime

Stoniton

Manchester

Naraga

Faulcon I.

Oyster P.

Plum I.

Fishers I.

Meriticks Bay

Gardners I.

Chapter two

Debate and Delay

Deliberation about location, materials, and funding delayed completion of Lyme's second meetinghouse. Initially expected to take twelve months, the project required twelve years.

And concerning placing the meeting house that it be left to be determined by the General Court in May next and that either side shall have a deputy to prefer and allege the same into said court.

Lyme's population had doubled when inhabitants agreed in 1680 to replace the original meetinghouse. That effort began when Joseph Peck (1641–1718), Edward DeWolfe (1646–1712), and Richard Lord (1647–1727) agreed "to provide and saw all the timber for the frame of such a meeting house as shall be concluded to be built by the town between this and Michaelmas next, twelve months." As compensation the town offered the privilege of cutting timber from common land and permission to operate a sawmill on what would later be called the Eight Mile River. Given the growing scarcity of timber and the demand for barrel staves for sugar plantations in the West Indies, the arrangement offered mutual benefits.

Three years passed before residents agreed in 1683/4 that the dimensions of the proposed meetinghouse "shall be 40 foot long and 26 foot wide and 14½ foot between joints." Plans moved forward again in 1685 when the town offered twenty-two acres of upland to sawmill owner Edward DeWolfe in return for his providing boards and eighteen-inch chestnut or cedar shingles "to cover the meetinghouse which is to be built." Disagreement over the site then stalled the project. At the town's request, the General Court agreed to resolve the dispute and sent two representatives to Lyme to hear opposing opinions.

Wolston Brockway, an early settler whose property adjoined the site of the original meetinghouse, testified to Lyme's deputy Matthew Griswold that the replacement should occupy the place previously decided. "Before Lyme meeting house was built," Brockway recalled, "the place that the inhabitants agreed upon and accordingly staked out for to set our meeting house upon was on a hill just above Richard Smith's [1620–1682] his now dwelling house." But "not long after the first place was staked out," Brockway's "uncle Waller" informed him that "the stakes for the meeting

After joining the landscape painters gathered in Old Lyme in 1903, New York artist Edward Rook painted eight different impressions of the repurposed mill on the site of the town's first gristmill built in 1678.

house overlapped slightly" on his own land. Brockway then "protested against the standing of the meeting house on the aforesaid place," and William Waller, formerly a town constable and representative to the General Court, "carted the timber unto the place where the meeting house now standeth." The Court, siding with Brockway, decided that the original hillside location of the meetinghouse should not change.

While discussions of "what will be needful for the finishing of the meeting house" continued, Lyme's inhabitants attended to other needs. They measured, surveyed, and allocated whatever land had not been distributed. They built roads, bridges, fences, livestock pounds, and public landings. They exported barrel staves and imported "salt and Barbados goods on reasonable terms." They authorized the building of a warehouse whose owner would "supply the town of Lyme with salt and certain woods upon reasonable terms," and they prohibited the cutting of timber on common land and the "transport of the

Weathered headstones in a cemetery on Meetinghouse Hill recall the names of early colonists who settled in the area called Between the Rivers. Today a country club and golf course occupy the former site of Sabbath meetings.

same out of the town" because "all sorts of timber grow scarce among us." They also managed the operation of the gristmill to keep it "in repair continually for to grind the town's corn all winter and summer," and they decided the length of the school year, authorizing two dame schools "for teaching young children and maids to read and whatever else they may be capable of learning, either knitting or sewing." In 1685 they decided to erect "a pair of stocks & scaffold to answer the laws within a month at the meeting house."

Work on the town's public building resumed after a decision in 1687 to "take care of the meeting-house timber & to procure the meeting house perfectly finished." Authorization to purchase boards and timbers for "the seating and the sealing of the meetinghouse with all speed" came a year later, and approval in 1690 to raise the pulpit brought the project near completion. A controversy about whether to pay for seats with a special tax or by selling common land then required three separate votes. The interior seating had apparently been completed two years later when a town meeting in April 1692 required that "all bachelors and boys from eight years old and upwards shall be catechized by Mr. Noyes once a fortnight on the Lords day in the meetinghouse." On weekdays "all maids and girls" would be catechized "as Mr. Noyes shall see meet to order."

A granite marker placed on Meetinghouse Hill by postmaster Benjamin Franklin's survey team in 1753 gave the distance between Lyme and the active customs port of New London as fourteen miles.

CHAPTER THREE

Gathering a Church

By the time a town meeting in 1693 established a church and called its serving minister to office, Moses Noyes had preached in Lyme for almost three decades.

At a town meeting it was desired and agreed upon with the inhabitants of this town, as agreed by a unanimous vote, that there may be a church gathered in this town and Mr. Noyes called to office if it may be obtained according to rules of Christ.

No one knows why it took twenty-seven years to establish a church in Lyme. So unusual was the long interval between the minister's arrival and his call to office that his successors offered wide-ranging explanations. Rev. William B. Cary (1841–1923) speculated in 1876 that the difficulty of dealing with "wild and jealous tribes of Indians" caused the delay. Rev. Arthur B. Shirley (1902–1968) argued in 1893 that the shrinking of Saybrook's congregation after its minister left for Norwich in 1659 brought objection to a separate church in Lyme. He assumed that Mr. Noyes had spent the intervening years "directing the labors of the negro slaves upon his farms and performing such ministerial labors as the situation allow[ed]."

When local writer Kendall Banning photographed Old Lyme's historic sites in the 1930s, he titled his view of Meetinghouse Hill *The Road to Eden*.

Other Connecticut towns installed ministers with far less delay, thereby authorizing them not only to preach the Gospel but also to administer the sacraments and admit as church members those who "owned the covenant" and offered a public profession of faith. In New London, Simon Bradstreet (1640–1683/4), a Harvard schoolmate of James and Moses Noyes, started preaching in 1666 and four years later was "formally inducted into the pastoral office by ordination." In Stonington, James Noyes began preaching in 1664 and was called to office when the town organized a church ten years later. Lyme's inhabitants initially approved a similar interval.

Not quite ten years after the minister's arrival, a town meeting in 1675/6 voted unanimously that "there may be a church gathered which may be for the glory of God and edification of each other according to the laws of the Commonwealth." The report of the meeting entered in the town

A Sunday afternoon tradition for Charles Ludington's family began with a stroll among the gravestones in Duck River Cemetery followed by a walk to scenic Meetinghouse Hill.

book explained that Lyme was in "want of being in a church way" and remained "without the administration of all the ordinances of Christ," even though "from the first settlement, which is now ten or eleven years," it had been "under the ministry of the word." When the town did not implement the decision, the sacraments remained unavailable in Lyme. Records of Saybrook's church do not survive, but its historian surmised that Lyme inhabitants were "subjected to the necessity of crossing the river for participation in the ordinances of baptism and the Lord's Supper." New London's church records show that Rev. Simon Bradstreet baptized several inhabitants of Lyme. Among them were the children of John Borden (1635–1684), baptized in 1670, not long after a Lyme town meeting approved "a sufficient highway to Borden's house."

Lyme's deputies, in an effort to implement the town meeting decision, appealed to the General Court in 1678 "in behalf of Mr. Noyes and other Christian people" for "liberty to organize into a church society." The Court "countenance[d] them in their regular proceedings" and offered "encouragement in so good a work," requiring only that they "take the approbation of neighbor churches therein and attend the laws of this colony." As the decision languished, Mr. Noyes continued preaching, participated actively in town affairs, and supplemented his landholdings. He also decided to marry.

Ruth Pickett Noyes (1653–1690) grew up in a New London family of means and perhaps some notoriety. She was fourteen when her father, John Pickett (1629–1667), died on a return voyage from Barbados, leaving a substantial estate. Her mother soon remarried, and her stepfather Charles Hill (1629–1684), also a New London merchant, went "to and from Barbados." Ruth was seventeen when Simon Bradstreet baptized "Mr. Pickett's children, John, Mary, Ruth, Mercy, William," together with "Mr. Hill's child Jane" and "Widow Bradley's daughter Lucretia." A year later, in 1672, a "negro servant of Charles Hill" appeared before the county court "for shooting at and wounding a child of Charles Haynes." The General Court in Hartford in 1675 ordered Charles Hill to pay damages of £35 for a wound inflicted "by the accidental discharge of a gun in the hands of Mr. Hill's negro servant." The ruling noted that "the negro belonged to the estate of Mr. John Pickett, deceased."

Ruth was twenty-two when her mother's widowed sister Elizabeth Brewster Bradley (1637–1708) appeared in court in New London in 1673 for "a second offense in having a child out of wedlock, the father of both being Christopher Christophers, a married man." The court sentenced Widow Bradley "to pay the usual fine of £5, and also to wear on her cap a paper whereon her offence [was] written, as a warning to others, or else to pay £15." Christophers (1631–1687), the child's father, owned wharves and warehouses in New London jointly with Ruth's stepfather Charles Hill.

No record of Ruth Pickett's marriage to Moses Noyes has been found, but she likely did not move to Lyme until after the minister's six-month enlistment in 1675 in King Philip's War, for which he received as compensation a parcel of land in the town called Voluntown. A list of English volunteers indicates that his brother James and his cousin Nicholas both served as chaplains, but Moses Noyes's role in the bloody campaigns that cleared native inhabitants from large areas of New England is not specified. Whether he had already built a dwelling on his home lot not far from the sawmill in 1678 when the birth of his first child, Moses Noyes Jr. (1678–1743), was entered in town records is not known. The "three

House of Rev. Moses Noyes house drawn from
description of Enoch Noyes.
well and barn
correct
Lyme
Conn
about
1818

Curious about the dwelling of Lyme's first minister, local artist Ellen Noyes Chadwick relied on her father's recollection to create a pencil sketch of Rev. Moses Noyes's parsonage.

scores of upland lying by mile brook" laid out for Moses Noyes was not recorded until 1688, a decade after his son's birth, but the parcel may have been allotted to the minister twenty years earlier in the first division of town land.

While Mr. Noyes waited to be called to office, the town appointed representatives each year to collect his rate. Not everyone fulfilled that obligation, and collecting the minister's salary became such an urgent concern in 1679 that a town meeting pledged to "gather all the arrears which are due to Mr. Noyes from the time of his first coming among us" and also threatened to restrain any who refused to comply. A subsequent meeting in 1683/4 pledged "to use all lawful means to gather in the arrears of the rates due to Mr. Noyes for all the years past forthwith." The town further stiffened the power of its rate collectors in 1685 by giving them "as full power to get and gather the rate and all arrears of such rate to Mr. Noyes as the constable has to gather the country rate."

Moses Noyes was almost fifty when a town meeting determined in 1693 that a church was "desired and agreed upon with the inhabitants." A unanimous vote then decided again that "there may be a church gathered in this town." This time the decision specified that "Mr. Noyes [be]

A simple gravestone in Duck River Cemetery marks the burial place of Ruth Pickett Noyes, the first minister's wife, who died at age thirty-six.

called to office if it may be obtained according to rules of Christ." Whether neighboring clergymen gathered for an installation procedure is not known, but town records thereafter referred to the long-serving minister as "Reverend Noyes." A year later the General Court invited the "Reverend Mr. Moses Noyes" to deliver a sermon in Hartford to accompany the annual election of representatives.

Ruth Noyes did not live to see her husband called to office. Her death in 1690 at age thirty-seven left Lyme's minister with four children ranging in age from three to thirteen. Moses Noyes did not remarry, and the care of his children along with the work of his household likely fell to Arabella, an enslaved black woman whom he later bequeathed to his younger daughter Sarah. Three years after the death of the minister's wife, Rev. James Noyes informed Judge Samuel Sewall (1652–1730), a mutual friend in Boston, "I heard but now that my brother Moses is well & his family."

The Wonders of the Invisible World:

Being an Account of the

TRYALS

OF

Several Witches,

Lately Excuted in

NEW-ENGLAND:

And of ſeveral remarkable Curioſities therein Occurring.

Together with,

I. Obſervations upon the Nature, the Number, and the Operations of the Devils.

II. A ſhort Narrative of a late outrage committed by a knot of Witches in *Swede-Land*, very much reſembling, and ſo far explaining, that under which *New-England* has laboured.

III. Some Councels directing a due Improvement of the Terrible things lately done by the unuſual and amazing Range of *Evil-Spirits* in *New-England*.

IV. A brief Diſcourſe upon thoſe *Temptations* which are the more ordinary Devices of Satan.

By *COTTON MATHER*.

Opinions on Blasphemy

When a special court session convened in Hartford to hear evidence against an outspoken New London dissenter, Lyme's minister joined other Connecticut clergymen to offer testimony.

The opinions of four ministers were taken as to the blasphemous nature of said expressions . . . [and] in every one of the expressions evidenced against him there is a high and abominable profanation of the name of Christ.

Congregational ministers responded harshly to heresy and deviance in their struggle to eradicate the influence of Satan. Like witchcraft suspicions, dissenting beliefs occasionally reverberated in Lyme, and a year after preaching the election sermon in Hartford, Moses Noyes returned in 1695 to testify at a special Superior Court session about an ongoing challenge to New London's church.

A quarter of a century earlier, in 1670, Matthew Griswold had arranged for his eldest daughter, Elizabeth Griswold (1652–1727), to marry John Rogers (1648–1721), the eligible son of a propertied New London merchant. An encounter with a Baptist sect in Rhode Island four years later prompted the conversion of Elizabeth's husband. His dissenting beliefs, outspoken and confrontational, caused her, with her father's influence, to petition the General Court in 1676 for a release from her "conjugal bond to her husband."

Before succeeding John Winthrop Jr. as Connecticut's governor in 1708, Rev. Gurdon Saltonstall, shown here in a portrait by an unknown artist, served for two decades as New London's minister.

Even before that request was granted, the Court allowed Elizabeth to live with her father in Lyme because she was "under so great distress and hazard." The Court also took the unusual step of permitting her two children to join her, having judged that John Rogers, who had "utterly renounce[d] all the visible worship of New England, and professedly declare[d] against the Christian Sabbath as a mere invention," was "so heterodox in his opinion and practice."

The language and behavior of Elizabeth's estranged husband grew increasingly defiant. Supported by family members and a small group of dissenters who became known as Rogerenes, he advocated direct confrontation with the established church. To compel his submission to established authority, the Court ordered him fined, whipped, placed in the stocks, and held in irons in the depths of winter in New London's unheated jail. Still he refused to moderate his speech, observe the Sabbath, or refrain from promoting baptism by full immersion.

Court hearings had already spanned two decades when Moses Noyes joined Rev. Gurdon Saltonstall (1666–1724), Simon Bradstreet's successor in New London, and two other clergymen to offer their opinion on the "blasphemous nature" of John Rogers's expressions. The previous year he had driven a wheelbarrow into New London's church to protest observance of the Sabbath, and the ministers testified that statements from the accused evidenced "a high and abominable profanation of the name of Christ." Rogers was found guilty of evil speaking against the ordinances of God and sentenced to pay a fine, remain in prison until he pledged "non-disturbance of the people of God," and stand with a rope around his neck on a ladder leaning against the gallows for a quarter of an hour.

Ministers in Massachusetts had resorted to even harsher means to safeguard the established church. "The devil is now making one more attempt upon us," Rev. Cotton Mather (1663–1728) wrote in August 1692 after the last of a series of witchcraft executions in Salem. Witchcraft, he declared, "if it were not seasonably discovered would probably blow up, and pull down all the churches in the country." The struggle against witchcraft involved Moses Noyes's family members, Harvard schoolmates, and childhood

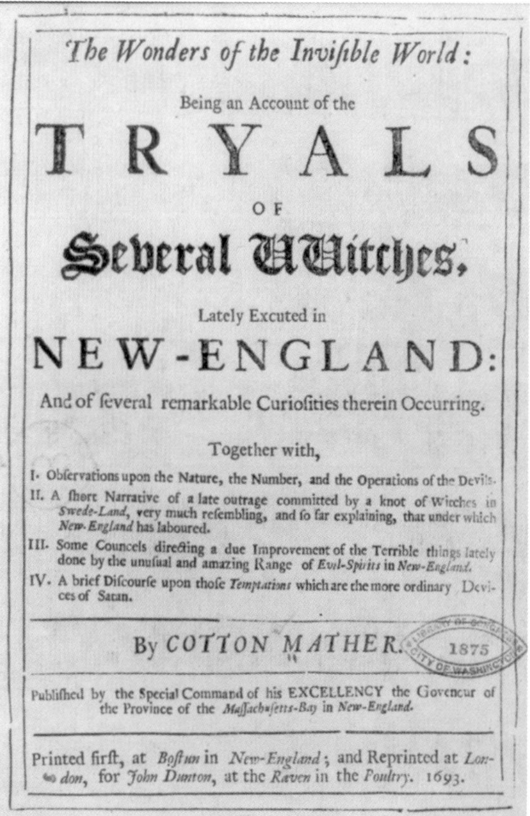

The Wonders of the Invisible World:

Being an Account of the

TRYALS

OF

Several Witches,

Lately Excuted in

NEW-ENGLAND:

And of several remarkable Curiosities therein Occurring.

Together with,

I. Observations upon the Nature, the Number, and the Operations of the Devils.

II. A short Narrative of a late outrage committed by a knot of Witches in *Swede-Land*, very much resembling, and so far explaining, that under which *New-England* has laboured.

III. Some Councels directing a due Improvement of the Terrible things lately done by the unusual and amazing Range of *Evil-Spirits* in *New-England*.

IV. A brief Discourse upon those *Temptations* which are the more ordinary Devices of Satan.

By *COTTON MATHER*.

Published by the Special Command of his EXCELLENCY the Govenour of the Province of the *Massachusetts-Bay* in *New-England*.

Printed first, at *Bostun* in *New-England*; and Reprinted at *London*, for *John Dunton*, at the *Raven* in the *Poultry*. 1693.

In a treatise on witchcraft, Rev. Cotton Mather denounced Satan's assault on New England's churches and approved the execution of witches, but suggested caution in the use of "spectral evidence."

friends. Not only his brother-in-law Rev. John Hale (1636–1700), the long-serving minister in Beverly, but also his cousin Rev. Nicholas Noyes, ordained in Salem after preaching in Lyme's neighboring parish, witnessed the August executions and lent their authority to the court proceedings. Samuel Sewall, a wealthy Boston merchant who had recently kept the Sabbath in Stonington with Rev. James Noyes, served as one of the nine sentencing judges. He recorded in his diary the names of the "five unfortunates [who] were executed at Salem for witchcraft" and also noted the "very great number of spectators" present: "Mr. Cotton Mather was there, Mr. Sims, Hale, Noyes, Chiever, &c." The accused, Judge Sewall added, all "said they were innocent," but "Mr. Mather says they all died by a righteous sentence."

Moses Noyes's sister Sarah Noyes (1656–1695) had married his Harvard schoolmate John Hale in 1684 and was pregnant with their fourth child when she faced witchcraft accusations in November 1692. By then doubts about the reliability of spectral evidence had ended the witchcraft trials, and Mrs. Hale was never formally charged, but when she died three years later at age thirty-nine, her demise was said to be "hastened by the excitement through which she had passed." After his wife's death, Rev. Hale wrote *A Modest Enquiry into the Nature of Witchcraft* to reexamine the assumptions and acknowledge the mistakes of Salem's witchcraft persecutions. A few months later Judge Sewall made a public apology for his actions in a petition read on a fast day. Stating that he "desire[d] to take the blame and shame of it," he asked "the pardon of men and especially desire[d] prayers that God, who has an unlimited authority, would pardon that sin."

Lyme's minister had not yet been called to office when witchcraft suspicions gripped Massachusetts Bay parishes. But in May 1695 when his sister died in Beverly, Rev. Moses Noyes traveled to Hartford to defend the established church against a different threat by condemning John Rogers's blasphemy.

A Modeft Enquiry
Into the Nature of
Witchcraft,
AND
How Perfons Guilty of that Crime may be *Convicted*: And the means ufed for their Difcovery Difcuffed, both *Negatively* and *Affirmatively*, according to *SCRIPTURE* and *EXPERIENCE*.

By John Hale,
Paftor of the Church of Chrift in *Beverley*, *Anno Domini* 1697.

When they fay unto you, feek unto them that have Familiar Spirits and unto Wizzards, that peep, &c. To the Law and to the Teftimony; if they fpeak not according to this word, it is becaufe there is no light in them, Ifaiah VIII. 19, 20.
That which I fee not teach thou me, Job 34. 32.

OSTON *in* N. E.
B. Green, and *J. Allen*, for
under the Town Houfe. 1702

When Rev. Moses Noyes's brother-in-law Rev. John Hale reconsidered Salem's witchcraft persecutions, he urged readers that "it is our duty, in all humility, and with fear and trembling to search after truth." Courtesy of Historic Beverly.

gulis Has præsentes perlecturis
Nobis Notum sit, quod Iohanne
n, Primum in Artibus gradum
bavimus, quam approbavimus: quem
prævio approbatum, Nobis placet
n Liberalium Baccalaurei adornare
hoc Instrumentum in membrana
n sit. A Gymnasio Academico
alend. Octobr. 1703.

Abrah: Pierson Rect:

Moses Noyes Thomas Buckingham

Noadiah Russel

Inspectores

CHAPTER FIVE

On Elderly Childbearing

In a Sabbath sermon delivered to young scholars at the Collegiate School in Saybrook, Moses Noyes elaborated on the biblical story of Abraham to offer guidance about marriage and childbirth.

Hence we learn that men may have children when they are old. Oh! methinks some of my hearers are ready to enquire, can men have children when they are old? we fear they cannot. I answer men may have children when they are old; Abraham was an hundred years old.

Only one of Rev. Moses Noyes's sermons survives. Preached at the Collegiate School in Saybrook on a "holy day of Christian Sabbath" in 1707, it preserves the voice of Lyme's minister speaking from the lectern. Noyes had by then served for four years as a trustee of the school, which despite his objection moved a decade later to New Haven and became Yale College.

Connecticut's General Assembly had chartered the Collegiate School in 1701 to instruct the colony's youth in the arts and sciences and fit them "for public employment both in church and civil state." The group of founding ministers, which included Rev. James Noyes, requested prior advice from several Boston colleagues. Rev. Cotton Mather responded with a detailed

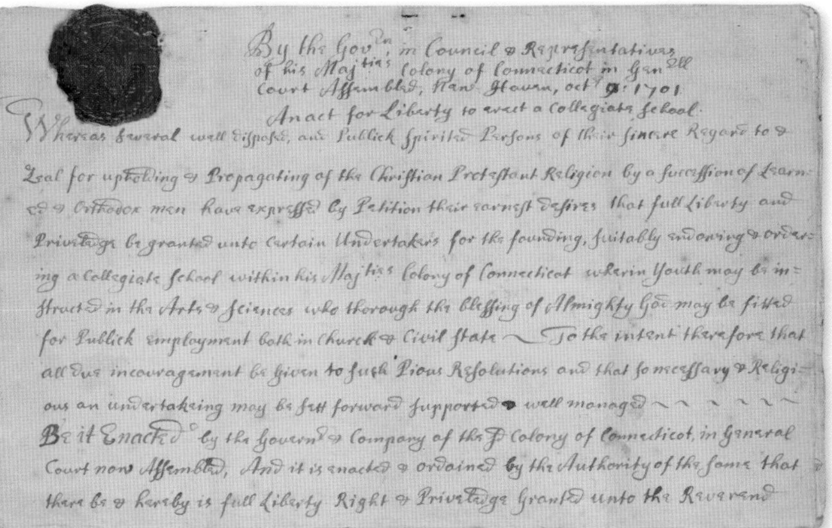

By the Govr in Council & Representatives of his Majties Colony of Connecticot in Genll Court Assembled, New Haven, octr 9: 1701
An act for Liberty to erect a Collegiate School.
Whereas Severall well disposed, and Publick spirited Persons of their sincere Regard to & Zeal for upholding & Propagating of the Christian Protestant Religion by a succession of Learned & Orthodox men have expressed by Petition their earnest Desires that full Liberty and Priviledge be granted unto Certain Undertakers for the founding, suitably endowing & ordering a Collegiate School within his Majties Colony of Connecticot wherein Youth may be instructed in the Arts & Sciences who thorough the blessing of Almighty God may be fitted for Publick employment both in Church & Civil State ~ To the intent therefore that all due incouragement be given to such Pious Resolutions and that so necessary & Religious an undertaking may be sett forward supported & well managed ~
Be it Enacted by the Governr & Company of the sd Colony of Connecticot in Generall Court now Assembled, And it is enacted & ordained by the Authority of the same that there be & hereby is full Liberty Right & Priviledge Granted unto the Reverend

After Connecticut's General Court passed "An Act for the Liberty to Erect a Collegiate School" in 1701, Nathaniel Lynde deeded a building and two acres in Saybrook "for the liberal education of youth that by God's blessing may be fit for public service."

"Scheme for the College," and Judge Samuel Sewall promised a later "essay." He sent instead "a sheet to discourage our trading to Africa for men," a three-page pamphlet published in Boston the previous year. Viewed today as America's first antislavery tract, *The Selling of Joseph: A Memorial* expressed Sewall's opposition to the African slave trade and the practice of slavery in the American colonies. Whether the "sheet" influenced the thoughts of Connecticut ministers preparing to educate the colony's future leaders is not known.

When Rev. Moses Noyes preached to students at the college six years after its founding, his topic was childbearing. Offering a literal interpretation of a passage in Genesis describing Abraham as a hundred years old when his son Isaac was born, he advised the young scholars in Saybrook that both men and women could conceive children at an advanced age. Addressing them as "my brethren, my dear brethren," he also explained that while men could "beget" sons, they could not themselves bear children, for "they have not the proper organs for the business." He then

Newly elected as a trustee of the Collegiate School in 1703, Moses Noyes signed the diploma of John Hart, age twenty-one, who graduated alone that year at Saybrook.

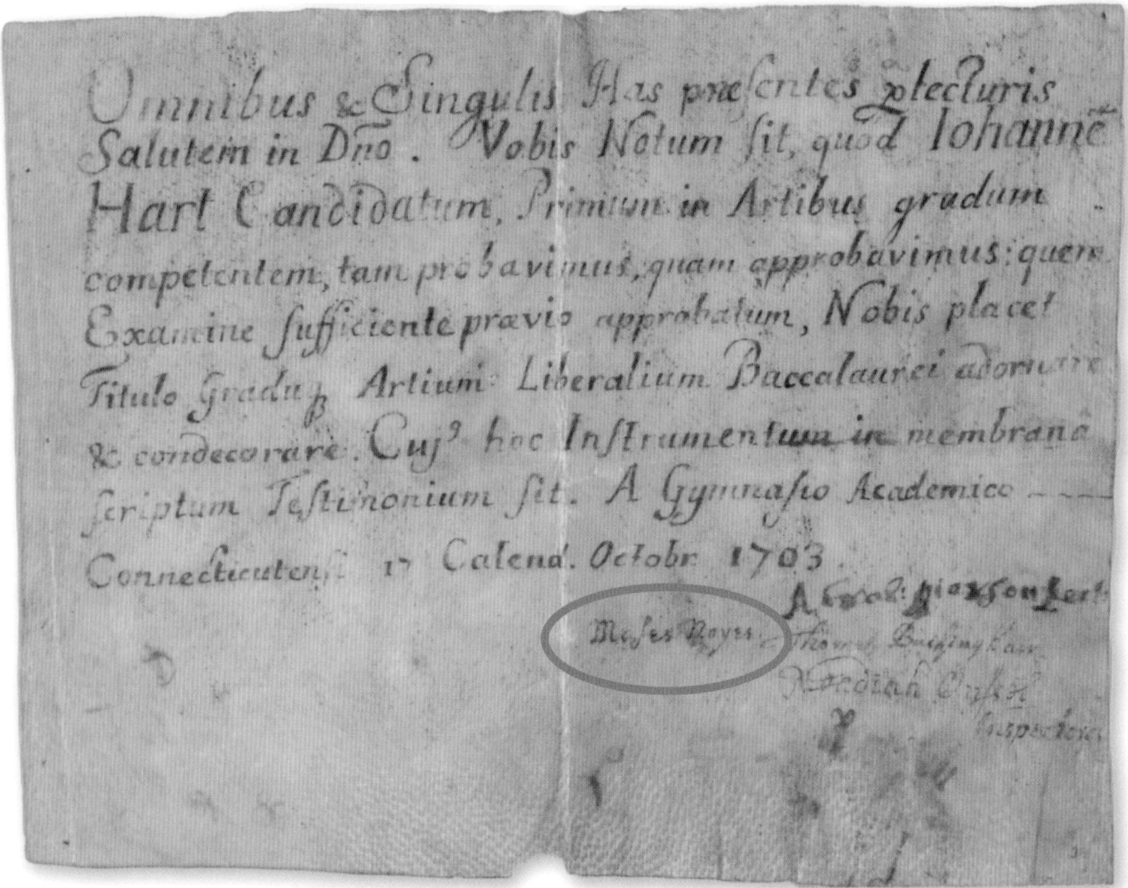

Omnibus & Singulis Has praesentes perlecturis Salutem in Dno. Nobis Notum sit, quod Iohanne Hart Candidatum, Primum in Artibus gradum competentem, tam probavimus, quam approbavimus: quem Examine sufficiente praevio approbatum, Nobis placet Titulo Gradus Artium Liberalium Baccalaurei adornare & condecorare. Cujus hoc Instrumentum in membrana Scriptum Testimonium sit. A Gymnasio Academico Connecticutensi 17 Calend. Octobr. 1703.

Moses Noyes

recommended that the future ministers and government officials "marry wives younger than themselves" since men could conceive over a longer span of years than women.

Demographic data are scarce for early Connecticut towns, where marriage age varied widely, but Moses Noyes's guidance reflected his own experience. Like his brother James, he had married at about age thirty-four and had chosen a wife ten years younger. Both Matthew Griswold and Richard Ely, a generation older than Lyme's minister, married at around age thirty-six and also chose younger wives, but some of Noyes's contemporaries married earlier. Joseph Peck (1640–1718), two years older than Moses Noyes and a church deacon, was about twenty-one when he married Sarah Parker (1636–1726), some five years his senior.

With an apology that he may have "tired the patience" of the Collegiate School students, Noyes, then sixty-three and a grandfather, concluded his sermon with words of reassurance. "Men and women too may have no reason of discouragement," he advised, "for they may have children when they are exceeding old." He ended his lecture with a warning about "the necessity of having midwives" and an additional reminder about the importance of good midwives. Deaths in childbirth were common, and while his own four children had lived to adulthood, the seventh and last child of his brother James, named Moses, died in 1692 at age five weeks.

When Noyes delivered his remarks on child-bearing in 1707, the eldest son of his sister Sarah Hale served as senior tutor at the Collegiate School and wrote down "in short hand" the words of his uncle's sermon. James Hale (1685–1742) had graduated from Harvard in 1703, a year after the publication of his father's treatise on witchcraft, and served for two years as a tutor in Saybrook. He settled in 1718 as the founding minister in Ashford, Connecticut, and several of his family members later moved to Vermont, where Rev. Moses Noyes's curious sermon on childbearing appeared in print in 1785.

1703.

The XLIst Year.

Revd Cotton Mather, D.D. 3d Pastor of the 2d ch: in Boston, (Old N

[...]ied February 13. 1725. Aged 65.

Qui bene vivit, semper orat. Gerson.

Votum Christianorum confessio Nationum. Tert.

I found this number of the Rev. Cotton Mather's Diary among the Collections of Thomas Walcott Esq. at Boston. Aug. 7. 1834.

Christopher Columbus Baldwin.
Librarian of ye Amer. Ant. Society.

Chapter six

Lessons from a Wayward Son

An elaborate narrative about the remarkable adventures of the Griswold family's disobedient son provided Boston minister Cotton Mather with material for a sermon.

In this time two Godly ministers came to see my family and one of them, then putting up a fervent prayer with us on the behalf of my absent child, he was directed into such expressions that I was persuaded that the prayer was not lost, and that my poor son was then in some remarkable distress.

Sometimes Moses Noyes's voice can be heard indirectly. A letter that Matthew Griswold Jr. (1652–1716) composed in 1712 after the death of his eldest son conveys the guidance of Lyme's minister. Echoing the biblical parable of the prodigal son, the lengthy narrative relates the "remarkable circumstances" of a wayward youth who strays and suffers before reuniting with his father. Mr. Griswold sent the sermon-like story to Rev. Cotton Mather in Boston.

The letter's context leaves little doubt that the "two Godly ministers" who prayed with the Griswold family at its time of affliction were Moses Noyes and Azariah Mather (1685–1736), age twenty-seven at the time and Cotton Mather's cousin. Ordained in Saybrook in 1710, he had succeeded James Hale as tutor at the Collegiate School, and Cotton Mather had noted in his diary, "I have a Kinsman who is Minister of Saybrook, and who has also an Opportunity to do good unto the College there." While Matthew Griswold Jr. had no personal acquaintance with Cotton Mather, Azariah Mather had recently received several notes of encouragement from his influential relative, along with a request for assistance "in dispersing books of Piety thro' the Colony."

"Sir," Mr. Griswold wrote, "Though I am an utter stranger to you, yet, considering that it ought to be the chief and continual care of every man to glorify God, I thought it my duty humbly to present unto you the following narrative, desiring you to improve it as God shall direct." The letter began with an account of his eldest son Matthew Griswold 3rd (1689–1712), age seventeen and described as "weakly" since childhood, disobeying his father and "escaping" from his house to go to sea. How he reached the West Indies, presumably on a coastal trading vessel, is not explained,

Cottonus Matherus
S. Theologiæ Doctor Regiæ Societatis Londinensis Socius,
et Ecclesiæ apud Bostonum Nov-Anglorum nuper Præpositus.
Ætatis Suæ LXV, MDCCXXVII.
P. Pelham ad vivum pinxit ab Origin. Fecit et excud.

London portrait artist Peter Pelham launched his reputation as an American engraver by reproducing his own painting of Cotton Mather, just months before the Boston minister's death at age sixty-five in 1728.

The sandy point where Matthew Griswold 3rd allegedly returned after a harrowing five years at sea appears as a sun-drenched site for summer bathing two centuries later in William Chadwick's *Bathers at Griswold Beach.* "Moonlight drives to Griswold's beach are in order this week," reported Old Lyme's hometown newspaper the *Sound Breeze* in August 1893.

but the narrative of loss and redemption provides extended detail about the missing son's spiritual tests. After barely surviving a severe storm at sea, the young Griswold acknowledged his dependence on providential mercy, but harsher lessons followed.

Impressed aboard a man of war in Jamaica, he obtained release after punishing months of service, only to fall in "with a privateer, on board whereof he was exposed unto eminent hazard of his life, in an hot engagement, wherein many were killed." After that desperate fight "God caused him to take up solemn resolutions to reform his life, and he resolved to return as soon as might be to his father's house," but the consequences of his disobedience had not yet concluded. Captured first by the French and then by the Spanish, marched in chains without food or water, sickened by fever, ague, and smallpox, the prisoner faced a threat of hard labor in the mines unless he became a papist.

Taken aboard a Spanish galleon, where he was bled by the ship's doctor, the runaway youth from Lyme then "lay for dead." The Spanish captain, having no son of his own, offered kindness and assistance if the young Protestant would accept baptism into the Catholic faith, but even when close to death, the disobedient son resisted temptation and "put his trust in the providence of God." Surmounting additional challenges and aided by the charity of strangers, he eventually returned home in gravely ill health after a five-year absence. Three weeks later, having manifested true penitence, Matthew Griswold 3rd, age twenty-two, died in his father's house.

The elaborate tale sent to Cotton Mather resembles a shorter account of misfortunes at sea that Richard Ely's eldest son William Ely (1647–1717) allegedly encountered on a voyage from Barbados to Lyme. That story, related at an Ely family reunion in 1878, described a brigantine dismasted in a furious gale with William the "only soul on board" to survive after "the ill-fated vessel sank to rise no more." Floating on a yardarm and "lashed in fury by the raging storm," William was picked up on the third day by a Spanish cruiser exploring the shores of New England. He later landed "on the coast not far distant from the mouth of the Connecticut River," where "he sought and soon found the rude hamlet of his father." Richard Ely "with joy unspeakable" then "embraced his son, who related the story of "his voyage, his rescue, and his escape from a watery grave."

The Ely shipwreck story, said to describe an incident in Richard Ely's life some twenty-four months after he moved from Boston to Lyme, concludes with the father and son offering up prayer and thanksgiving "for this Divine interposition." It adds that Mr. Ely ascended daily for weeks and months "to the height of a neighboring hill and there alone, with outstretched arms, poured forth his gratitude to the Divine Master for the preservation of his child." Whether Moses Noyes contributed to the shorter narrative about trials at sea, said to demonstrate the religious feeling that imbued Richard Ely's soul and to "illustrate the fervency of his devotion and piety," cannot be determined, but the families had close ties. In 1713, a year after the death of Matthew Griswold 3rd, Moses Noyes Jr. married Richard Ely's granddaughter.

A note from "your sincere Friend & Servt Cotton Mather" acknowledged the receipt of Matthew Griswold's letter. The Boston minister noted in his diary his "inclination" to publish a sermon based on the letter he had "received from a gentleman in Connecticut, concerning the remarkable circumstances of his own prodigal and repenting son." Such a sermon was "urgently called for," he added, and would "prove of manifold use." When his sermon *Repeated Warnings: Another essay to warn young people against rebellions that must be repented of* appeared in print in Boston in 1712, it included the letter from Lyme.

In a simple string-bound diary kept between 1681 and 1724, Rev. Cotton Mather recorded observations about his sermons and ministerial duties, comments about current events like the witchcraft trials in Salem, and news of his family and friends.

Grave of Samuel Pierpont, Pastor of t[illegible]
of Lyme, Conn , who was drowned
necticut River. Body found an[illegible]
on Fisher's Island, N. Y., April
1723.
Fisher's Island, N. Y.

Chapter seven

Finding a Successor

The shocking dismissal of Yale's rector and senior tutor in 1722 disrupted Lyme's search for a minister to assist the elderly Moses Noyes.

It was an awful stroke of Providence in taking away Mr. Pierpont, in whose assistance I promised myself much benefit to the place, & much ease & comfort to myself, & it is the more afflictive, because our young men are feared to be infected with Arminian & Prelateral notions; so that it is difficult to supply his place. It was a wrong step when the Trustees, by the assistance of great men, removed the College from Saybrook, and a worse when they put in Mr. Cutler for rector. . . . Had Mr. Pierpont lived, I hoped this summer to have liberty to come into the Bay."

Moses Noyes's letter to Samuel Sewall in 1723 has a melancholy tone. The minister's acquaintance with the Boston judge stretched back to their youth when Sewall had prepared for college in the Noyes family home in Newbury. Decades later Noyes voiced to his friend a sharp sense of loss after the sudden death of his young assistant. Concern about the influence at Yale of "Arminian" notions, both Anglican tendencies and other departures from strict Calvinism, compounded his sense of personal affliction.

Thirty years had passed since the establishment of Lyme's church, and Noyes could no longer fully perform the work of the ministry or preach the gospel to those who lived far from the meetinghouse. By the time he drafted a will in August 1719 stating his readiness to leave "this contentious and quarrelsome world," the town had attempted to secure a successor. The initial choice was Samuel Russell Jr. (1693–1746), age twenty-four, a former tutor at the Collegiate School and son of a founding trustee. In February 1717/8 a Lyme town meeting decided "to go and treat with Mr. Russell, Jr., to come and assist Mr. Noyes in the work of the ministry." To attract the young candidate, it approved £70 in bills of credit, along with the future use of the parsonage farm and the sale of "one hundred pounds worth of land for the settling of Mr. Russell." A year later, in October 1719, a town meeting authorized

John Smibert's portrait of Samuel Sewall captures Rev. Moses Noyes's childhood friend from Newbury, who unlike his colleagues refused to wear a periwig, just months before the esteemed Boston judge died in 1729. Photograph ©2019 Museum of Fine Arts, Boston

"Mr. Noyes and Mr. Russell, the ministers of this town," to preach on the Sabbath to those living in Lyme's north section and "to proportion time as they see fit."

Mr. Russell's assistance ended abruptly a month later. The town paid the young minister a full year's salary and "acquitted" him from the £200 provided for his settlement, then voted to hire a replacement "for three months on probation." It also directed a committee to "advise with Mr. Noyes concerning another minister." Two weeks later, after a majority vote at a town meeting chose Yale's senior tutor Daniel Browne (1698–1723), after Lieutenant Richard Lord (1647–1727) traveled to New Haven to "treat with Mr. Daniel Browne concerning his coming to Lyme to preach in said Lyme." No further mention of the second candidate appears in town records. Mr. Browne may have declined, or Moses Noyes may have raised doubts about the Yale scholar's theological views.

The search had spread over three years when the town reiterated its readiness to hire "another minister to help and assist Mr. Noyes in the work of the ministry." Inhabitants then agreed in January 1720/1 that "Mr. Samuel Pierpont (1700–1723) shall be hired to assist Mr. Noyes in the work of the ministry for half a year." To assure the third candidate's acceptance, the town appointed a committee to "go to Mr. Noyes and get his advice." Financial entanglements complicated the arrangements. Samuel Russell had used the £200 previously provided for his settlement to purchase land, and the town argued its right to dispose of that land as "a settlement for another minister." In June 1722 it granted the land to Mr. Pierpont, "the now assisting minister in the town society, if he lives to be ordained in said town society."

An ongoing dispute about the "use and improvement of the parsonage lot" also needed resolution. Moses Noyes had previously insisted on passing the farm to his heirs rather than to a succeeding minister, but a letter entered in the record book by town clerk Moses Noyes Jr., a month after the hiring of Samuel Pierpont, resolved the controversy. "To the town of Lyme for the preventing of causeless content[ion]," the elder Noyes wrote, "I have thought meet to signify to you that I have accepted and do accept . . . to leave the parsonage farm to the next incumbent." Denying that he had "designed any damage" to his successor, the minister claimed there was not "any shadow of grounds to suspect I desire or intend any other [outcome]."

Samuel Pierpont's ordination took place in December 1722, presumably in the meeting-house, "to the great satisfaction of Mr. Noyes and the people." Three months later, in "an awful stroke of Providence," the new minister drowned while crossing the Connecticut River, allegedly after courting a young woman in Middletown. The *Boston News-Letter* carried the story of his disappearance: "Essaying to pass over Connecticut River, towards Lyme, a league above Saybrook ferry, in a canoe, with an experienced Indian waterman; a sudden and unusual storm came down upon them, overwhelmed and drowned them." In April, Pierpont's remains washed ashore and were buried on Fishers Island. The next month the *Boston News-Letter* printed an elegy for the young minister composed by Samuel Sewall in Latin.

When Moses Noyes wrote to his friend in Boston, he remarked that Samuel Pierpont's assistance would have "brought much benefit to the place" while assuring his own "ease & comfort." Relief from ministerial duties might even have allowed him, late in life, to pay another visit to "the Bay." Meanwhile, fears that young men at Yale College had been "infected" by Arminian notions

Grave of Samuel Pierpont, Pastor of the first Church of Lyme, Conn , who was drowned in the Connecticut River. Body found and buried on Fisher's Island, N. Y., April 28th, 1723.
Fisher's Island, N. Y.

Rev. Samuel Pierpont's "lonely grave" on a bluff on the south shore of Fishers Island became a destination for sightseers, and a postcard ca. 1910 showed the slab of red sandstone that marked his burial place. The inscription "Here lies the body of ye Rev. Mr. Samuel Pierpont pastor of ye first church in Lyme" was re-carved in 1924, and the grave marker was later moved to the dooryard of St. John's Church.

made Mr. Pierpont's loss the more "afflictive," and Noyes worried how to "supply his place." The decision for the Collegiate School to leave Saybrook had been wrong, the minister wrote, but choosing Timothy Cutler (1684–1765) as rector was worse.

Cutler and senior tutor Daniel Browne had together overseen instruction at Yale, and less than a year after Lyme inhabitants voted to hire Browne as assistant minister, he joined the rector in openly declaring his Episcopal beliefs. At a commencement meeting in October 1722, college trustees relieved Cutler of his duties and accepted the resignation of Browne. Within a month both had left for London, where Cutler accepted orders in the Church of England and Browne died of smallpox in April 1723. As a result of Yale's shocking "apostasy," future rectors and tutors were required to affirm their opposition to "Arminian and prelateral corruptions" and declare their acceptance of the Saybrook Platform. A group of twelve Connecticut ministers drawn from the four counties in the colony, among them Moses Noyes and James Noyes, had drafted that detailed confession of faith and formulation of church governance and ecclesiastical discipline in 1708.

A finely detailed wood engraving by Thomas Nason conveys the graceful simplicity of the Congregational church built in 1841, overlooking Hamburg Cove, to replace the original meetinghouse in Lyme's north parish.

When Moses Noyes wrote to Judge Sewall in 1723, his congregation was shrinking. A second church society on the town's east side had been established in 1719, and a third parish in the north section would follow in 1724. How members of the original church viewed the diminished size of their parish is not known, but remarks by Jonathan Parsons (1705–1776), who succeeded the elderly minister after his death in 1729, have an edge of criticism. Noyes "often lamented the errors that he feared were creeping in among us," which made him "backward to have a colleague," Parsons wrote. After "being left of many on each side . . . that used to be his special charge, he went on preaching to that part of the town which is called the first parish as health and strength permitted, till he died."

ors & administrators that ... premeses un to the sd
& defend the within bargined premeses against the Lawfull
s heirs and assignes for ever & for the more
nges of any other what so ever
nfermation of this act and deed I the sd Joseph Peck
set my hand affix my seal this 13th day of January
year of our Soveraim Lord George an - Dom 1725
e above sd molata negro Girl doe freely Consent
le & further being Come to years of discretion doe
have power put and binde my self and my heirs to the
eirs for the Term of our naturall Lives in testemoney
re by set my hand & affix my seal the day and year ab
hand signed sealed & delivered in presence

Joseph Peck

her
Temperance
mark
negro molat

Children of oxford and Temprance the two
Richard Lord jun I say the birth of the children
Temprance are as foloweth
was born the 23 day of october 1726
7th day of may 1728
was born y 30 day of october 1732

---

n & Temprance molata Girl the two servants
Lyme ware married together by ye Revd mosses noyes the 21 day of Januy 172

Chapter eight

Oxford and Temperance

After 1694 not only magistrates but also clergy had the legal right to perform marriages in colonial Connecticut. The only known marriage conducted by Lyme's first minister united a "negro man" and a "molato girl."

Oxford negro man & Temprance molato girl the two servants of Richard Lord of Lyme were married together by ye Revd Moses Noyes the 21 day of January 1725/26.

Formalizing the bond of an enslaved couple was likely unprecedented in Lyme when Moses Noyes, age eighty-two, married two servants of Lieutenant Richard Lord, age seventy-five. The union of Oxford and Temperance 1725/6 appears in the land records alongside a deed detailing Temperance's purchase. When Lord died a year later, the married couple passed to his son Richard Lord Jr. (1690–1776), described in a later family history as a "genial man" with a "large household and many slaves."

The couple's passage through Lyme left faint traces. Oxford, born in 1706, may have been a son of Moses Noyes's servant Arabella, with whom he was later baptized and admitted to the church, or a grandson of Moses, Richard Ely's servant, or he may have been purchased elsewhere, in Boston or New London. Temperance was the daughter of a "Negro" man and a Narragansett woman named Jane who had been captured at age two in King Philip's War. Until a week before her marriage, Temperance served Joseph Peck Jr. (1680–1757), son of the first deacon in Lyme's church.

An account book kept by Deacon Peck's son recorded varied financial transactions. In 1715 he sold large quantities of sugar by the pound and rum by the pint and quart, along with wheat, oats, and beef. He delivered wood by the sled load, provided hay storage in his barn, and hired out his plow, harrow, and ox team. He also hired out a slave. In 1718 he entered charges of one shilling for a "black boy one day" and three shillings for a "black boy one day [with] harrow." The black boy may have been "Jack man servant of Joseph Peck." Twenty years later church records noted the death of Peck's servant.

(170)

Deed of Sale from Joseph Peck to Richard Lord Junr

Know all men by these presence that I Joseph Peck of Lyme in the Colloney of Conecticut and County of new London in newengland Yemon for the Consideration of the sum of Sixty pounds in Bills of Publick Credit of the Colloney of Conecticut to me in hand paid by Richard Lord Junr of Lyme in the County and Colloney afore sd before the ensealeing and delivery of these presents the Receipt whereof I do here by acknowlidge and am fully satisfied contented & paid have therefore Alineated Assigned made over & sould un to the sd Richard Lord his heirs & assignes A Certain molato Negro Girl named Temperance after the maner of a negro slave to serve the sd Richard Lord his heirs and Assignes from the day of the date of these presents during the Term of her natural Life and I the sd Joseph Peck doe here by declare that un till the ensealing here of I am the sole proprieter and Lawfull owner of the sd negro Girl & have in my self Good Right & Lawfull authority alieneate and sell the sd negro Girl & I the sd Peck doe further Covenant & promise for my selfe and my heirs Executors & administrators that we & each of us shall and will for ever warant & defend the within bargined premeses un to the sd Richard Lord his heirs and assignes for ever against the Lawfull Claims or Challenges of any other what so ever & for the more full & perfect Confermation of this act and deed I the sd Joseph Peck have here un to set my hand affix my seal this 13th day of January Anno Domi 1725 and in the 12th year of our Soverain Lord George [illegible]

I Temperence the above sd molata negro Girl doe freely Consent to the above sd sale & further being come to years of discretion doe freely so far as I have power put and binde my self and my heirs to the sd Lord and his heirs for the Term of our naturall Lives in testemoney here of I doe here by set my hand & affix my seal the [illegible] as witness my hand Signed sealed & delivered in [illegible] of us

Samuell marvin
Edmund Dorr

[illegible]ph Peck
her
[illegible] mark
a negro molato

June 23 1725

Janu 13 1725/6

The birth of the Children of oxford and Temperance servants of mr Richard Lord junr I say the birth of the sd oxford and Temperance are as followeth
Zachary their son was born the 23 day of october
Luke was born ye 14th day of may
Jordan their son was born ye 30 day of october 173[illegible]

Janu 21 1725

Oxford negro man & Temperance molata Girl the two servants of Richard Lord of Lyme ware married together by ye Revd moses Noyes the 21 day of January 1725

When Joseph Peck Jr. sold the "molato" girl Temperance a week before her marriage, she "freely" consented to her purchase by Richard Lord.

When and where Peck acquired his enslaved servants is not known, but in January 1725/6 he sold "a certain molato Negro girl named Temperance, after the manner of a negro slave," to serve Lieutenant Richard Lord "during the term of her natural life." The deed stated a purchase price of "sixty pounds in bills of public credit of the colony of Connecticut" and included the young woman's consent. "I Temperance the above said molato negro girl do freely consent to the above said sale & further being come to [my] years of discretion do freely so far as I have power put and bind myself and my heirs to the said Lord and his heirs for the term of our natural life." Below Joseph Peck's signature, "Temperance negro molato," age twenty, marked an *X*.

Whether Temperance gave birth to a daughter, perhaps fathered by the manservant Jack, before her sale to Richard Lord cannot be established. But in May 1729, three years after her marriage to Oxford, Joseph Peck Jr., "in consideration of the sum of twenty five pounds," sold to Benjamin Reed of Lyme "one certain molato girl of about three years old called Jane, to have and to hold, possess & enjoy as his own proper estate free and clear to him and his heirs . . . during her natural life." The coincidence of names suggests that Temperance at age seventeen may have given birth to a child she called Jane after her own mother, and that the child remained the property of Joseph Peck Jr.

During the nine years that Richard Lord Jr., a justice of the peace for New London County, owned Temperance and her family, Rev. Jonathan Parsons baptized Oxford and three of the couple's five children, including infant Joel, in February 1734/5. Six months later Judge Lord sold the two adults, both age twenty-nine, together with Joel, age seven months, "all sound and in good health to the best of my knowledge," for £180. The deed of sale to John Bulkley (1705–1753), the son of Colchester's minister and also a justice of the peace, confirmed Richard Lord's "good right, full power, and lawful authority to sell said man,

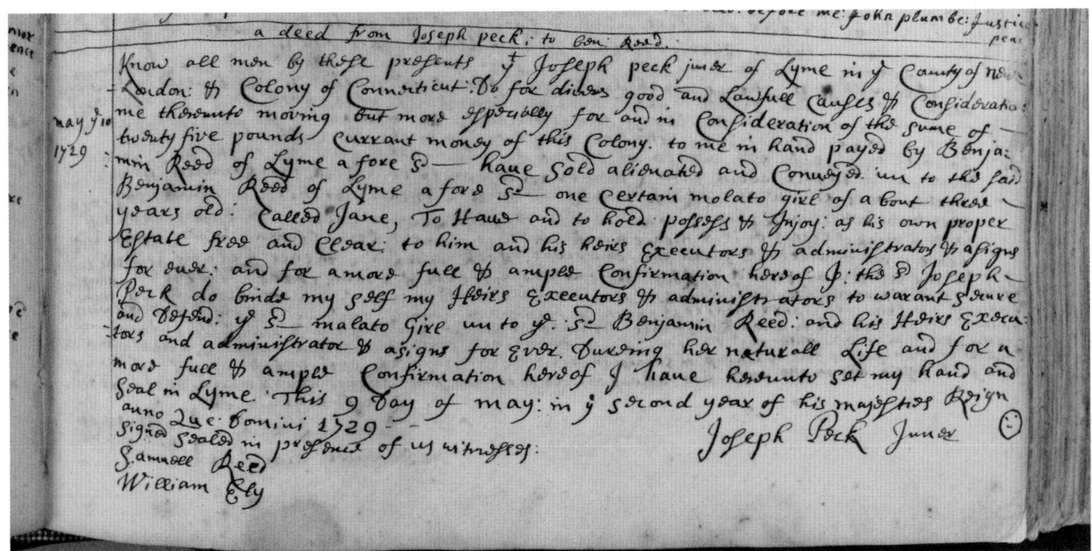
a deed from Joseph peck: to Ben: Reed.

may ye 10 1729

Know all men by these presents that I Joseph peck junr of Lyme in ye County of New London: & Colony of Connecticut: for divers good and Lawfull Causes & Considerations me thereunto moving but more Especially for and in Consideration of the sume of twenty five pounds Currant money of this Colony. to me in hand payed by Benjamin Reed of Lyme afore sd — have Sold alienated and Conveyed unto the said Benjamin Reed of Lyme afore sd one certain molato girl of about three years old: Called Jane, To Have and to hold possess & Enjoy: as his own proper Estate free and Clear: to him and his heirs Executors & administrators & asigns for ever: and for a more full & ample Confirmation hereof I: the sd Joseph Peck do binde my self my Heirs Executors & administrators to warant secure and defend: ye sd molato Girl unto ye sd Benjamin Reed: and his Heirs Executors and administrator & asigns for ever. During her naturall Life and for a more full & ample Confirmation hereof I have hereunto set my hand and Seal in Lyme This 9 day of may: in ye second year of his majesties Reign anno Domini 1729 —
Signed Sealed in presence of us witnesses:
Samuel Reed
William Ely
Joseph Peck Junor

The three-year-old "molato" child named Jane sold by Joseph Peck Jr. for £25 may have been the daughter of his enslaved servant Temperance.

The map that appeared in Richard Ligon's *A True and Exact History of the Island of Barbados* in 1657 included illustrative vignettes showing English planters hunting wild boars and chasing runaway slaves.

woman and child, as servants, during the term of their natural lives." It also obligated him and his heirs forever to defend Oxford, Temperance, and Joel as Judge Bulkley's "slaves against all . . . endeavors of said slaves to free themselves." The couple's four older children, born into hereditary slavery, remained the property of Judge Richard Lord in Lyme.

Enslaved people served other "consequential families" in town. A week before Parsons's ordination in 1731, Renold Marvin (1698–1761), later a church deacon, purchased from New London merchant John Bradick (1675–1733), then living in Lyme, a "Negro boy" named Caesar, about fifteen years of age, to be held as a "servant slave" for the term of his natural life. The deed of sale, witnessed by Joseph Peck Jr., was entered in the land records. Marvin's "Negro woman servant" Chloe died in 1748.

After Rev. Parsons's enslaved child servant Cato, age ten, died in 1734, the minister baptized his maidservant Phillis six years later. He also baptized Lucy, servant of David Deming (1681–1745/6), a retired minister living in Lyme who had assisted "in preaching in times past." Parsons may have acquired Cato and Phillis from his father-in-law Judge John Griswold (1690–1761), a son of Matthew Griswold Jr., and described as a man of "great wealth." Judge Griswold's estate inventory after his death in 1761 listed among other property a "Negro girl" named Phillis. The deeds to two "Negro" men "sold and delivered to him during his life" were found among his papers. A family history states that in all probability those were "only a representation of his household-slaves."

Rev. George Griswold (1692–1761), also a son of Matthew Griswold Jr. and the founding minister in Lyme's second parish, purchased a servant in New London in 1730. The bill of sale noted that he paid £80 "current money of New England" to New London merchant and ship captain Joseph Coit (1698–1787), who sold "unto the said Mr. George Griswold, in plain and open market in New London . . . a Negro woman called or known by the name of Cornelia . . . for and during her natural life."

Bristo, the servant of Rev. George Beckwith (1703–1794), the founding minister in Lyme's third parish, became involved in May 1756 in an extended court case following an accusation that he sexually assaulted a white woman "in a bye and secret place." The Superior Court in New London sentenced Bristo "to suffer the pains of death," but "soon after said condemnation" the alleged victim, Hannah Beebe, "openly and freely declared said Bristo to be innocent of said crime and that her said complaint was wholly false and groundless." The court overturned the conviction in November and released Bristo from the county jail. Two decades later, in 1777, Beckwith advertised in the *Connecticut Gazette* for the return of London, "a runaway Negro man, age about 25."

Unlike Lyme's ministers, Rev. James Noyes in Stonington acquired native captives as servants. In October 1676 he wrote to colonial official John Allyn (1631–1696) detailing his "considerable expense, in powder & lead & provisions & tobacco," while serving the previous year as a chaplain in King Philip's War. He noted that "the worshipful John Mason" (1600–1672) knew something of his "constant pains and charge" and had already sent him "a young girl of 14 years of age," along with "her child of 5 years of age" and the girl's mother, "an old woman that [was] sick." James Noyes had also received a forty-year-old man whose limbs had been lame for two years and "would do [him] no good." He requested instead "a young man & woman."

Seeking assurances that the captives already sent, if they "proved a pest to us," could be sold "to [the] English," or some other way be found "to rid our hands of them," Stonington's minister asked for "a good young lad of about 16 years of age." His letter advised that he "knew of some that could do [him] service." Among the young males who moved at night from wigwam to wigwam to avoid being sold in Barbados, a suitable servant could be found.

Concerning the DEATH *o*

Righteous

Had at *Lyme,*

Occasion'd by the Decease of the R

Mr. Moses Noye

The First Pastor of the Church of C
in that Town.

Who dyed November 10*th.* 17
In the *Eighty Sixth* Year of hi

By Azariah Mather
Pastor of a Church of CHRIST in *Sa*

CHAPTER NINE

A Dark House

After Rev. Moses Noyes died in November 1729, Saybrook's minister delivered a eulogy in Lyme's meetinghouse. He offered not only praise for a learned teacher and valued friend but also warnings that ongoing controversy in the parish could erupt into open strife.

I must now offer a word to this Church & Society, you have lost an excellent and eminent pastor, What shall I say? . . . His doctrine once distilled as the dew and the rain, but now you will see him and hear him no more. This bereaved flock surely mourns, his study mourns, his very books mourn, as it were, leaving none so able to look into them; his family mourns, his pulpit mourns, this is a dark house and desk now. You must allow me to share with you in tears.

When Rev. Azariah Mather delivered a sermon "occasioned by the decease of the Reverend Mr. Moses Noyes," he offered words of consolation from the pulpit to the "bereaved flock" in Lyme's meetinghouse. The "eminent pastor" who had served the town for sixty-three years would be heard no more. "This is a dark house and desk now," Saybrook's minister, age forty-three, lamented. He had viewed Moses Noyes as both a mentor and a father, he wrote in his *Discourse Concerning the Death of the Righteous*, and his remarks reflected his personal experience.

The printed version of the funeral sermon in 1731 opened with Mather's note of condolence to Moses

To preserve Rev. Moses Noyes's gravestone, church members removed it from Duck River Cemetery in 2007 and substituted a replica. Today a glass case in the church fellowship hall protects the original monument.

Noyes Jr.: "Sir, At the instance of many & your solicitation in particular, I have adventured to let come forth to the light some things, delivered upon the death of your deceased & excellent parent." While the *Discourse* offered lofty praise for the elder Noyes's character, learning, and godliness, it also warned that "sparks of contention" in the parish were "ready to break out into a flame."

The choice of a successor loomed over the "dark house" when Mather brought the sparks of contention into the light. Concerned with discord among church members, he made no reference to the dissenting beliefs of Baptists, which two years earlier had filled Noyes with "a pious Zeal to withstand the designed propagation of their Errors." More pressing was the loss of the minister's doctrine that "once distilled as the dew and the rain." While some had "censured" Noyes for being "backward to have a colleague," his only intent, the sermon affirmed, had been to safeguard his congregation. "I must tell you he knew not where to find one he could safely leave his poor flock with," Mather advised, and it was only the deceased minister's "lenity, patience and charity" that had "let the sparks die, which . . . some men had blown up to a dangerous flame." After the death of the righteous, Saybrook's minister warned, sometimes "great disorders follow in towns, churches, state & families."

Lyme's Ecclesiastical Society moved quickly to secure a successor. Two months after Noyes's death, it invited Jonathan Parsons, a recent Yale graduate studying theology in his native Springfield with Rev. Jonathan Edwards (1703–1758), "as a probationer for settlement." It voted three months later to "continue Mr. Parsons in the work of the ministry" and allocated the "just sum" of six shillings to Renold Marvin (1669–1737) "for his service in bringing Mr. Parsons, the present minister, into the Society." Surviving documents do not reveal whether the Society sought a successor whose beliefs departed from those of Moses Noyes, but Jonathan Parsons later made the difference explicit. "In that day, he wrote, "I was greatly in love with Arminian principles."

To secure the candidate's acceptance, the Society offered a generous settlement. It agreed to pay the new minister's salary either in money or in "wheat at seven shillings per bushel, or rye at five shillings per bushel, and Indian corn at

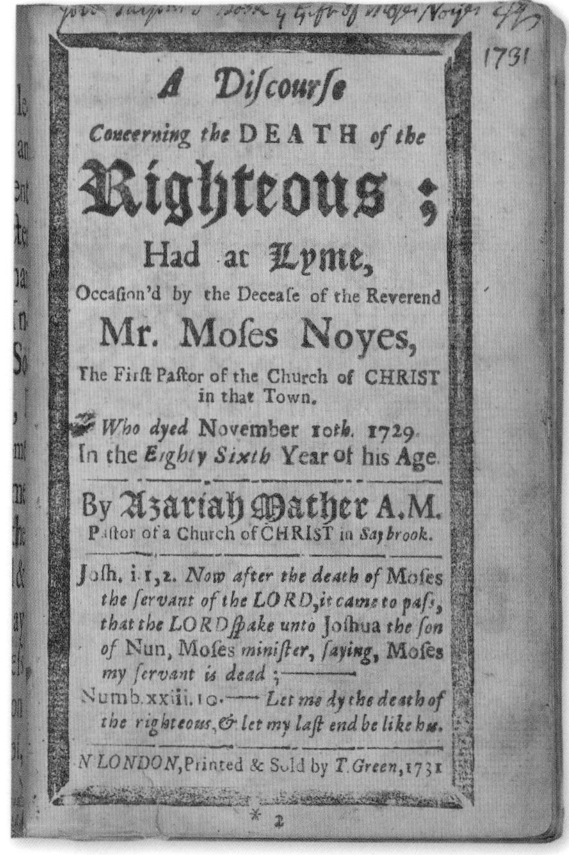
A Diſcourſe
Concerning the DEATH of the
Righteous;
Had at Lyme,
Occaſion'd by the Deceaſe of the Reverend
Mr. Moſes Noyes,
The Firſt Paſtor of the Church of CHRIST in that Town.
Who dyed November 10th. 1729.
In the Eighty Sixth Year of his Age.
By Azariah Mather A.M.
Paſtor of a Church of CHRIST in Saybrook.
Joſh. i. 1,2. *Now after the death of* Moſes *the ſervant of the* LORD, *it came to paſs, that the* LORD *ſpake unto* Joſhua *the ſon of* Nun, Moſes *miniſter, ſaying,* Moſes *my ſervant is dead;* ——
Numb. xxiii. 10. —— *Let me dy the death of the righteous, & let my laſt end be like his.*
N. LONDON, Printed & Sold by T. Green, 1731

In a eulogy for Lyme's long-serving first minister, Rev. Azariah Mather warned that sparks of contention smoldering in the parish could soon burst into flame.

four shillings per bushel, pork at five pence per pound, beef at three pence per pound." When the Society unanimously confirmed the choice of Mr. Parsons "for the settled minister and pastor" in August 1730, it allocated a parcel of fourteen acres "with the house erected thereon," along with the income from the parsonage farm and a yearly salary of £100, for as long as the minister remained single. The previous month Parsons, age twenty-four, had sent a second courtship letter to his mentor's sister Hannah Edwards (1713–1773) in Springfield, who declined his request.

On a "fair, cold, and windy day" in March 1731, New London farmer and justice of the peace Joshua Hempstead (1678–1758) noted in his diary that he "went to the ordination of Mr. Jonathan Parsons in Lyme first Society." The minister later explained that he had "refused to take the oversight of the church" for seven months while struggling with doubts about the validity of "Presbyterian" ordination. When those uncertainties had not resolved on the eve of his ordination, he made clear that he would not be guided by the Saybrook Platform but would take only "the general platform of the Gospel for [his] rule." Church records note that ministers from New London, Killingworth, and Saybrook's newly separated west parish conducted the ordination of Moses Noyes's successor. Rev. Azariah Mather, who had delivered the ordination sermon in Lyme's north society for Rev. George Beckwith two years earlier, did not participate.

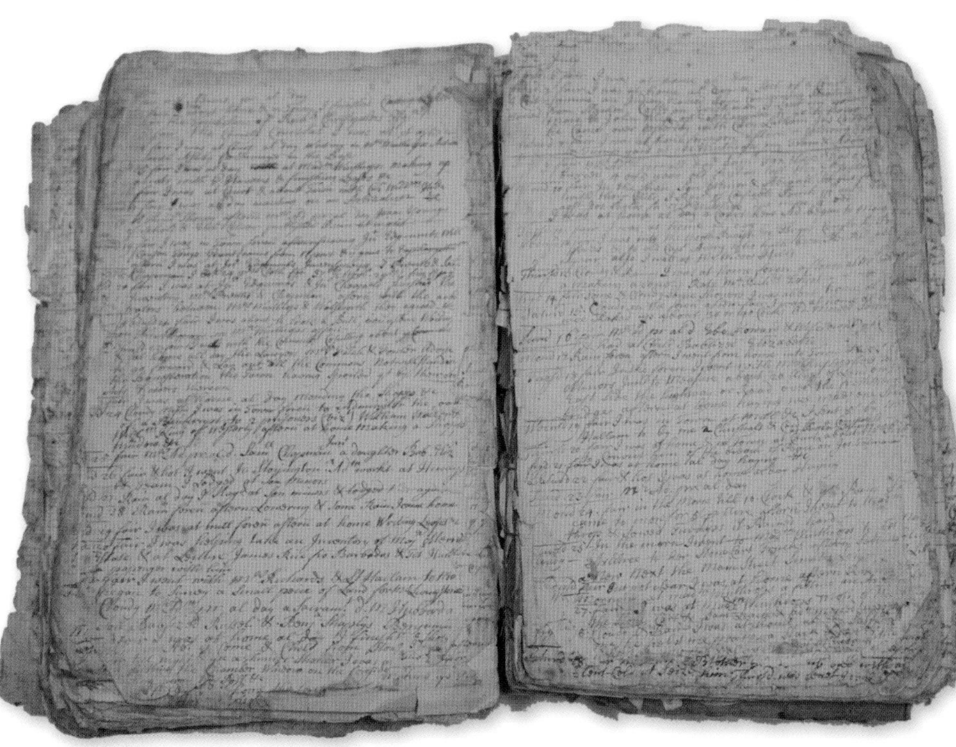

Over almost four decades Joshua Hempstead chronicled his activities in a diary that includes vivid details about weather conditions, farm labor, marriages, church services, and court decisions in New London and the surrounding region.

God governs by his Providence — —

Ps. 33. 11. — ye Counsel of ye Ld Standeth fore[ver]
[tho]ts of his ht to all Genera[tio]ns.

In ye Psalm, David, or whoever was ye Author, exhorts ye
[...] ye Consid[eratio]n of ye many Benefits, wch ye whole race of Manki[nd]
[espe]cially ye Ch[urc]h, Ld Chs. favoured by G, & wch wod celebrat[e]
[...] praises, & excite ym to fear, faith, & ye other gratfu[l]
[...] to be given to G. & yt is done by various Argumts; ye [...]
[...] takn fro ye justice, goodn, Providence, wisd & powr of [...]
[sh]ines forth in Crea[tio]n & constant preserva[tio]n of ye wld: [...]
[...] he says is so gret, yt ye Sit & thots of it may well m[ake]
[...] Earth tremble: ye Second is takn fro human [...]
[...] ordains, dispenses & governs by his admirable goodn, [...]
[...] ye David, ye malice of wicked men, ye most be[...]
[...] be instituted, shd be confounded & overturnd; bu[t]
[...] ye Ch & all G's people seem to be destitute of al[l]
[...] & Surrounded wth ye most potent Enemies, who wth gr[...]
[...], & endeavor to blot it out forever, yet it [...]
[...] covered by ye hand of G, who often makes it [...]
[...] Strength so great, as to overturn ye Counsel of [...]
[...] forever, ye thot[s] [...]

Chapter ten

Confessions

Continuing records of Lyme's first church start in 1731 when Rev. Jonathan Parsons began documenting meetings and keeping detailed lists of baptisms, admissions, and dismissals. The record book opens with a sequence of confessions.

April 4th James Beckwith, son; made a confession for his sin of drunkenness, whereupon he was received into the charity of said church and to all the privileges of it.

Tho. Huddson made confession for his sin of drunkenness . . . and unbridled feelings, which satisfied the church.

April 11th Jn Alger made confession for his sin of fornication which put him into charity.

June 6th Widow Deborah Mather confessed her sin, in declaring herself guilty of the sin of fornication, which established her in the charity of the church.

An almost indecipherable notebook stitched with string lists two baptisms, a marriage, and an "owning of the covenant" in Lyme in 1724, but no other records from Moses Noyes's ministry survive. The sturdily bound ledger that today preserves an account of church meetings, said to be "a true copy of the old record," begins in April 1731 and opens with a list of confessions. Acknowledgments of drunkenness, "rash speaking," and fornication all found acceptance by "the first assembly of Christians, in Lyme." Even the confession of blacksmith Zechariah Sill (1717–1783) for "giving way to passion, evil speaking, and intemperate drinking" was duly accepted by church brethren. The conduct of David Deming, a Harvard-educated minister who moved to Lyme in retirement, required fuller consideration.

The town had employed Mr. Deming, age fifty-four, as a schoolmaster, and in 1734 the Ecclesiastical Society's treasury paid him "twenty shillings and two pence for his assistance in preaching for time past." Later that year he faced criminal charges in the New London County Court following reports of his "lascivious carriage" with Elizabeth Greenfield

The parsonage of Rev. Jonathan Parsons, much altered after his son Marshfield Parsons added a rear ell for a coaching inn and Deacon Daniel Noyes later built a two-story front addition, stood a mile west of the hillside meetinghouse on the road to the ferry.

(1723–1814), age ten, which included "exposing her most private parts." Accusations surfaced after a neighbor, alerted that Mr. Deming's conduct with schoolchildren was "unsuitable," observed him dismiss other students and call Elizabeth back inside. Susannah Loveland (1715–1752) testified that the schoolmaster stood the child on a desk, raised her clothes, and placed his hand on her "privates." As word spread and parents withdrew their children from school, Deming claimed he thought Elizabeth was afflicted with worms and had stroked her belly so the worms would fall out.

The former minister pleaded not guilty at a court hearing in January 1735/6 when bond for a trial appearance was set at £50. Later that month the church suspended him from communion and appointed a committee to "wait upon and address Mr. David Deming of said Lyme, in the name of said Church, and persuade and urge him to offer some reflections upon himself for his conduct respecting Elisabeth Greenfield, daughter of Archibald Greenfield (1692–1769), about whom there has been much discourse."

The letter of confession was entered in church records. "My conduct has been very grievous to my good brethren, of this and some other churches," the confession stated. "I do solemnly reflect upon myself with sorrow . . . and

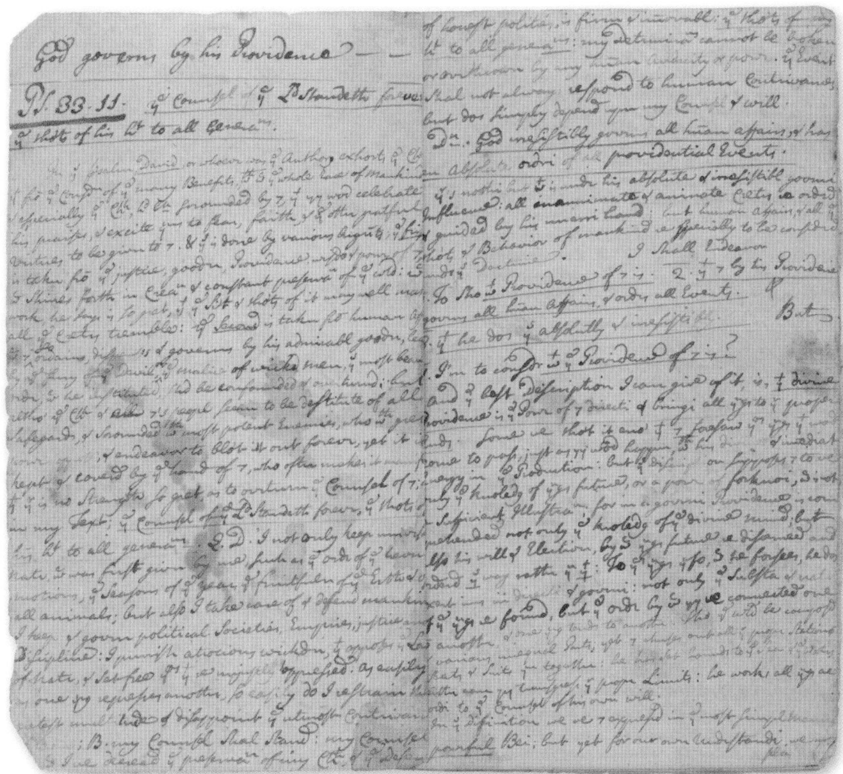
God governs by his Providence —

Ps. 33.11.

Before a verdict had been reached in the case against David Deming, Rev. Jonathan Parsons likely delivered, in the hilltop meetinghouse, the unsigned sermon "God governs by his providence," dated February 22, 1736.

heartily ask their charity and the charity of you all, as well as of all other churches, and also I ask your prayers that I might in whatever state or employment I engage—be more careful to allow the doctrine of God my Saviour, by a good and unspotted life and conversation." The case finally resolved two years later after Elizabeth reversed her prior statement that Deming had three times touched her private parts and claimed instead that Susannah Loveland's testimony was false. The court, citing conflicting evidence, found Deming not guilty, and church members in 1737 "restored [him] to the communion."

Two years earlier the General Court had resolved debate about the location for a larger meetinghouse. An urgent memorial in 1735 protested the inconvenience of the meeting-house for those who lived on the east side of the parish, but the Court affirmed that its committee "could not find any place in said society that on all accounts would so well accommodate the greatest part of the inhabitants of said society as the hill on which the old meeting house now stands." It "proposed that a new house be erected about four rods northwards of the old meeting house," and in April 1738 the Ecclesiastical Society approved the collection of a tax, exempting only Baptists, "towards building the meeting house in this Society."

Construction began six months later when the Society hired two builders "to frame the

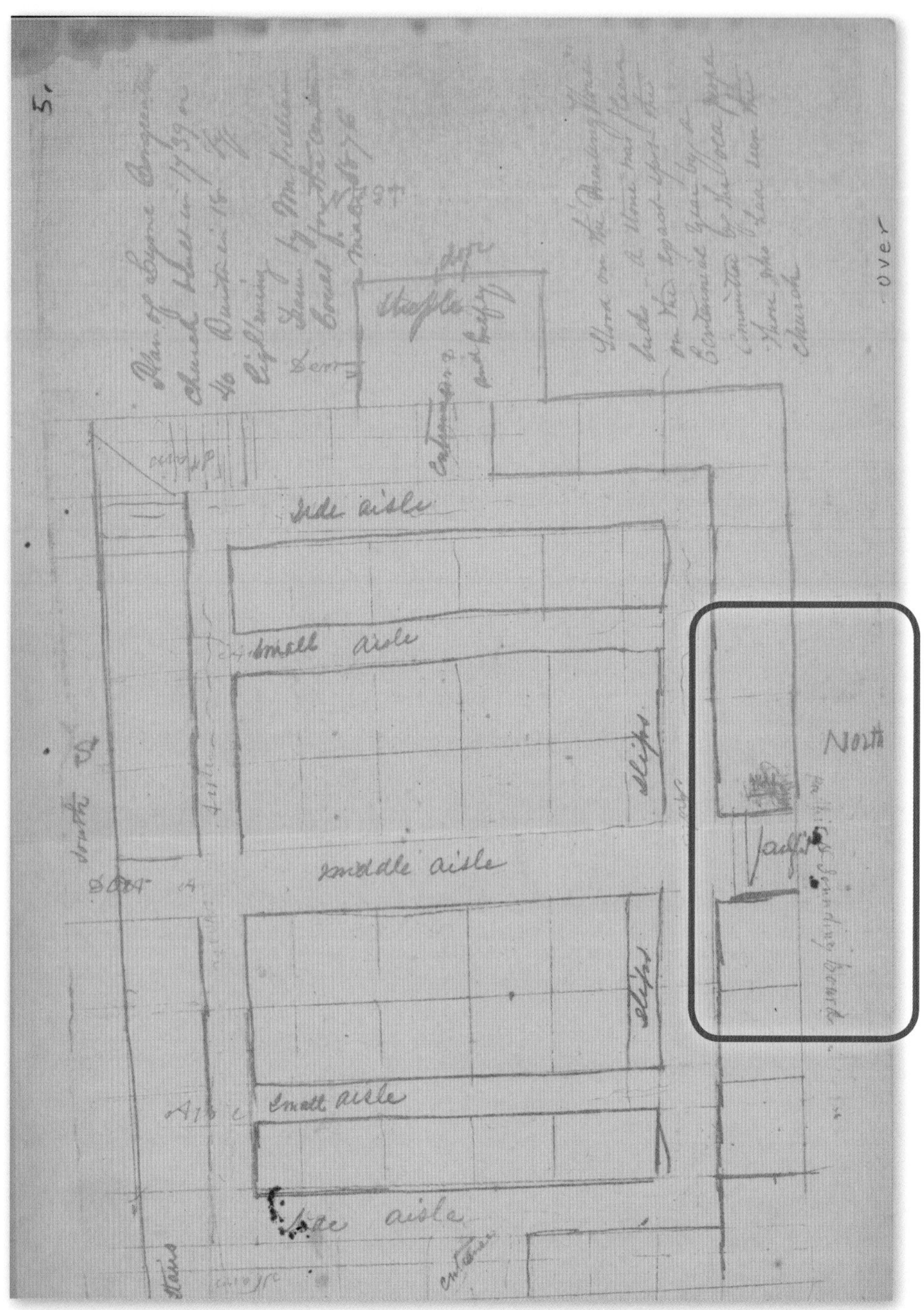

When Old Lyme celebrated America's centennial in 1876, church treasurer William Coult drew from memory at age seventy-nine the floor plan of the town's third meetinghouse, where he had attended services as a youth. His pencil notes locate the steeple and belfry above the west-facing entrance and the pulpit with sounding board on the building's north side.

meeting house on reasonable terms." It also appointed a committee to provide £100 worth "of good white pine and white wood boards," along with "window frames and nails and fittings for said house . . . done at the cost of the Society." After a vote to "pull down the old meeting house and improve what timber and body that will be proper towards building the new meeting house," Uriah Roland (1710–1760) offered the use of his dwelling for interim Sabbath worship. Four months later the theft of building materials halted construction.

Pews and galleries had not yet been installed or a steeple erected when the building committee decided in January 1739/40 to "proceed not further than to finish what they have agreed with." It tasked Benjamin DeWolfe (1695–1742), the Society's clerk and an experienced carpenter, "to take care that no boards and timber shall be carried away from the meetinghouse" and to "find out all such as he can that have carried timber and boards away already." The loss of materials coincided with complaints about the minister.

Criticism of Parsons brought an admission by William Borden (1674–1747), age fifty-five, in December 1739 that he had "at sundry times and places with an apparent heat and vehemence of Spirit" denounced "greedy ministers" who "accepted a certain sum to preach the gospel." He had also criticized the choice of "young men of a college education" to preach at the neglect of "the age[d] and experienced brethren of the church among them." Claims about the minister's "ill conduct toward said Society in general" and allegations that he had defamed the Ecclesiastical Society "publicly in the meetinghouse" prompted an effort in 1739 "to proceed against the Rev. Mr. Jonathan Parsons." But church members followed "the desire of the pastor" and voted instead to suspend Mr. Borden from communion and admonish him "for his obstinate continuances in the scandalous sin of defamation."

As confessions continued in the unfinished meetinghouse, David Lord (1715–1785) in 1738 acknowledged abusing and violently striking a man. The next year, John Peck (1716–1785) and his wife Catherine Lay Peck (1715–1810) confessed together to fornication. After Deacon Marvin confessed to intemperance in January 1741, six church members in rapid succession, including Lucy, the enslaved servant of Mr. Deming, confessed to fornication. In the coming months the Great Awakening, a sweeping religious revival movement that disrupted established churches with its fervent emotionalism, would dramatically alter religious practice in Lyme's first church.

A

FUNERAL SERM

Delivered at NEWBURY-PORT, Dec.

Occafioned by the DEATH of

Mrs. PHEBE PARSO

Confort of the

Rev. JONATHAN PARS

Chapter eleven

The Minister's Wife

The playful reputation of the minister's wife dates from 1876, more than a century after her death, when a magazine article celebrating Lyme's prominent families included a fanciful anecdote about her pranks in the meetinghouse.

His wife was given to practical jokes. One evening as he was about to leave the house for the weekly prayer-meeting—after taking a last look in the mirror to satisfy himself that every particular hair was stroked the right way—she playfully threw her arms about his neck, passed one hand over his face, and kissed him. As he entered the church he was nettled by a ripple of smiles which ran through the congregation, and he noticed that some of the brethren were eyeing him suspiciously. Presently it was whispered in his ear that his face was blackened.

The vivid details in a whimsical narrative about Phoebe Griswold (1716–1770), who at age fifteen married the town's new minister, ten years her senior, are likely apocryphal. They seem to have originated a century after her death when Evelyn McCurdy Salisbury (1823–1917), a Griswold descendant eager to highlight the family's distinguished marriages and praise "the beauty and spirit of its women," provided a colorful anecdote to historian and journalist Martha J. Lamb (1829–1923). Mrs. Lamb included the charming story in her article celebrating Lyme's illustrious past, which appeared in the centennial issue of *Harper's Magazine* in 1876. The incidents she recounted became fixed in local lore and still shape the remembered past today.

Martha Lamb's purpose was to engage her magazine audience in an appealing portrayal of a historic Connecticut town. Her article describes how Parsons arranged his hair in front of a mirror, kissed his wife goodbye, and left for a weekly prayer gathering in the meetinghouse, where his smudged face elicited "a ripple of smiles." It details an additional occasion in the meetinghouse when his "fun-loving wife," who "was given to practical jokes," removed a page from his sermon, then "sat in the little square pew before him, quietly fanning herself, and enjoying his embarrassment

Historian Martha J. Lamb drew national attention to Old Lyme's scenic beauty and the achievements of its "consequential families" in an illustrated profile of the town that appeared in 1876 in the centennial issue of *Harper's Monthly.*

when he reached the chasm." The anecdote later became confused with fact, as if Mrs. Lamb were actually reporting the reaction of those gathered in Lyme's meetinghouse for a prayer meeting and a sermon in the 1730s.

Parsons's own accounts of his ministry in Lyme offer no hint of playfulness in his household. He described efforts to eliminate youthful frivolity in the parish and reported that young people, at his urging, "turned their meetings for vain mirth into meetings for prayer, conference, and reading books of piety." They then took pains, the minister noted, "to dissuade others from levity and frothy conversation." His accounts of his ministry mention his wife only once, when he described his severe mental struggle after settling in Lyme. "Sometimes I thought I must be in hell," he explained, and "I thought everyone that saw me must see my wretchedness." When "Mrs. Parsons, taking notice of something extraordinary, asked what was the matter," the minister told her that he "could not live so," then retired "unto a secret place in the field" where he remained on his knees alone with his Bible."

When Martha Lamb described Jonathan Parsons's manly and good-humored face looking down from a portrait, she likely referred to this "crayon" copy of a painting by John Singleton Copley showing the minister with the hint of a smile.

Although Martha Lamb portrayed Jonathan Parsons as an affectionate and indulgent husband, a grandson's memoir commented that his "natural temper was hasty and rather unlovely," and that "it cost him a struggle to keep it under, to the end of his life." But John Singleton Copley's (1738–1815) portrait of the minister in middle age seemed to confirm Mrs. Lamb's impression of his amiable temperament. Observing a pastel copy that showed Parsons in black robe and clerical collar with the hint of a smile, she remarked that a "fair, frank, manly, good-humored face looks down." She also claimed, without any known evidence, that his "passion for fine clothes, for gold and silver lace, and ruffled shirt fronts" caused distress among "some of the good Puritans in his church." Today those details allow Parsons to be described as Phoebe Griswold's "dandy of a husband."

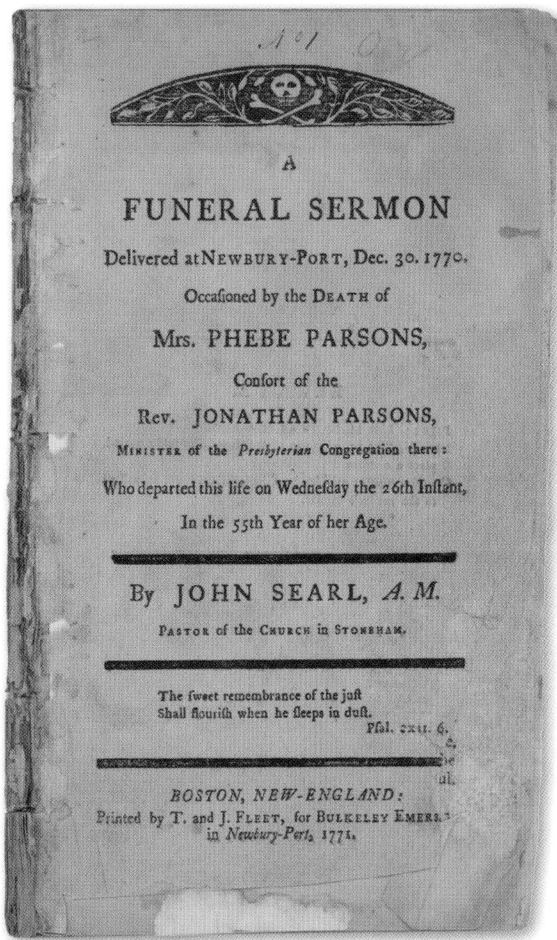
A

FUNERAL SERMON

Delivered at NEWBURY-PORT, Dec. 30. 1770.

Occaſioned by the DEATH of

Mrs. PHEBE PARSONS,

Conſort of the

Rev. JONATHAN PARSONS,

MINISTER of the *Presbyterian* Congregation there:

Who departed this life on Wedneſday the 26th Inſtant,

In the 55th Year of her Age.

By JOHN SEARL, *A. M.*

PASTOR of the CHURCH in STONEHAM.

The ſweet remembrance of the juſt
Shall flouriſh when he ſleeps in duſt.
Pſal. cxii. 6.

BOSTON, NEW-ENGLAND:
Printed by T. and J. FLEET, for BULKELEY EMERSON
in *Newbury-Port*, 1771.

The funeral sermon that Rev. John Searle preached in Newbury after the death of Phoebe Parsons in 1771 commended her knowledge and integrity and noted her keenness of wit.

Only the outlines of Mrs. Parsons's life can be established. She grew up in a prominent Lyme family, married young, and faced repeated tragedy when six of her thirteen children died before adulthood. Her response when bitter contention divided Lyme's church and when her brother Matthew Griswold (1714–1799), later Connecticut's governor, served as her husband's most outspoken advocate is not known. When Parsons's troubled ministry in Lyme ended in 1745, she moved at age twenty-nine to Newbury, Massachusetts, where she died a quarter of a century later in 1770. A funeral sermon praised Phoebe Parsons's exceptional capabilities. It commended her mental endowments, her Christian simplicity and integrity, her knowledge of divinity, and her rare acquaintance with church history. It also noted her liveliness and keenness of wit.

Chimney

12 …
Vi…
Oct…

Phebe & Pez a Mohegg
Wigwaum admirantis

B
C
D
K
K
K
12 f
4½ f
7 f 4 f
6 f
L
I
M
G
A
N
E
F
H

…a Table
…Shelf with Plates
… Chests
… Pots hanging
… Table
…Dresser

Chapter twelve

Out of Darkness

To bring the "natives of New England" living on a reserve in Lyme's east parish "out of their heathenish state," Jonathan Parsons joined his wife's uncle in a request for assistance from the General Court.

The humble memorial of us, the subscribers, shows that, whereas your Honors' memorialists, being ministers of the Gospel in Lyme in which town dwells about thirty families of Indians, natives of New England called the Niantics, the most of which continue in their heathenism notwithstanding all the good laws already made for the natives being Christianized.

Three years after his marriage, Parsons joined Rev. George Griswold in a "humble memorial" submitted to Connecticut's General Court. The petition requested assistance in an ongoing effort to Christianize thirty families of "Niantic Indians" in Lyme's east parish. Noting that "the younger sort of them" seemed "desirous of learning," the ministers urged education as "a leading step to conversion."

The memorial, written a century after the Pequot Wars, followed ongoing efforts to lead the "heathen" Niantics "out of darkness" and persuade them "to attend the public worship of God's house, and to desire a schoolmaster to teach their children and youths to read." The ministers argued that the chiefs resisted because they "would not be concerned with one religion or have a school unless that the English would deal honestly with them respecting their land." Three hundred acres had been allotted as a reserve for the Niantics, but the boundaries remained uncertain and unenforced. Incursions on Niantic land had brought Court intervention at least since 1663, when a committee was appointed "to determine the differences betwixt the Indians at Niantic and the English, respecting burning their fence, or any other complaints presented to them respecting those Indians." When Lyme's ministers reported the Niantics' protest in 1734 that "the English, their neighbors, had encroached on their property," they advised that if the chiefs "could have the bounds of their land settled, they would willingly hear a sermon." Their only requirement was to be "settled in the quiet and peaceful enjoyment of their land."

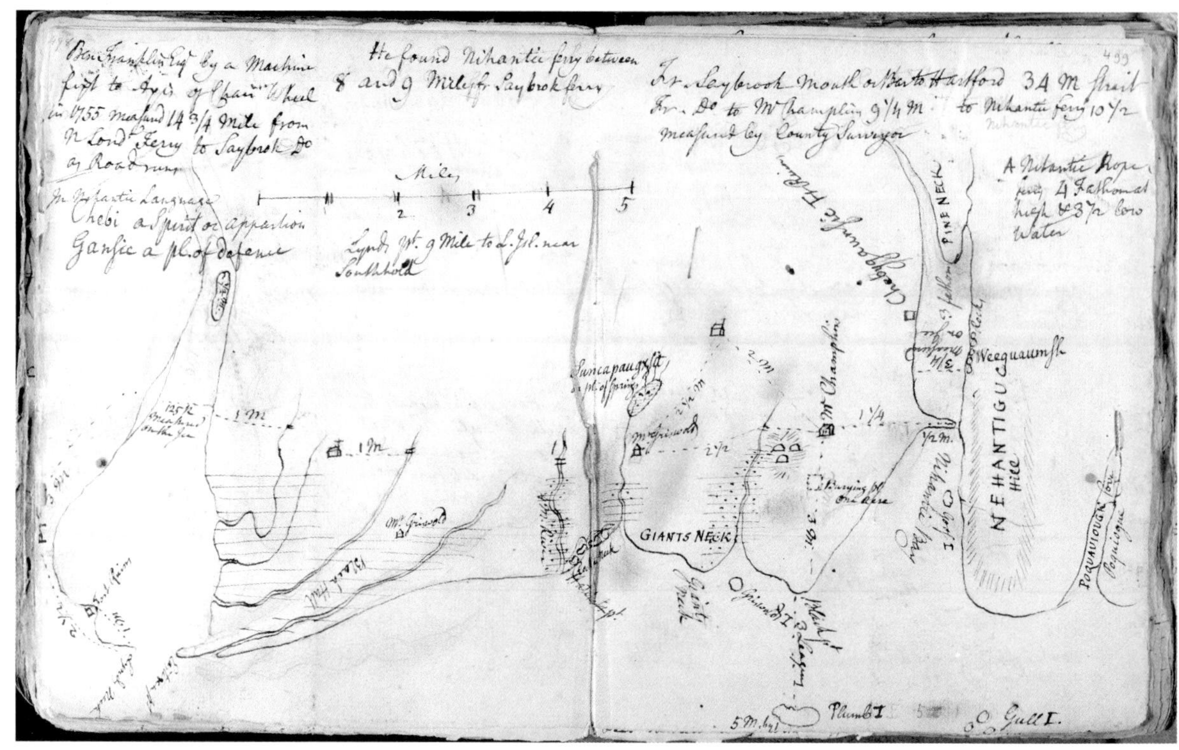

A detailed map of the Lyme shoreline drawn by Rev. Ezra Stiles located the meetinghouses in the west and east parishes, the houses of Matthew Griswold and George Griswald, and the wigwams and burying ground of the Niantics at Black Point.

The Court once again appointed a committee to "inquire into the wrongs complained of by said Indians," then specified boundaries and affirmed that "these shall always be and remain to be the bounds of the said Indian lands." Assured two years later in 1736 that "the said Niantic Indians desire their children may be instructed," the Court committed £15 from the public treasury to hire "some suitable person to instruct the said children to read, and also in the principles of the Christian religion." The next year Governor Joseph Talcott (1669–1741) confirmed that "our school of Indians at Niantic prospers."

In a letter published in the journal *Christian History* describing the Great Awakening's impact in Lyme's east parish, George Griswold reported in 1744 that religious concern among the Niantics had "increased for a considerable time." He described them as a "poor, ignorant people" who for ages past had lived "without God in the world" and "did not seem to have any thing of religion among them" but to be "generally given to Sabbath-breaking." But two rousing sermons delivered by the itinerant evangelist James Davenport (1716–1767) in 1741 had served as a catalyst for conversion. That year Parsons added the names of Nehemiah, Penelope, Hannah Jeffrey,

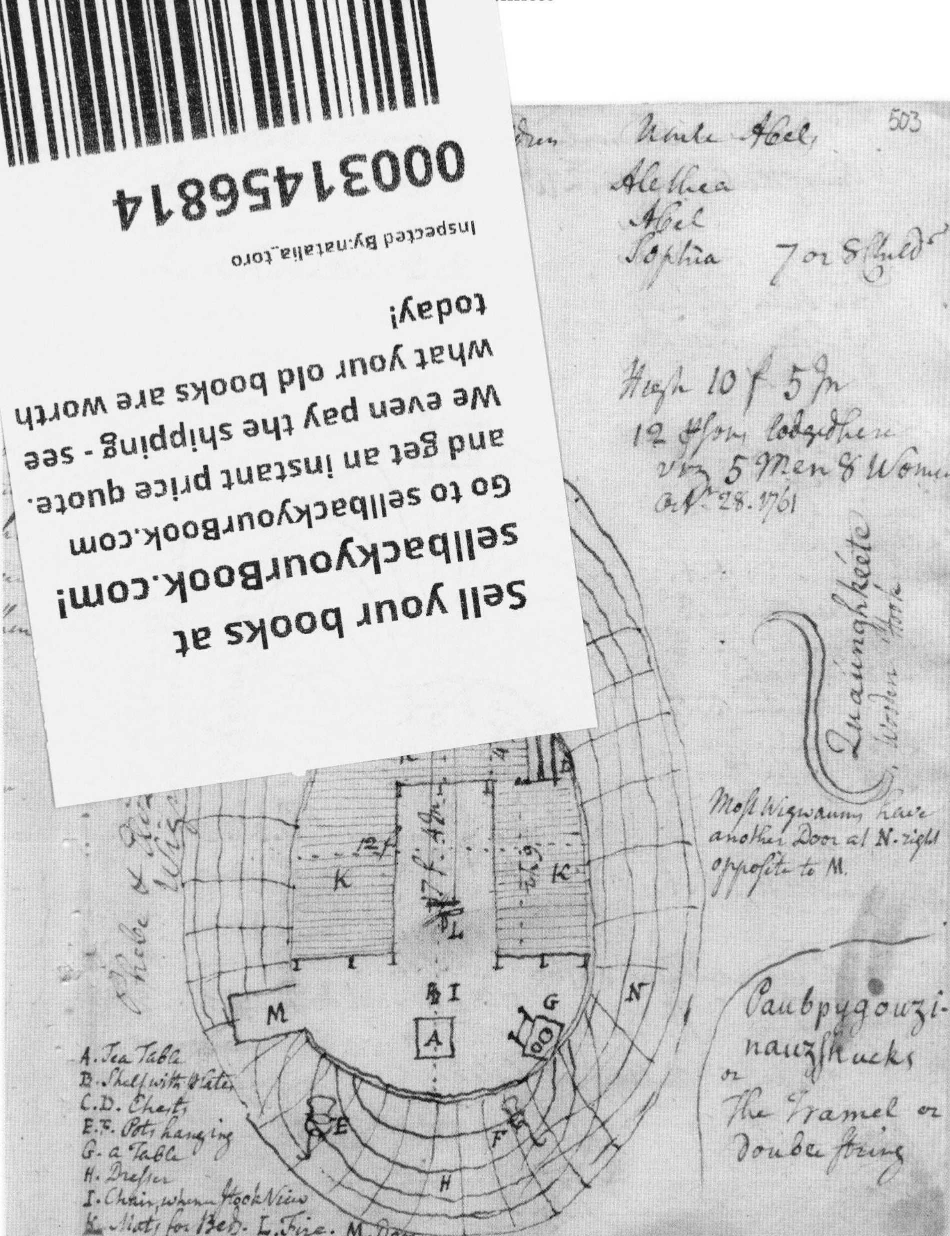

Ezra Stiles sketched the dome-shaped frame of Eliza and Phoebe Moheage's wigwam when he visited the Niantic reserve in 1761, and he described its earthen floor, central fire pit hearth, and raised platform for bedding and furnishings.

and Sarah Jeffrey to the baptismal list of Lyme's first church, and the following winter in the east parish "twenty or upward of this tribe of Indians," Griswold wrote, had been "hopefully converted." Some had reformed their "excessive drinking and Sabbath breaking," and there had been only "two or three instances of excess," which were followed by manifestations of "deep repentance."

To facilitate conversion, church members in the east parish made special accommodation for native customs in January 1744/5. After considering "the case of Ann Chesno, an Indian Woman," they voted "to admit her into the church without requiring a confession for putting away her Indian husband," agreeing that she had acted "according to the Indian law." That same year, when "Hannah Jeffrey, (Indian)" offered "a confession for the sin of drunkenness and laxity" in Parsons's west parish, it "was read and accepted" by Lyme's first church members. But by then, Griswold reported, "the great sense of divine things seem[ed] to be in a great measure abated among those Indians," and the school for native youth "had so little good effect, that it was given over."

When Scottish-born physician Dr. Alexander Hamilton (1712–1756) visited the Niantic reserve in 1744 while traveling on horseback through New England from Maryland to Maine, he noted in his diary seeing "thirteen or fourteen huts or wigwams made of bark" in "the Indian town of Niantique." The memorial from Lyme's ministers had reported thirty families of Indians in Niantic a decade earlier, but that number steadily declined. When Newport minister Rev. Ezra Stiles (1727–1795) visited the reserve in 1761,

Mercy Ann Nonsuch Matthews, shown here approaching age ninety, married in 1846 Henry Matthews, an accomplished Mohegan stonemason and basket maker who served as a deacon in the Mohegan church.

after the death of seven Niantic men serving with colonial troops in the French and Indian War, he counted "10 families besides 9 widows."

The population decline continued in the nineteenth century, and overseer Moses Warren (1762–1836) reported "less than thirty" Niantics left in 1825. The state passed a law "to protect the wood and lands of the Niantic Indians" in 1836, but thirty years later the population on the reserve had shrunk to nine. In 1870 the state declared the Niantics extinct and sold the three-hundred-acre tract on the Black Point peninsula. By then Mercy Ann Nonsuch (1822–1913), born on the reserve and "bound out" at age seven to the widowed Mrs. Ethelinda Caulkins Griswold (1778–1864), whose husband Thomas Griswold (1779–1817) was Rev. George Griswold's grandson, had married and lived elsewhere in a comfortable home surrounded by houseplants, a parlor organ, and two Bibles. "They may declare me extinct, that does not make me extinct," she said in 1871. "I am not extinct, I am not buried."

In 1858 Hartford artist Charles de Wolfe Brownell depicted the legendary rock ledge along the Connecticut River known as Joshua's Seat, part of an expanse of tribal land acquired by Richard Ely after the death of Attawanhood, called Joshua, in 1676.

WHITEFIEL

the celebrated Preacher, addressing one

that attended his m

Chapter thirteen

Great Danger

Inspired by the fervent message of a British evangelist who attracted rapt crowds on a tour of New England in 1740, Rev. Jonathan Parsons led a religious revival in Lyme that left his parish bitterly divided.

The parish is small, consisting of about 120 families, yet many days the past summer, I have had 20, 30, 40, 50, and sometimes 60 persons under deep concern with me in one day, inquiring the way to Zion. I hope since the 14th of May last, more than 140 souls have been savingly converted in this place. The same happy work has been carried on in the neighboring parishes of the town, especially one under the care of the Rev. Mr. Griswold, in a most wonderful manner.

Parsons's prayer and reflection during a period of mental struggle in his early ministry brought a sudden moment of revelation and, according to his grandson, an "undoubted alteration both in his doctrines and mode of preaching." After agonizing over his errors, the minister turned away from his Arminian beliefs and burned the sermons he had written in Lyme over the course of five years. An opportunity to hear British evangelist George Whitefield (1714–1770) preach in New Haven in 1740 accelerated his spiritual awakening. "The news of Mr. Whitefield's rising up with great zeal for holiness and souls, had great influence upon my mind," Parsons wrote.

George Whitefield, age twenty-six, enthralled crowds at each stop on his first New England tour, and news of his itinerary spread widely. When Nathan Cole (1711–1783), a farmer living near Hartford, learned that Mr. Whitefield would preach in Middletown, he dropped his farm tools in his field and rushed with his wife on horseback. "The land and banks over the [Connecticut] river looked black with people and horses all along the 12 miles," Cole wrote in his journal. "When I saw Mr. Whitefield come upon the scaffold he looked almost angelical; a young, slim, slender, youth before some thousands of people with a bold undaunted countenance." Although the

WHITEFIELD
the celebrated Preacher, addressing one of the numerous crowds
that attended his ministry.

Most of the portraits of George Whitefield in an album of engravings given to Charles Ludington in Old Lyme depict the celebrated evangelist in middle age with white wig and portly build, but one shows a slender, youthful preacher "addressing one of the numerous crowds that attended his ministry."

charismatic evangelist "came not by the way of Lyme," Parsons noted, his own parish members still became "more generally rous'd up to bethink themselves, and converse about religion."

More than a year later, in a letter to Rev. Benjamin Coleman (1673–1747), pastor of Boston's Brattle Street Church, Parsons praised the initial progress of the revival in his small parish of 120 families.

Describing the revival's "happy work," he reported in December 1741 that "20, 30, 40, 50, and sometimes 60 persons under deep concern" had met with him in a single day. Ecclesiastical Society records the previous year had already noted that "men and their wives" were seated together in the meetinghouse, and Parsons stated that "more than 140 souls have been savingly converted in this place."

Three years later he provided a more detailed account of the "very gracious revival of religion among us" in a letter to Rev. Thomas Prince (1687–1758) for publication in the recently launched revivalist newspaper *Christian History*. Calling attention to the "vast falsehoods that have been spread about the country respecting our opinions and practices in this place," Parsons asked that "you must suffer me to be a little more particular, than otherwise I would be." His second narrative, written in April 1744 and published in seven installments, opened with "some hints of the town, its settlement, &c. and my own settlement also." It recounted how his heart had "burned with love to and pity for the people of [his] peculiar charge" and how, believing them to be in "great danger," he had determined that his "errand" was "to lay open the state of their souls." He also expressed the hope that "above one hundred and eighty souls belonging to this congregation have met with a saving change."

Parsons emphasized again the frequency of gatherings in the meetinghouse. He described the rush of people who flocked to his study "daily and in great numbers, and deeply wounded," and noted that his sermons and prayer meetings held particular appeal for the town's youth. They had "left their sports, and grew sick of their youthful amusements," he wrote, but "some of middle age" had also appeared to be savingly converted. At a communion service in October 1741 when he "administered the sacrament of the Lord's Supper, to near 300 souls" amid many "signs of distress," some at the communion table had dissolved in tears, while others trembled in anguish.

Parsons detailed, in addition, the response to a sermon he had preached, in the manner he "thought proper to awaken and convince," to "a great

THE
Chriftian Hiftory,
CONTAINING
ACCOUNTS
OF THE
Revival *and* Propagation
OF
RELIGION
IN
GREAT-BRITAIN, AMERICA &c.
For the YEAR
1744.
BOSTON, N. E.
Printed by S. KNEELAND and T. GREEN,
for T. PRINCE, junr. 1745.

An announcement of the launch of *Christian History* in March 1743 promoted its "Authentic Accounts; from ministers and other creditable serious persons, of the revival of religion in the several parts of New-England." Subscriptions declined when the journal's firsthand accounts repeated similar details, and publication stopped two years later.

assembly" on Election Day in May 1741. The election of civic officials in the past had brought an occasion for "feasting, music, dancing, gaming, and the like," but during his lecture "some young women were thrown into hysteric fits." Many others "had their countenances changed," and "their thoughts seemed to trouble them, so that the joints of their loins were loosed, and their knees smote one against another." Overwhelmed by emotion, "great numbers cried out aloud in the anguish of their souls," and "several stout men fell as though a cannon had been discharged, and a ball had made its way through their hearts." After the sermon, "those that could not restrain themselves were generally carried out of the meetinghouse."

Displays of emotion had also greeted Parsons's labor "beyond the bounds" of his own parish, particularly in Norwich, Stonington, and Groton. When he preached to George Griswold's congregation in Lyme's east parish in May 1741, "the assembly in general, were in tears, and near one half, I suppose, crying out aloud in distress." Three years later when Parsons surveyed the achievements of the revival, he acknowledged that its fervent emotionalism had also provoked strong opposition. He mentioned the "unhappy case" of New London where "increased difficulties" had "produced an open separation" and where "Christians had such sharp contentions between them, as to part asunder from one another."

Nor had the "happy work" of the revival prevailed in Saybrook. There Rev. William Hart (1713–1784) in August 1741 had denied the use of his pulpit to Rev. James Davenport after the itinerant preacher declared Hart "unconverted." Parsons stated he had not known at the time that Mr. Davenport referred to the neighboring minister as unconverted. His *Christian History* report omitted mention of the impassioned sermon he delivered in Boston in 1742 defending Davenport after his arrest there for deliberately provocative preaching in the streets late at night. Also missing from the Lyme minister's

Wiſdom juſtified of her Children.

A

SERMON

Preached (in Part) at the publick Lecture in *Boſton*, on Thurſday Sept. 16. 1742.

By *Jonathan Parſons*, A.M.

And Miniſter of the Goſpel at *Lyme* in *Connecticut*.

Publiſhed at the Deſire of a Number of the Hearers.

Placet *Chriſto*, non Defectu Poteſtatis, ſed ex Abundantia Bonitatis ejus, in congregando Eccleſiam, cum Hominibus agere per Homines; Quibus res ſacras *ille* diſpenſat, et *Hæreſes* et *Hæreticos* repudiat. *Ezek.* iii. 17, 19.

BOSTON, Printed by *Rogers* and *Fowle* for *N. Procter* at the *Bible* and *Dove* in Fiſh-ſtreet. 1742.

Rev. Jonathan Parsons traveled to Boston in 1742 to deliver a sermon *Wisdom justified of her Children* defending the incendiary minister James Davenport, who had been jailed after his deliberately provocative preaching and his denunciation of fellow clergymen.

account was mention of Davenport's frenzied preaching in New London in 1743, when he exhorted followers to burn all books of history and theology, then urged them to create a sacrificial blaze and incinerate their worldly goods. "I greatly loved him for his eminent piety, but I can't justify all his measures," Parsons wrote, acknowledging that the itinerant preacher had "greatly prejudice[d] persons against religion."

In Lyme's north parish the great danger that concerned Rev. George Beckwith in August 1741 was not the problem of unsaved souls but the authorizing of anyone displaying a "divine impulse" to pass judgment on other brethren. In two strongly worded sermons Beckwith warned against following the "dictates of man's wild fancies" and denounced those "who usurped God's judgment and presumed to act in His place." A group from his congregation, together with a few from Parsons's west parish, funded the printing of the paired sermons. Influential among the contributors was Dr. Eleazar Mather (1716–1789), a Yale graduate and local physician who later quipped that Lyme had been favored during the Great Awakening "with the lights of several wandering stars, viz. traveling Tennant, singing Davenport . . . whining Whitefield."

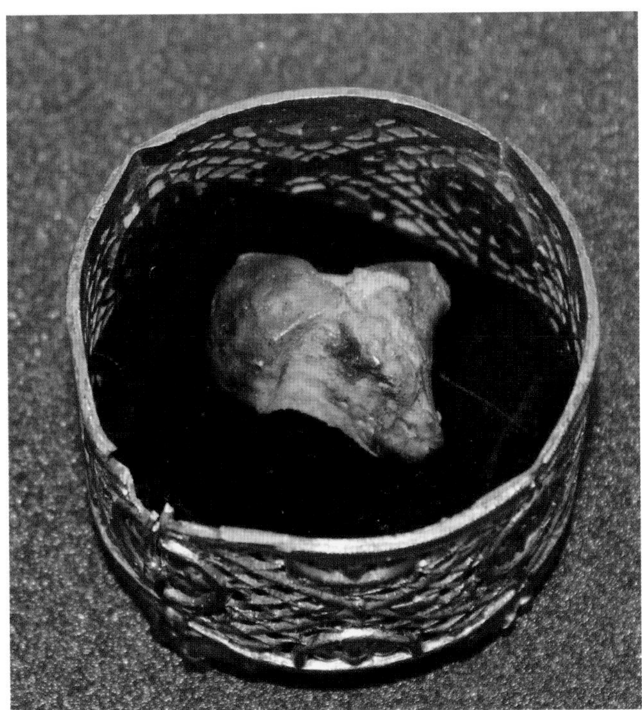

After George Whitefield died of chronic asthma in Newbury, he was interred in a crypt beneath the pulpit in Jonathan Parsons's church. Fervent admirers later removed pieces of his clothing and parts of his body, and today a glass case at the Methodist Center at Drew University displays what is said to be the famous evangelist's thumb.

By the time George Whitefield preached in Lyme's east parish in August 1745, sharp disagreements had long divided Parsons's church. On that return tour of New England, the British preacher traveled with his wife, and the *Boston Gazette* announced their planned appearances. It reported on August 20 that Mr. Whitefield "purposes to preach for the Rev. Mr. Griswold and Parsons of Lyme, and then go over to Long-Island," but the itinerary seems to have changed. Joshua Hempstead heard the visiting revivalist preach in Groton on August 10 and the next day went out "to Lyme East Society to hear Mr. Whitefield once more." His diary notes that Mrs. Whitefield on August 11 passed "thro New London near night to go to Lyme" in "a Shays & Chair & 2 horses besides, 4 in all," and that the couple lodged that night at the home of Solomon Miner (1713–1754), near Niantic's rope ferry. They then left for Long Island "& so to New York and Georgia." Had Whitefield also preached to Parsons's congregation, Joshua Hempstead almost certainly would have mentioned such a noteworthy appearance.

By then Whitefield had received continuing criticism in sermons, pamphlets, and press reports and chose not to appear in parishes where his message was not enthusiastically welcomed. Opposition to the revival in Parsons's troubled church would result in the minister's departure from Lyme in October, two months after Whitefield preached in the east parish. The controversial evangelist appears to have limited his preaching in Lyme to George Griswold's church, but a story about his address to a crowd from a rock in a field adjacent to Parsons's home nevertheless became inscribed in local lore. Today a low granite outcropping beside Old Lyme's fifth meetinghouse is alleged to be the site of a sermon by Whitefield.

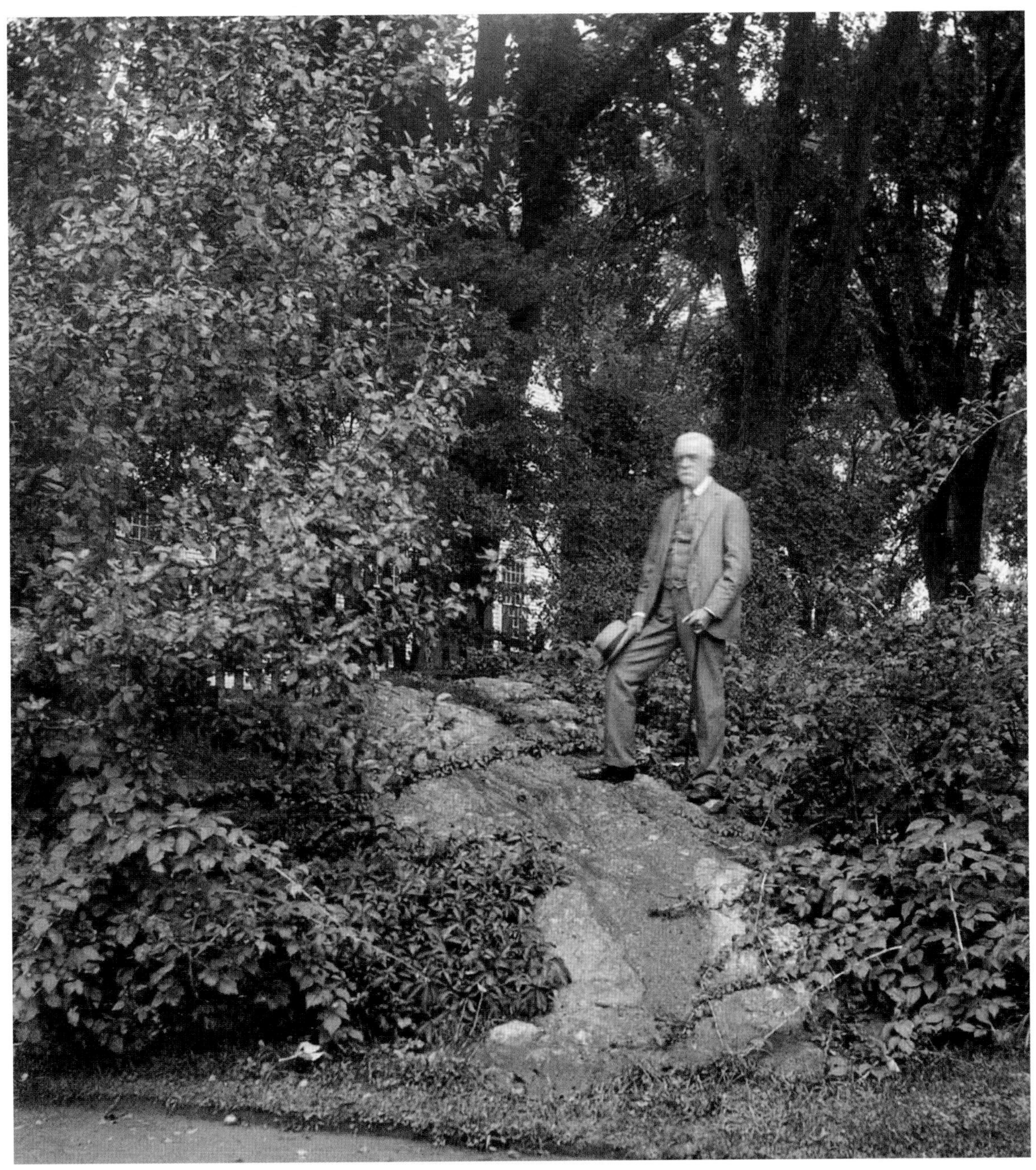

Charles Ludington posed ca. 1905 on the rock in his side garden in Old Lyme where George Whitefield was said to have preached to a large audience.

Wiſdom juſtified of her Children.

A

SERMON

Preached (in Part) at the publick Lecture in *Boſton*, on Thurſday Sept. 16. 1742.

By *Jonathan Parſons*, A.M.

And Miniſter of the Goſpel at *Lyme* in *Connecticut*.

Publiſhed at the Deſire of a Number of the Hearers.

CHAPTER FOURTEEN

Scandalous Reports

When the departure of Jonathan Parsons did not resolve the bitter divisions in Lyme's first church, a council of New London County clergymen sought to restore harmony in the meetinghouse.

Tis with regret of mind that we are obliged to treat a number of our brethren as offenders, but after much patience used and much pains taken to convince them of their ill conduct, they still continue to disturb the peace of this church by scandalous and false reports and unenforceable articles of complaint against the Reverend Jonathan Parsons and this church, tending unjustly to blemish the character of Mr. Parsons and this church & greatly injure the interests of religion in this place.

Voices in Lyme's meetinghouse were never more clamorous than during the Great Awakening. Near the end of his letter to Thomas Prince in 1744, Parsons noted "that there have been many things amiss." He wrote of "evil surmisings and perverse disputings" and denounced those who had "born false witness against the glorious work" of the revival. That disputing did not end with his removal to Newbury, and a year later his wife's brother Matthew Griswold (1714–1799), age thirty-two and an accomplished lawyer, defended him before a council of four New London County ministers reviewing the "sundry difficulties subsisting between this church and five of the brethren of the same church." Protesting the unjust blemishing of Parsons's character, Matthew Griswold lamented in September 1746 the great injury to "the interests of religion in this place"

The stridently opposed views in Lyme's west parish had erupted in 1743 after Deacon Marvin publicly denounced local mill owner Edmund Dorr (1693–1772), long an officeholding church member. Pointing his finger at Dorr, Marvin declared him no more a Christian "than any Indian in Niantic." The insult brought Edmund Dorr's protest in the meetinghouse that Marvin was "a censurable defamer," but church members supporting the minister insisted the deacon's offense "would not amount to a censurable evil." Captain Timothy Mather (1681–1755), age sixty-two and Rev. Moses Noyes's son-in-law, then assembled a fifteen-point complaint together with Edmund Dorr and three others and "publish[ed] the same in this town."

The document signed by the "Five Brethren" criticized the deacon's "insufferable arrogance." It also complained of Parsons's refusal to quiet the "crying out and talking" that had greatly disturbed those assembled for worship and the "rash judging and unchristian censuring

[that] have prevailed among us like an epidemical distemper." Circulation of the complaint followed Deacon Marvin's reiteration of his insult at a church meeting held in the minister's house. There, "in the face of said church in the solemn meeting," the deacon had again called Dorr an "unconverted creature" and declared he had "no reason to think him as a Christian." The conflict grew so heated that Parsons in November 1744 announced his desire for "liberation from said church." Members voted "to release said pastor," but Parsons deferred his departure in case the difficulties could be "made up."

The controversy that split apart Lyme's church drew the attention of a visitor. When Dr. Alexander Hamilton traveled through New England in August 1744 accompanied by his enslaved servant Dromo, he waited several hours at the house of Timothy Mather for ferry passage across the Connecticut River. He described in his diary "the opinions lately discussed here in religion." Noting that he found his host, who "condemned Whitefield's conduct in these parts very much," to be "a man of some solidity and sense," he expressed no patience for a group of townsfolk that arrived after dinner. Hearing them argue with little knowledge about opposing "points of religion," Dr. Hamilton compared them to "a rabble of clowns."

For another two years complaints and counter-complaints fed the controversy in Parsons's parish. Church members supporting the minister appointed a committee to denounce the Five Brethren's accusations and "demand satisfaction of Edmund Dorr for certain rash and slanderous expressions." When Dorr refused to retract his accusations, opposing members of the church invited a council of eight ministers to "prosecute its complaint." Not until October 1745 did the disputing factions agree to select a council of mutually chosen ministers to evaluate the "difficulties that do subsist between them" and to

Amid bitter controversy between "sundry aggrieved brethren" and the First Church in Lyme, "J. Parsons Pastor" recorded the decision that Deacon Renold Marvin need not withdraw from communion while church members "advise & consider further what shall be done."

a Qtn put to ye first Chh in Lyme, June 13. 1744. at a Meeting of ye Pastr & Chh, Viz. Whither ye Chh desire Deacn Reynold Marvin to withdraw from ye Communion, untill they can advise & consider further what shall be done respecting his insisting upon being present when Judgment is made up by ye Chh in his Case now laid before ye Chh.
& voted in ye Negative
a true Copy of a Qtn proposd to ye first Chh in Lyme, taken from Record Test J. Parsons Pastor

In this "old Mather house" torn down ca. 1885, a traveling Maryland physician learned in 1744 about disputes in Lyme's meetinghouse during the Great Awakening.

"advise, respecting the liberation of the Rev. Mr. Parsons from his pastoral charge of this church." The embattled minister left Lyme two weeks later.

For a year no entries appeared in church records, and the terms of the minister's release from his pastoral charge were not noted. His own account, according to his grandson, explained that the "contention became at length so sharp, that at his own request he was dismissed from his pastoral charge, by the advice of a council, in October, 1745," and left "by the advice of Mr. Whitefield." Rev. Ezra Stiles later noted that the "N. Lond. Consociation formerly dismissed Mr. Parsons of Lyme against Will of his Church." By then, nineteen dissident members of Newbury's established church, which Rev. Moses Noyes's father helped found more than a century earlier, had invited Parsons to serve as pastor of a new congregation. "I came to visit," Lyme's former minister wrote, "and as I thought the doctrines of Christ were run down in this part of the land . . . I did, by great importunity, consent to abide with them."

Not everyone in Newbury importuned Parsons to settle in January 1745/6, and his arrival caused "considerable opposition," along with efforts "to ascertain from the church at Lyme, Conn., the truth or falsity of some statements that had been circulated in regard to his theological views." Edmund Dorr had sent a letter in December to his family's minister in Roxbury, Rev. Nehemiah Walter (1663–1750), an influential voice among Boston-area clergy, to convey the Five Brethren's criticisms, but members of Newbury's small separated congregation ignored the opposition. At an installation ceremony in March 1746, Parsons pledged with uplifted hand, "I take this people to be my people."

The Mutual Council of clergymen that convened in Lyme's meetinghouse six months later heard opposing arguments, then distributed blame. It found that some of the Five Brethren's complaints could not be supported and that Edmund Dorr was guilty of "scandalous reflections." It also judged that Deacon Marvin had "great fault," and the church had erred in failing to censure him. In a plea for unity, the council urged Lyme's first church members "to forgive one another & bury all past offences, and embrace each other in Christian love."

Benj. Franklin Esq. by a Machine fixt to Axis of Chair Wheel in 1755 measured 14 3/4 Mile from N London Ferry to Saybrok Do as Road runs

He found Nihe 8 and 9 Miles fr.

Miles

1 2 3

In Nepantic Language
Chebi a Spirit or Apparition
Gansic a pl. of defence

Lynds Pt. 9 Mile to Southhold

1/2 M.

125 R measured on the Ice

1 M

1 M

Mr Griswold

Black Hall

Fort Grim

1 M

CHAPTER FIFTEEN

Difficulties among Ourselves

An agreement not to speak about past difficulties temporarily silenced the controversy in Lyme's meetinghouse, but old resentments lingered and new scandals loomed.

To prevent present difficulties among ourselves . . . we agree under our present circumstances to leave matters as they are, and say no more about them at present.

Lyme's church members agreed to ignore their differences when they invited Stephen Johnson (1724–1786), age twenty-two, to settle as Gospel minister. The Ecclesiastical Society had voted in May 1746 to apply to the New London Council "for advice concerning a minister to supply the pulpit in its present vacancy" and on the council's recommendation had asked Mr. Johnson to "preach the gospel to this Society for some Sabbaths in order for settlement." A Yale graduate from an established family in Newark, New Jersey, the candidate had recently married Elizabeth Diodati (1722–1761), daughter of a prosperous banker and broker in New Haven who "dealt in coin and plate." Three weeks before Johnson's ordination in December, church members agreed in the meetinghouse that "to prevent present difficulties among ourselves," they would not mention prior conflicts.

Commercial activity in Lyme expanded during Johnson's early ministry as the town's infrastructure developed. Richard Mather (1712–1790) and Elisha Sheldon (1709–1779), successful merchants and frequent officeholders in the Ecclesiastical Society, built a new wharf in 1751 near the toll bridge crossing the Lieutenant River. The town had recently rebuilt the bridge, which Dr. Hamilton noted in 1744 was "in very bad repair," and had made it "wide enough for a cart bridge." The town also constructed a ferry wharf and replaced the passenger ferry, and postal surveyors inspecting the mail route from New York to Boston in 1753 installed stone mile markers measuring the distance from the meetinghouse and the ferry to the active customhouse port of New London. Among those attracted to the developing town was the enterprising Scots-Irish immigrant John McCurdy (1724–1785), who

Scene on Lieutenant River, Lyme, Conn.
W. F. Clark

Today the banks of the Lieutenant River are valued for their scenic vistas and the tidal marshes that offer habitats for birds and marine life, but in 1750 this tributary of the Connecticut River served as an important local transportation route. Its wharves, warehouses, and shipyards had long disappeared when W. F. Clark's general store sold this postcard in 1910.

integrated himself into the local community by marrying in 1752 the youngest daughter of Judge Richard Lord. Four years later Lyme, with a census count of 2,762 whites, 100 Negroes, and 94 Indians, ranked fourteenth in population among Connecticut towns.

Difficulties in the parish did not resolve after the Great Awakening, and those who had withdrawn from the first church after Jonathan Parsons's departure continued to "set up a worship by themselves in opposition," despite "repeated pains" by the new minister. A committee accompanying Rev. Johanson used additional arguments "to convince said brethren of their unwarranted and sinful practice in separating and making a schism." The committee used "like arguments and endeavors with the sisters in the church in like circumstances," but the separated members, including the outspoken former deacon Renold Marvin, refused to "return to their duty."

Stephen Johnson had preached for a decade when Matthew Griswold suddenly raised again the disputes of the previous ministry. Church records curiously include two versions of a complaint he submitted objecting to the letter Edmund Dorr had sent more than a decade earlier to Rev. Nehemiah Walter in Roxbury. The longer entry notes in March 1757 Dorr's demand that

Griswold produce the original letter rather than a copy. After church members "maturely considered" the pleas of both parties, they decided "the copy exhibited [was] not sufficient for them to admit the proofs upon, desired by the complainant."

The record book does not reveal why Jonathan Parsons's brother-in-law chose that moment to recall earlier controversies, but the Great Awakening's conflicts had recently been revisited in an unsigned letter. The letter writer, who claimed to be "considerably acquainted with the difficulties Mr. Parsons met with while he lived in Connecticut," denounced the "mean and wicked artifices that were used to render him vile in the sight of the world." The anonymous letter, which appeared in print in Boston in 1757, insisted that Lyme's former minister had

Rev. Stephen Johnson's house stood alongside the "highway" that crossed Meetinghouse Hill to connect Lyme with New London. This "old Johnson house" would be demolished soon after the photograph was taken ca. 1930.

proceeded judiciously throughout the difficulties and scandals that disrupted his church.

By then a more immediate scandal loomed. Rumors circulated that on Election Day in 1756 Stephen Johnson had engaged in adultery with a neighbor, Hannah Lay (1720–1784), wife of town clerk John Lay Jr. (1714–1792), a prominent Ecclesiastical Society member. Uriah Roland, a representative to the legislature two years earlier and recently clerk of the Society, made the adultery accusation public in 1758. Johnson declared the charge false and denounced Roland for trying to "blacken, ruin, & defame . . . his good name, fame, & credit & to put him out of his ministry." After he also sued his accuser for defamation, the case played out in public view over two years in the county and superior courts.

The New London court summoned for testimony a cluster of influential church members and two enslaved servants. While Johnson's supporters indignantly defended the minister's reputation, Mr. Lay's servant Charles London told the court in 1759 that he had seen his mistress with the minister naked on a bed. The court found Uriah Roland guilty of defamation but awarded Johnson only a fraction of the damages he requested. After the minister appealed, the superior court upheld the verdict but did not increase the compensation. A month later Lyme voters reelected Roland to Connecticut's legislature, but he was then excluded from serving, replaced by Matthew Griswold.

Contentious meetings in the first parish that year considered the "unhappy difficulties subsisting between said Mr. Johnson and some of this society," then sought to "agree on terms of reconciliation, if possible." The appointment of a committee "to inquire into the grounds of the reports spread concerning the Reverend Mr. Stephen Johnson" prompted a "solemn protest" read in the meetinghouse. That lengthy statement, likely written by Matthew Griswold, repudiated the "vile reports which appear to be groundless and maliciously spread and carry a vile reflection

Stephen Johnson's corner "roundabout" chair, fashioned by an unknown cabinetmaker, stands today behind the pulpit in Old Lyme's fifth meetinghouse.

on Mr. Johnson, as though he was not sufficient to manage his own private affairs and is the more injurious as Mr. Johnson has been grossly injured & abused in them, [and] has put himself under the protection of the law that he might vindicate his innocence and seek redress."

As the controversy continued, the Society appointed another committee in January 1760 to confer with the minister about calling "a proper Ecclesiastical Council to consider and advise whether it be not most likely to preserve the interests of religion that the said Mr. Johnson be dismissed from his pastoral charge in this place." The committee was tasked with making a report "of their doings" at the Society's next meeting, but a one-year gap in the record book followed, and the resolution reached with the minister is not known. Johnson ended his efforts to recover additional damages in 1762 after Uriah Roland's death and later that year married as his second wife an accomplished widow from Gardiners Island, Mary Gardiner Blague (1714–1772).

By the time Stephen Johnson spoke out boldly in the press in 1765 in support of colonial liberty, the controversy over his fitness to serve as Gospel minister in Lyme had subsided. His friend Rev. William Gordon (1728–1807), pastor of Roxbury's third church, later praised his patriotic defiance in words that obliquely recalled the minister's personal difficulties. "The Rev. Mr. Stephen Johnson of Lyme," Gordon wrote, "vexed and grieved with the temper and inconsiderateness of all orders of people, determined if possible to rouse them to a better way of thinking."

... on a Sense over Bre-
thren, that this is a melancholy
& alarming Truth I trust the
e all pretty fully convinced.
e did indeed hope better things
long as ~~[struck out]~~ any Place for
pe was found. But lamentable
perience has shewn that all our
pes were without Foundation.
Flames of war have already
gun to rage with merciless
ury in a neighbouring Province
I have already repeatedly re-
ived the unwelcome News of
e confused Noise of the Warri-
& of Garments rolled in Blood.
bers of our Brethren slain & wounded in the Field, &
st Numbers have been oblig'd
leave their houses & their For-

Chapter sixteen

Slavery or Independence

Rev. Stephen Johnson published in 1765 a series of bold letters in a New London newspaper after Britain imposed new taxes on its American colonies, then delivered a forceful fast-day sermon warning that the impending calamities posed the dire alternative of slavery or independence.

The calamities which impend over us, and which we are now to deplore and deprecate, are the heaviest the churches and inhabitants of this land have ever felt, from any earthly power, and threaten (in our apprehension) no less than slavery and ruin to this great people, in this widely extended continent. . . . In short, if there be left to the colonies but this single, this dreadful alternative,—slavery or independency,—they will not want time to deliberate which to choose.

A decade before the first shots were fired in the American Revolution, Rev. Stephen Johnson, age forty-one, warned of the dangers ahead. In December 1765, on a day reserved by Connecticut's General Assembly for fasting and prayer, he preached a sermon urging legislators to defend their liberty. His fast-day sermon described the "shocking ill effects and terrible consequences" that would result from "the enslaving of a free people."

Britain's imposition of new colonial taxes had roused strong opposition in Connecticut. With the Stamp Act pending in Parliament and hostility to British authority mounting, Rev. Naphtali Daggett (1727–1780), a Yale professor of divinity and later the college president, published under the pen name "Cato" a widely circulated letter in the *New London Gazette* in August 1765, denouncing stamp tax collectors in the colonies. A month later Lyme's minister, likely encouraged by the urgent anti-British views of Scots-Irish merchant John McCurdy, followed Daggett's example. Johnson used the name "Addison" when he published in the *Gazette* on September 6 the first of six anonymous letters overtly encouraging opposition to British authority. "My dear

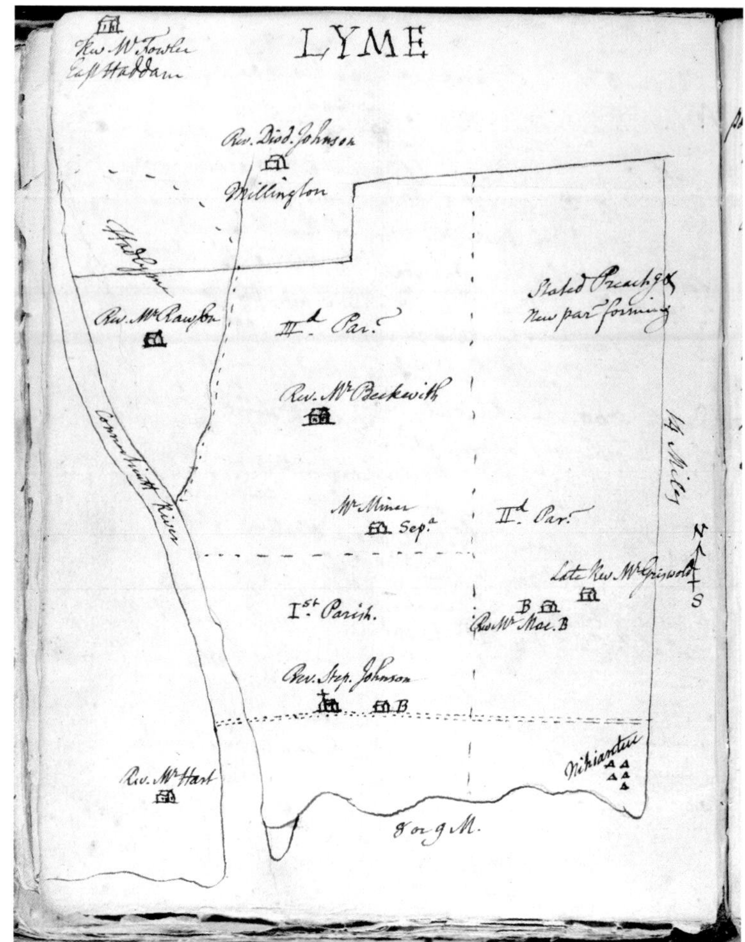

A map of Lyme's parishes drawn by Rev. Ezra Stiles in 1768 locates Lyme's meetinghouses during Rev. Stephen Johnson's ministry. It also shows two Baptist churches, a separatist church in the third parish, and the wigwams of the Niantics in the second parish.

friends," he declared, "it is the most critical season that ever this colony or America saw, a time when every thing dear to us in this world is at stake."

Insisting on the colonists' right to economic and political freedom, Lyme's minister anticipated a future need for armed resistance. "If the B——sh Parliament have right to impose a Stamp Act," he wrote, "they have a right to lay on us a poll tax, a land tax, and why not tax us for the light of the sun, the air we breathe, and the ground we are buried in?" A month later, on October 4, he asked, "Do not those measures tend to a very fatal Civil War? I hope, in the mercy of God, things may never be pushed to this bloody, this dreadful, issue!"

Passions had already flared in Lyme in August when the local Sons of Liberty staged a mock trial for the Connecticut colony's stamp tax collector Jared Ingersoll (1722–1781). According to a report in the same issue of the *Gazette* that published Johnson's initial letter, the Sons accused "the Stampman" of "treachery to his country," then pronounced him guilty before "the good people of the colony" and dragged his effigy through the street. The political theater ended with a public hanging and a "funeral ceremony performed by the blacks in the place," which brought "a universal satisfaction in the countenances of all present."

A political cartoon engraved by Paul Revere shows a stamp collector's effigy dangling from an elm tree near the Boston Common in August 1765. That same month Lyme's Sons of Liberty dragged a likeness of Connecticut's "Stampman" Jared Ingersoll behind a cart, hanged it from a fifty-foot gallows, and buried it in a funeral ceremony "performed by the blacks in the place."

Most if not all "blacks in the place" remained enslaved in 1765, but Johnson's defense of the God-given gift of liberty ignored those held in bondage. By then he had baptized fourteen enslaved people in the meetinghouse—six owned by Matthew Griswold. The same issue of the *Gazette* that published his first letter and reported the Stampman's fate also advertised a slave for sale in New London: "To be sold. A likely Negro boy, about 13 years of age, has been in the country about twelve months, speaks pretty good English. Enquire of the Printer."

Five years later when Johnson delivered a sermon in Hartford on Election Day in 1770, he warned citizens only briefly about being "reduced to abject slavery." With his friend Matthew Griswold serving as Connecticut's deputy governor, his topic was the importance of civic virtues at a time when liberty was threatened. His sermon, *Integrity and Piety the Best Principles of a Good Administration of Government*, elaborated on the need for governance based on the "spirit of righteousness," but it also urged a sense of responsibility among the clergy. "Is there not an important service which we owe to the state, to the support of government, and to the welfare of our country," he asked. "To us it belongs to cry aloud and spare not to shew them their transgressions."

Rev. William Gordon later noted that once "the eyes of the public began to open, and fears were excited," Stephen Johnson stepped back from political controversy, and "other writers engaged in the business." Personal circumstances may have contributed to his changing focus. His wife, Mary Blague Johnson, died in 1772, leaving two young children from his second marriage; and his eldest son, Rev. Diodate Johnson (1745–1773), a Yale graduate for whom he had preached an ordination sermon in nearby Millington, died the next year at age twenty-eight. Although other New England clergymen like Rev. Samuel Hopkins (1721–1803) in Newport began to "cry aloud" about human bondage, Stephen Johnson remained silent. "For shame," Rev. Nathaniel Niles (1741–1828) declared in Boston in 1774 in a *Discourse on Liberty*. "Let us either cease to enslave our fellow men, or else let us cease to complain of those that would enslave us."

As antislavery sentiment spread in New London County, Rev. Levi Hart (1738–1809), a Yale graduate ordained a decade earlier in Preston, denounced the hypocrisy of calling for liberty while holding other human beings in servitude. "Is it not high time for this colony to wake up," he asked in a sermon delivered in Farmington,

For a portrait by Newport artist Samuel King in 1770, Ezra Stiles held a "preaching Bible" and posed in a "Teaching Attitude." He included as background "Books to [his] Taste" and a medallion of his own design that conveyed his erudition.

"and put an effectual stop to the cruel business of stealing and selling our fellow men?" A letter to the *Norwich Packet* had recently denounced those who opposed political bondage while ignoring conditions of human servitude. Addressing "all you who call yourselves Sons of Liberty in America," the anonymous writer asked: "Are we not guilty of the same crime we impute to others?" Signing his letter "Honesty," he warned: "How preposterous our conduct! How vain and hypocritical our pretenses! Can we expect to be free, so long as we are determined to enslave?"

Support for slave owning had not diminished in Lyme's first parish, and Deputy Governor Matthew Griswold had advised Rhode Island's governor Joseph Wanton (1705–1780) the previous year that slaves who considered themselves illegally held in bondage deserved "to have a day in court," even though such proceedings were "not greatly favored in law by people of consideration" in Connecticut. "Negroes who have been manumitted in this Colony," Griswold wrote in 1773, were "ignorant of the art of honest living," and freed slaves had "frequently become strowling vagrants, united with thieves & burglars & proved very troublesome and dangerous inhabitants." Although few in Lyme had emancipated their servants, Mrs. Mary Noyes Ely (1705–1773), widow of William Ely Jr., made provision that year for Warwick (1723–1793), after her death, to be "free to be his own man to all intent and purposes." In 1773 she bequeathed to her "Negro man for forty years" a cow, a calf, a sow, and two small pigs "to be his own estate for ever."

Stephen Johnson never addressed the contradictions of slavery, but a letter he wrote from Lyme in 1774 to the national synod of Presbyterian churches suggests his awareness of the clergy's growing concern. His letter asked that a bequest from his recently deceased son Diodate be used "for propagating the gospel in the southern colonies." At the same meeting his friend Rev. Ezra Stiles, together with Rev. Samuel Hopkins, presented to the assembled delegates a request about "taking negro missionaries to Africa . . . in consequence of which the question of negro slavery came to be considered."

The census count in 1774 showed more people enslaved in Connecticut than in any other New England colony, with almost a third living in New London County. In Lyme the census listed 3,860 whites, 124 Negroes, and 104 Indians and provided the aggregate number of 228 "total blacks" in town. The size of the colony's enslaved population led the legislature to ban the future importation of "Indian, Negro or Molatto Slaves." The ruling in October 1774 noted that "the increase of slaves in this Colony is injurious to the poor and inconvenient."

Winnsimit
Penny Ferry
n. Putnam's Camp
Part of Winter Hill
Charles Town
Ferry Boat
Phipps's Farm
BOSTON
Castle
Dorchester Neck
Roxbury Hill
Dorchester

Chapter seventeen

Revolutionary Chaplain

Rev. Stephen Johnson took leave from his pastoral duties in Lyme to serve for six months as chaplain for a Connecticut regiment camped in Roxbury and during that interval courted his third wife.

At the same meeting voted that this Society consent that the Reverend Mr. Stephen Johnson accept of the appointment of the General Assembly to be chaplain to Col. S. M. Parsons' regiment.

At the start of the Revolutionary War, news of fighting in Lexington reached Lyme at one o'clock in the morning on April 21, 1775, when an express rider passed through town. Later that day sixty local militiamen led by Captain Joseph Jewett (1732–1776) marched to Boston in response to the Lexington alarm. A week later Connecticut's legislature confirmed in a special session that "sundry acts of hostility and violence have lately been committed in the Province of the Massachusetts Bay, by which many lives have been lost, and that some of the inhabitants of this Colony are gone to the relief of the people distressed." Urgent military preparations included the appointment of Samuel Holden Parsons as colonel of the Sixth Regiment and approval of Rev. Stephen Johnson, age fifty, as chaplain. Ten days later Lyme's Ecclesiastical Society granted its minister leave and appointed a committee to supply the pulpit during his absence.

The company that Colonel Parsons personally commanded included some one hundred foot soldiers, mostly farm boys from Lyme. Dispatched from New London in mid-June, they marched rapidly through Norwich and Providence and reached Boston, according to Private John Ely (1758–1847), age seventeen, on June 18, "the next day after the battle of Bunker Hill." Private Ely later recalled in a pension application that the company had encamped "on the high grounds of Roxbury, the smoking ruins of Charlestown lying there before us." He described being "on the lines in Roxbury" and initially "terrified with the noise of cannon balls flying over and the bursting of shells." Three days after their arrival, Colonel Parsons sent news to his wife that only

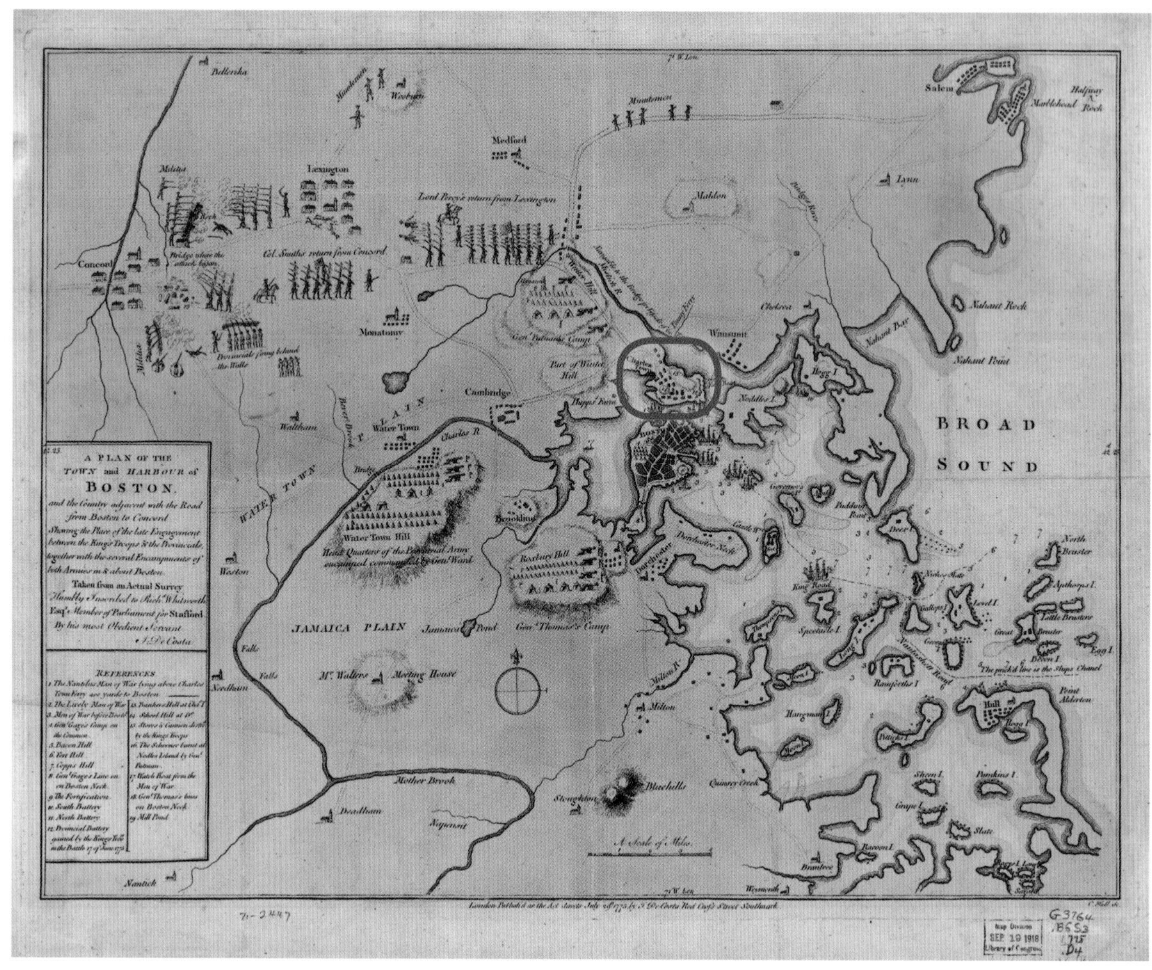

A British “Plan of the Town and harbour of Boston” indicated the strategic importance of the elevated land called “Bunkers Hill” at Charlestown and the proximity of British troops to the camp at Roxbury where Stephen Johnson served in 1775 as chaplain of Connecticut’s Sixth Regiment. The map also located “Mr. Walters Meeting House” in Jamaica Plain.

one private in his company, John Saunders from Lyme, had been wounded in their first engagement. He assured her that he intended to keep their son Willie (1762–1802), age thirteen and the company’s fifer, “out of danger if I can.”

Stephen Johnson’s name does not appear on the list of those who marched from Lyme or among the regimental officers that John Ely remembered from the early encampment at Roxbury. An unsigned sermon titled *A Discourse for a Fast*, possibly written in Johnson’s hand and preached at Milford, Connecticut, on July 20, 1775, may confirm that he had not yet left for Boston. The sermon, discovered among the papers of

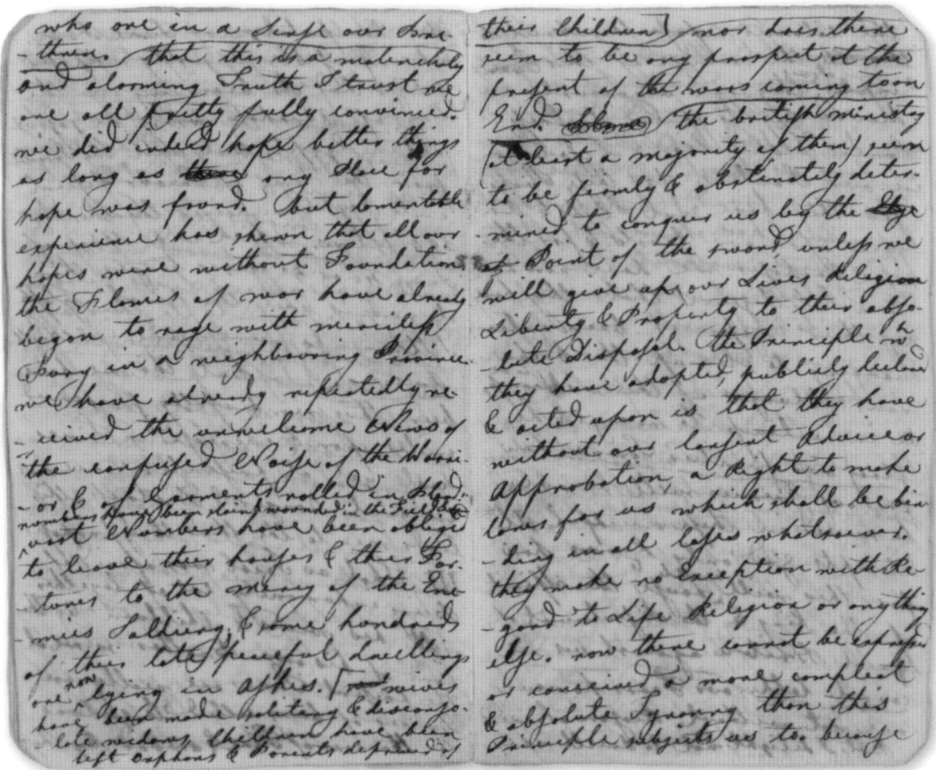

An unsigned sermon, possibly written by Rev. Stephen Johnson, warned in 1775 that the British seem "determined to conquer us by the point of the sword, unless we will give up our lives, religion, liberty & property to their absolute disposal." A pencil note reveals that Enoch Noyes loaned the sermon for display at Lyme's Centennial Exhibition at the Pierpont Hotel a century later.

Johnson's son-in-law Rev. Matthew Noyes (1764–1839), suggests the urgent voice of Lyme's minister when it describes the recent "danger & distress." It laments that "the flames of war have already begun to rage with merciless fury in a neighboring province" and that "numbers have been slain & wounded in the field & vast numbers have been obliged to leave their houses & their fortunes to the mercy of the enemies' soldiery." It concludes by praising God that "hitherto he has evidently helped us & smiled before us under our present calamities." A note in pencil confirms the importance of the Revolutionary-era sermon to later Lyme residents. It states that Enoch Noyes (1789–1877), a nephew of Rev. Matthew Noyes and his wife Mary Johnson Noyes (1768–1851), loaned the fast-day sermon for the "Centennial Exhibition, Old Lyme, 1876."

Stephen Johnson was "in camp at Roxbury" on October 6, 1775, when he wrote to Deputy Governor Matthew Griswold about improving conditions. "The camp more healthy," he wrote. "Have lost by sickness but 6 men out of our regiment." Two months later, after a half-year

Local tradition claims that George Washington slept at John McCurdy's house when he stopped in Lyme en route from Boston to New York in April 1776. A photograph of the McCurdy house shows improvements made almost a century later in 1866 when men, pulleys, and oxen moved the aging dwelling back from the street.

term of enlistment, the chaplain received a military discharge along with others in Colonel Parsons's company. No further details of his military service have been found, but letters written from Lyme the following spring make clear that while in Roxbury he courted his third wife, Abigail Leverett (1730–1817), age forty-five, the granddaughter of a Massachusetts governor and daughter of a wealthy Boston silversmith and merchant.

The minister's correspondence with Mistress Leverett preserves his personal voice. On April 16, 1776, he wrote to explain his delay in setting a marriage date. General George Washington had passed through Lyme a week earlier, following the British withdrawal from Boston, and the minister waited to learn "the effect of the application of the General and field officers for me to join the regiment and attend service in the Army this campaign." At an Ecclesiastical Society meeting that "lasted till late," he wrote, Colonel Parsons had "solicited them for another meeting to clear my way," but "they declined it." He thus saw "nothing at present in the way but we may proceed on as we proposed," and he would "like to come and have the matter completed."

Impatient in Lyme three weeks later, Johnson urged that they move ahead with their plans despite Mistress Leverett's lingering illness. "I have received Mr. [William] Gordon's [letter] informing of the continuance of your indisposition," he wrote on May 8, "for which I was sorry on your account and my own, as it renders me somewhat doubtful what to do." Reminding her that he could not leave his "pulpit unsupplied &c. &c.," he encouraged her to join him in Lyme before the heat of summer. "A long journey moderately pursued I think most likely to confirm your health, especially when attended with good and agreeable company &c." Aware that she hesitated about travel over difficult roads, he wrote at length about his effort to find a suitable carriage. He would have chosen one of the "good and cheap ones in Boston, second hand," except that he "did not know but [he] should go into service in the Army," and he had not yet found one at a reasonable price "in Middletown, New London &c." With a carriage secured and an invitation sent to William Gordon, Stephen Johnson and Abigail Leverett married in Roxbury on May 28, 1776. According to local lore the two-wheeled horse-drawn buggy purchased in Boston became "famous in Lyme."

A letter to "Madame Johnson" from a friend in Newton confirmed in June the couple's safe arrival in Lyme and expressed hope that her "reception among that people . . . [was] truly delightful." The letter enclosed an inventory of furnishings sent by wagon and apologized that a large desk and easy chair had not been included because "the waggoner don't choose to take in anything but what he can stow with safety." A month later in July the friend sent wishes for marital happiness to the minister and his new wife in Lyme.

By then the need to raise additional troops for the looming battle in New York had become urgent, and Colonel Samuel Selden (1723–1776), a deacon in the Hadlyme parish who owned a large estate along the Connecticut River, sent an impassioned letter from Lyme on July 7, 1776, to militia captain Joshua Huntington (1751–1821) in Norwich. Asking that Connecticut regiments be sent "without a moment's delay," Selden conveyed a sense of dire emergency. "Rouse the people to see their danger," he wrote. "Stir them up by all that is dear in this life. Our wives, our children, our prosperity, our liberty

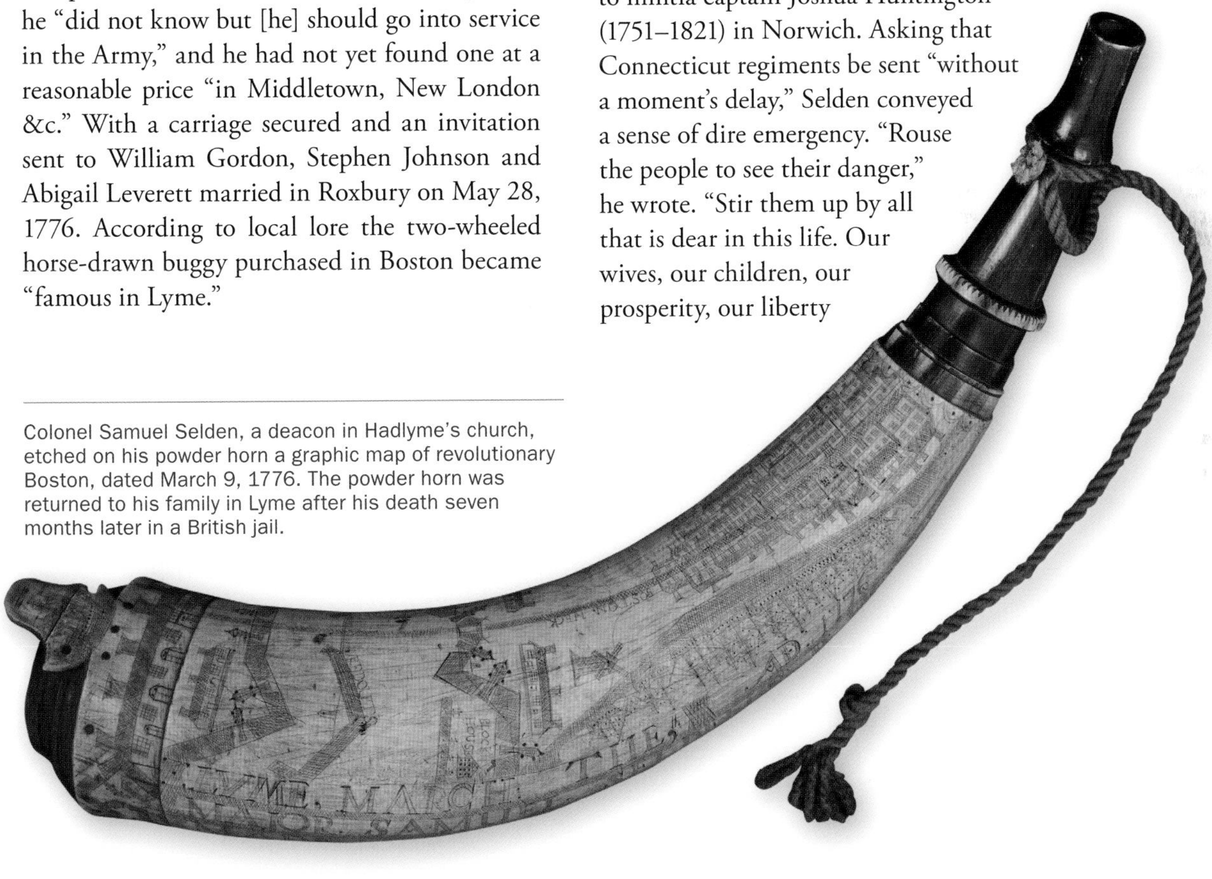

Colonel Samuel Selden, a deacon in Hadlyme's church, etched on his powder horn a graphic map of revolutionary Boston, dated March 9, 1776. The powder horn was returned to his family in Lyme after his death seven months later in a British jail.

is at stake . . . for if we can't defend ourselves at New York I fear all is gone." A month later Captain Joseph Jewett died in the attempt to stop the British advance on Long Island, and in October Colonel Selden, age fifty-three, died of fever in a British prison.

Colonel Samuel Parsons had been preparing for the expected British attack on Long Island when his father died in July 1776 "after a long and somewhat distressing sickness." Thirty years after his departure from Lyme, Rev. Jonathan Parsons led a large congregation in Newbury's Old South Presbyterian Church. A funeral sermon preached by Rev. John Searle praised Parsons's learning, piety, and eloquence. It also remarked that his congregation in Connecticut had been misguided in not recognizing his "true character."

Jonathan Parsons had reserved the right to occupy with his wife and unmarried daughters half of his former parsonage in Lyme rent-free, but after Phoebe Parsons's death in 1770, he gave all his remaining property in town to his eldest son. Within a year he married Lydia Clarkson (1731–1778), widow of a successful New Hampshire merchant. When Jonathan Parsons died five years after his second marriage, he was buried in the vault beneath his pulpit, where Rev. George Whitefield had already been interred. Devoted followers of the British evangelist could "descend into the crypt and gaze upon the remains of the eloquent preacher." Fifteen years later Rev. Joseph Prince (1723–1791), a fervent admirer of Whitefield, would also be interred in the Newbury crypt.

Gaps in the church record book make it unclear whether Sabbath services continued in the meetinghouse in 1776 when Stephen Johnson resumed his pastoral duties. Lyme's shoreline remained vulnerable to raiding parties, regimental troops kept watch along the coast, and urgent town meetings, noting "the present alarming state of our country," procured provisions for those who enlisted. Few records of the minister's activities during the war years survive, but in 1777, when finding a successor for Rev. Naphtali Daggett as Yale's president was considered urgent, given "the calamities of the times," Johnson, a Yale trustee, visited Rev. Ezra Stiles in New Haven and secured Stiles's consent to serve.

In 1780 Lyme's meetinghouse required repair "with all convenient speed" after a fire "accidentally alighted in the roof of said house." The Ecclesiastical Society authorized "twenty pounds States money to be divided to such of those persons as dangerously exerted themselves to extinguish said late fire," then rebuilt the steeple deck and purchased a new bell. During the repairs Johnson delivered an ordination sermon in Saybrook, and a personal reminiscence confirms his continued preaching in the meetinghouse after the construction. William Hall (1778–1865), son of Deacon Abel Hall (1743–1816) and briefly a partner with New York shipping merchant John Griswold, described in a newspaper column how as a child he rode in 1786 at age eight "on Sabbath on horseback behind his father, a deacon of the church," to hear one of Stephen Johnson's last sermons. "The word 'salvation,'" Hall wrote, "echoed in his heart for fourscore years."

Near the end of his life, Johnson completed a 360-page theological discourse expounding his views of salvation. In *The Everlasting Punishment of the Ungodly*, published in 1786, he denounced "the ill-judged and ill-concerted labors of some learned men" who had penned recent tracts claiming that "all men shall be saved." Endeavoring to "make clear the fallacy of their reasonings," he fervently defended his conviction that "the Supreme Judge of the world . . . [will] sentence us to everlasting life or punishment according to our characters formed in this state." While "laboring under bodily disorders" in October 1786, Johnson drafted a will distributing his property to his wife Abigail and other family members. A month later he died at age sixty-three. Among the many items listed in his estate inventory were a Bible, a beaver hat, a wig, a cloak, a greatcoat, a silver watch, a "stand of arms" with musket and bayonet, and the "riding chaise" purchased a decade earlier in Boston.

Stephen Johnson's brief but courageous promotion of the cause of liberty in 1765 achieved lasting recognition. A century later the distinguished historian George Bancroft (1800–1891) stated that among the Calvinist ministers who "nursed the flame of piety and civil freedom . . none did better than the American-born Stephen Johnson, the sincere and fervid pastor of the first church of Lyme." Letters, sermons, court documents, and a scholarly treatise offer a fuller portrait of his forty-year ministry.

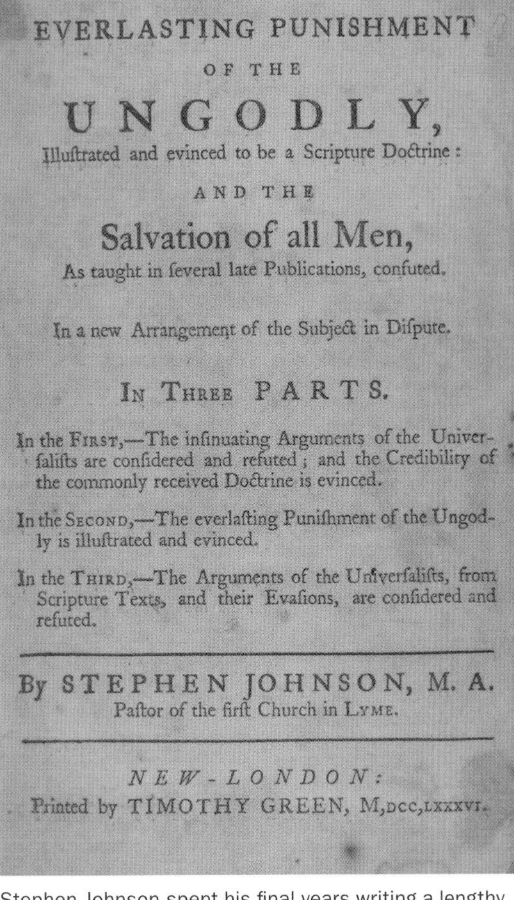
THE

EVERLASTING PUNISHMENT

OF THE

UNGODLY,

Illuſtrated and evinced to be a Scripture Doctrine:

AND THE

Salvation of all Men,

As taught in ſeveral late Publications, confuted.

In a new Arrangement of the Subject in Diſpute.

IN THREE PARTS.

In the FIRST,—The inſinuating Arguments of the Univerſaliſts are conſidered and refuted; and the Credibility of the commonly received Doctrine is evinced.

In the SECOND,—The everlaſting Puniſhment of the Ungodly is illuſtrated and evinced.

In the THIRD,—The Arguments of the Univerſaliſts, from Scripture Texts, and their Evaſions, are conſidered and refuted.

By STEPHEN JOHNSON, M. A.

Paſtor of the firſt Church in LYME.

NEW-LONDON:

Printed by TIMOTHY GREEN, M,DCC,LXXXVI.

Stephen Johnson spent his final years writing a lengthy treatise to refute contemporary theological views about universal salvation. Lyme's minister believed that eternal punishment awaited those who sinned without repentance.

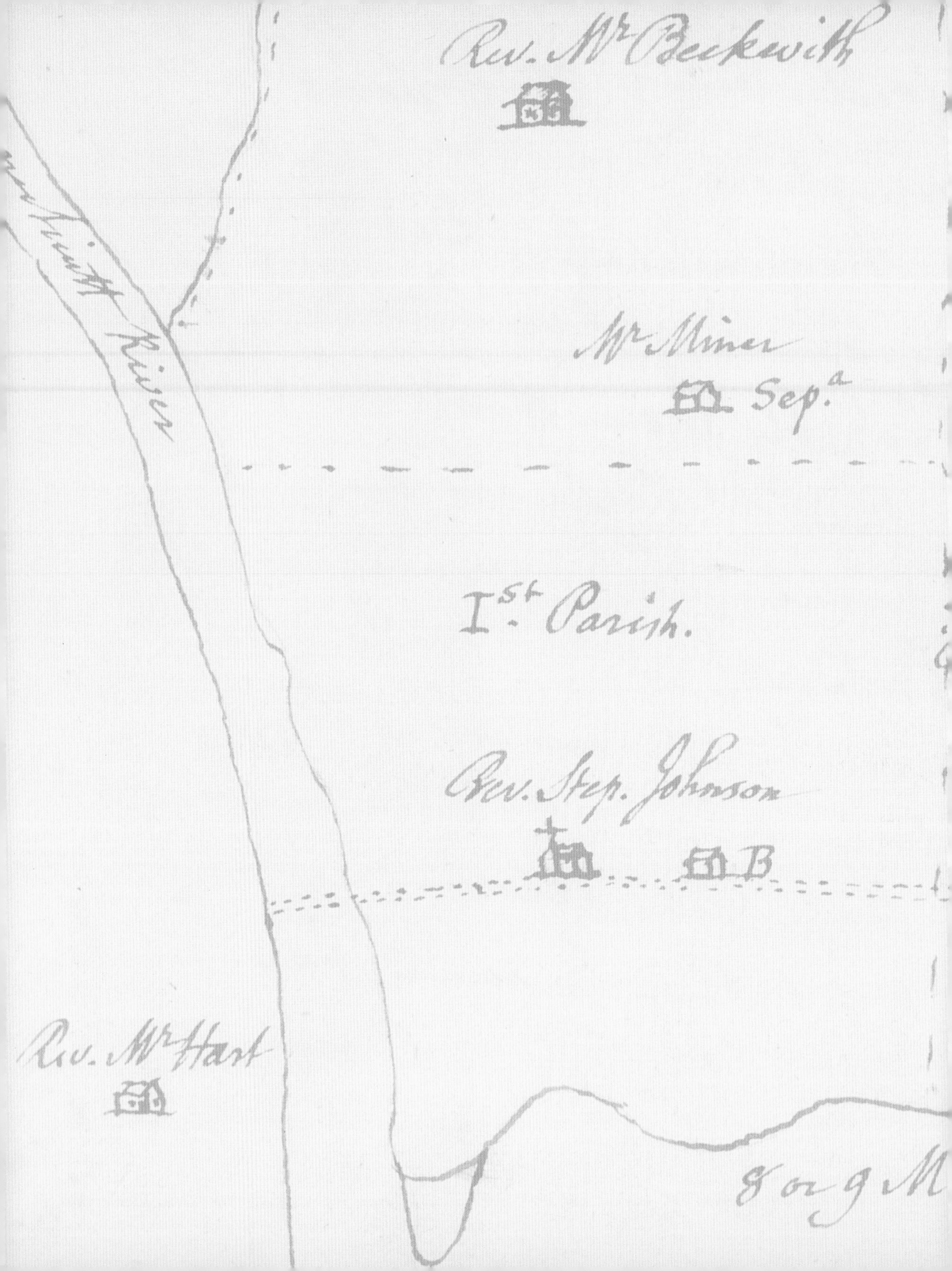

Rev. Mr Beckwith

necticutt River

Mr Miner

Sep.a

1st Parish.

Rev. Step. Johnson

B

Rev. Mr Hart

8 or 9 M

CHAPTER EIGHTEEN

Invitations

During the early years of the new Republic, Lyme's Ecclesiastical Society issued invitations to four Connecticut ministers over the span of three years before a candidate accepted its call.

Voted that the Society Committee apply to Mr. Channing to supply the pulpit, also to confer with him whether there is a probability of his settling as minister.

The Ecclesiastical Society waited only two weeks after Rev. Stephen Johnson's death in October 1786 before inviting Mr. Henry Channing (1760–1840) to supply the pulpit. A Yale tutor raised in Newport, Channing, age twenty-six, was then preaching as a candidate in New London and the next year would marry Sarah McCurdy (1762–1798), John McCurdy's third daughter. Since July the young minister had prayed daily in New London's jail with a "mulatto" child accused of murder.

Mr. Channing was said to be "indefatiguable in his attention" to Hannah Ocuish (1774–1786), a twelve-year-old "mulatto girl" who had confessed to the murder of a neighbor child. The badly

When Ralph Earl painted Sarah McCurdy Channing's portrait in New London's parsonage in 1793, he included a view of the Thames River from a parlor window.

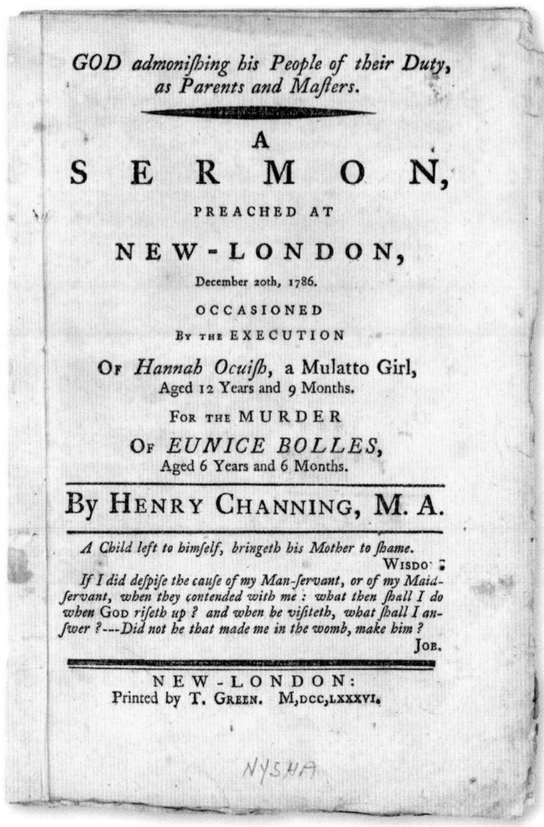

GOD admoniſhing his People of their Duty, as Parents and Maſters.

A

S E R M O N,

PREACHED AT

NEW-LONDON,

December 20th, 1786.

OCCASIONED

BY THE EXECUTION

OF *Hannah Ocuiſh*, a Mulatto Girl,
Aged 12 Years and 9 Months.

FOR THE MURDER

OF *EUNICE BOLLES*,
Aged 6 Years and 6 Months.

By HENRY CHANNING, M. A.

A Child left to himſelf, bringeth his Mother to ſhame.
WISDOM.

If I did deſpiſe the cauſe of my Man-ſervant, or of my Maid-ſervant, when they contended with me: what then ſhall I do when GOD *riſeth up? and when he viſiteth, what ſhall I anſwer?---Did not he that made me in the womb, make him?*
JOB.

NEW-LONDON:
Printed by T. GREEN. M,DCC,LXXXVI.

NYSHA

The sermon that Rev. Henry Channing delivered in New London before the execution of a "mulato" girl convicted of murder expressed compassion for the accused child but supported the court's verdict.

beaten body of Eunice Bolles, age six, had been discovered on the Norwich road covered by heavy stones. Because Eunice had previously reported Hannah, an indentured mulatto servant, for the theft of strawberries, the murder was viewed as retaliation. Judge Richard Law (1733–1806) considered Hannah's age before sentencing but argued that sparing her would uphold the idea that children could commit vicious crimes with impunity. A large crowd gathered near a gallows erected at the rear of New London's meetinghouse to watch the execution. The *Connecticut Courant* reported that the child "seemed greatly afraid."

A few hours before the sheriff placed a noose around Hannah's neck, Channing delivered an execution sermon reflecting on "the melancholy event, which we are now called to contemplate." His sermon described a "poor prisoner" who had been "left to heathenish darkness." It also condemned a "crime which freezes the mind with horror" and implored parents to guide and protect their children. Amid ongoing newspaper coverage of the case, Lyme church members applied to Channing three weeks before the execution to settle as their minister. He chose to remain in New London, where Rev. Ezra Stiles, his former pastor in Newport, delivered an ordination sermon in May 1787.

Lyme's Ecclesiastical Society then applied unsuccessfully to three other candidates, all of them Yale graduates. In July members "voted that this church make choice of Mr. Lemuel Tyler [1761–1810], raised in Northford, "to take the charge of this church as their Gospel Minister." A year later, in August, they voted to give Mr. David Hale (1761–1822), age twenty-seven and the younger brother of revolutionary patriot Nathan Hale (1755–1776), "a call to settle." In May 1789 they offered a generous settlement to Mr. Stanley Griswold (1763–1815) from Torrington, age twenty-six, if he would "settle as the Pastor of this Church." Each candidate chose ordination elsewhere in Connecticut, but in October 1789 Edward Porter (1765–1828), age twenty-four and raised in Farmington, accepted an invitation to settle in Lyme.

Matthew Griswold, who "went to farming" after "leaving the chair of governor," led the Ecclesiastical Society committee that conferred with the candidate. It offered Mr. Porter "two hundred pounds as a settlement, one fourth part to be paid in money and the other three fourths to be paid in pork, beef, live cattle, wheat, rye, Indian corn,

Ellen Noyes Chadwick's *View of Ferry Point*, which hangs today above a mantel in the Florence Griswold House, shows warehouses clustered near Old Lyme's ferry landing before the first railroad bridge spanned the Connecticut River.

oats and West India goods at cash price." After his ordination he would receive an annual salary of eighty pounds "so long as he shall remain."

To assure a reliable source of revenue, the Society decided two years later "that the pews in the Meeting House be sold for the year 1792 in open meeting and to the highest bidders." The auctioning of pews reflected the entrepreneurial spirit that brought growing prosperity to Lyme in the early years of the new Republic. After the death in 1785 of John McCurdy, one of Connecticut's wealthiest inhabitants, younger merchants purchased his warehouses and added to his wharves. They also commissioned coastal vessels from a shipyard established at the mouth of the Lieutenant River by Samuel Hill (1745–1818). By the time Edward Porter accepted an invitation to settle as minister in 1789, Samuel Mather Jr. (1745–1809) had registered in New London the first of fifteen ships he would commission from the Hill shipyard, a seventy-nine-ton sloop named *Peggy* designed for the West Indies trade.

Mather had acquired land, houses, warehouses, wharves, and cargo vessels, and in 1790 he owned four enslaved persons. As his ventures prospered, he built the town's largest dwelling just north of the McCurdy family's home, and when he died in 1809, his estate inventory included a wide range of furnishings. It also itemized goods in several storehouses that included lumber, farm implements, hardware, household provisions, casks of rum, and newly popular luxury items like exotic teas from China and silk gloves and shawls for fashionable women. A later church historian described Samuel Mather as Lyme's "merchant prince" and speculated that his wife and daughters were likely the best-dressed women in town.

Use of the first society's meetinghouse changed during Edward Porter's ministry when Lyme's inhabitants decided in 1792 to hold town meetings "for the future" equally in the town's parishes. Whether the location of separate justice court hearings also rotated as the population dispersed is not known. A faded notebook preserves records of the "justice court holden in Lyme" between 1790 and 1806 but does not indicate the venue. At those hearings Judge William Noyes

The stern gaze captured in James Martin's pastel portrait of Judge William Noyes seems to confirm his reputation for strict discipline and the punishment of Sabbath-breakers who traveled through Lyme.

(1728–1807), a church deacon whose household, according to the census, included three enslaved servants in 1800, resolved mostly small claims controversies requiring judgments about debts and the assigning of costs and damages. Occasionally Judge Noyes ordered corporal punishment for offenders, and in 1790 he decided that Abraham Wade would pay three times the value of twenty-five yards of cloth stolen from Abner Lord Jr. (1760–1821), sentencing him also to "be given to the officer to lay on eight stripes." Three years later Judge Noyes fined Atwell Tucker for "wickedly and profanely cursing Abel Rogers of said Lyme" and ruled that on failure of payment Tucker would "be set in the stocks two hours."

In 1792, when town meetings rotated among Lyme's meetinghouses, illness interrupted Edward Porter's brief service. Unable to perform his pastoral duties, he submitted a letter in August requesting "dissolution of the connection in which as Pastor and Church we stand related." The next month an Ecclesiastical Council gathered in the meetinghouse and "maturely deliberated upon so disagreeable and important [an] event." Agreeing that the termination served "the interest of religion and the good of Christ's Church and people in this place," the council approved Porter's dismissal "from his pastoral care and labor" owing solely to "bodily indisposition."

Having sold his Lyme property, Porter, his health recovered, accepted a call in 1795 to serve as pastor in the newly industrializing town of Waterbury. Two years later he again fell ill and requested dismissal from his pastoral duties because of "long and painful afflictions [that] incapacitate me for the great work I have undertaken among you." He never returned to the ministry but instead joined a brother in a profitable clock manufacturing business. One contemporary described the Porter brothers as "shrewd Waterbury retailers." In 1812 a question about Edward Porter's "integrity as a business man" led to his excommunication from Waterbury's church, where he had remained an active member. He then returned to his family home in Farmington, where his younger half-brother Rev. Noah Porter (1781–1866) served as minister for sixty years. His niece Sarah Porter (1813–1900) established a pioneering girls' boarding school there in 1847, and his nephew Rev. Noah Porter Jr. (1811–1892) became president of Yale College in 1871.

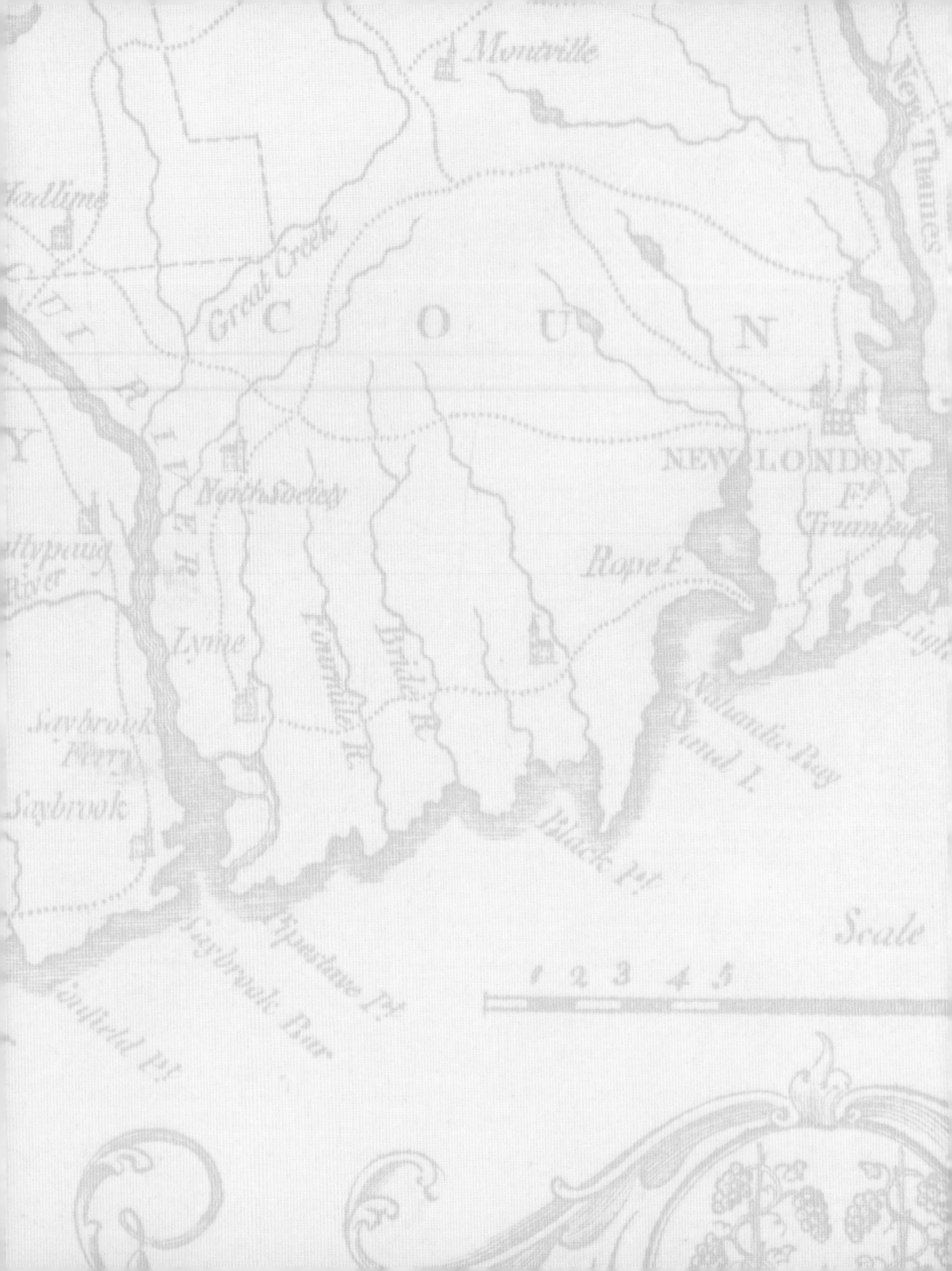

Montville
New Thames
Hadlime
Great Creek
C O U N
NEW LONDON
Ft. Trumbull
North Society
Lyme
Fourmile R.
Bride R.
Rope F.
Niantic Bay
Goud I.
Black Pt.
Saybrook Ferry
Saybrook
Saybrook Bar
Pipestave Pt.
Scale
1 2 3 4 5

Chapter nineteen

Silver Tankard

As Lyme prospered between America's two wars with Britain, the purchase of a silver tankard and flagons for the communion service and a Bible to be kept in the meetinghouse reflected a shift away from the building's secular use.

Voted that the sum of eighty five dollars fifty cents be appropriated to procure a silver tankard for the use of the Church, & that the treasurer be directed to pay the said sum of eighty five dollars & fifty cents, out of monies belonging to the Church.

A century after the organization of Lyme's first church in 1693, members set aside their preference for candidates educated at Yale and invited a recent Dartmouth graduate to settle as their pastor. A cordial letter from Deacon William Noyes to Lathrop Rockwell (1769–1828), age twenty-five and raised in Lebanon, Connecticut, advised him in October 1793 that a meeting approving his invitation had been "held and finished without any opposition and all good natured." Fourteen clergymen gathered in the parlor of Samuel Mather Jr.'s spacious home in January 1794 to question the candidate about theology and doctrine on the eve of his "solemn service of ordination."

Lathrop Rockwell brought a different voice to Lyme's meetinghouse as the century ended. In a funeral sermon for Governor Matthew Griswold in 1799, he offered a "last tribute of respect, to one, who has been useful in life, a private and public blessing in his day and generation." Old attitudes revived briefly the next year when eight Society members, in an echo of past controversy, voiced their opposition to a tax that would help pay the minister's salary. "In our opinion the Society is in an alarming, critical situation, respecting our ministerial affairs," they wrote.

The minister responded judiciously to a proposal "to dissolve the covenant which exists between him and said Society." Recommending that the Society consider "such measures as they deem expedient," he offered to discuss the resolution of differences once members who withdrew in protest rejoined the Society. "I did not judge it prudent for me to advise or intermeddle with difficulties in the Society," Rockwell stated. "If

The stagecoach route through Lyme in the early years of Rev. Lathrop Rockwell's ministry appears on the map that Amos Doolittle made from an "actual survey" for Benjamin Trumbull's *Complete History of Connecticut* in 1797.

any person had any thing against me personally, it was their business to let me know what it was—that their objections may be removed." Only trivial objections emerged, like a complaint from Jasper Peck Jr. (1737–1821) that the minister had passed by his house when he was ill without stopping.

As discontent subsided, Society meetings focused on renovating Lyme's third meetinghouse, where Sabbath services and town meetings had been held from the time of the Great Awakening's revivalism through the difficult years of the Revolution. Not only the exterior walls but the steeple needed repair in 1802, and the Ecclesiastical Society approved a tax to paint the aging

On the eve of his ordination, Lathrop Rockwell answered questions from a council of ministers in the home of Samuel Mather Jr., Lyme's wealthiest merchant.

building, install new windows and sashes, and replace the steeple with a cupola. Members then voted to purchase a costly silver tankard and flagons for the communion service, as well as a Bible that for the first time would be "kept in the meeting house."

Soon after the minister's arrival, growing opportunities for trade had prompted two of Rev. George Griswold's grandsons to leave their family farm in the east parish and seek commercial gain in the growing port of New York. Nathaniel L. Griswold (1773–1847) and his brother George Griswold (1777–1859) had established a flour store on New York's waterfront in 1794 that brought rapid success shipping flour to the West Indies and importing large quantities of sugar and rum. A decade later John Griswold (1783–1856), a grandson of Rev. Stephen Johnson, followed his cousins to New York and in 1804 became a partner in a South Street shipping firm that owned and chartered vessels built in Connecticut River shipyards. When President Thomas Jefferson issued an embargo three years later that stopped all trade with foreign ports, three hundred ships lay at anchor in New York harbor. Griswold vessels were likely among them.

Strong opposition in Connecticut to a second war with Britain led its new governor, Roger Griswold (1762–1812), Governor Matthew Griswold's son

Lathrop Rockwell conducted a private tuition school in his parsonage preparing boys for college; fourteen names appear on a handwritten list of "Boys at Mr. Rockwell's in 1809 & 10."

and a cousin of the New York merchants, to issue a proclamation in August 1812 refusing to send state militia into federal service. Two months later Governor Griswold, age fifty and already ill with cancer, died in office. Britain's ongoing blockade of Long Island Sound during the War of 1812 crippled the economy of coastal towns like Lyme, disrupting trade and transport and affecting not only shipbuilders and merchants but mill owners, carpenters, tanners, farmers, fishermen, and their families.

Lathrop Rockwell served as a chaplain in Connecticut's Thirty-Third Regiment when British warships patrolled near the mouth of the Connecticut River in 1813. Wary Lyme residents constructed earthen breastworks on a hill overlooking the river, but the town escaped attack. When British seamen rowed upriver in small boats under cover of darkness in April 1814, they passed by those defenses to target instead the shipbuilding town of Essex, then called Pettipaug. Governor Roger Griswold's son Charles Griswold (1791–1839), a young attorney, watched the conflagration across the river as merchant ships and privateers burned in the Essex harbor. "I was at Higgins' wharf in the afternoon of that day," he wrote to a cousin in Norwich. Later he watched from his home in Black Hall as British soldiers rowed back to their vessel. "I was on our beach when the boats went out of the river & saw their blue lights."

The auctioning of pews continued to raise revenue for the Ecclesiastical Society during the war years. Those in the parish with economic means purchased places of prominence in the meetinghouse, but age, gender, and race also influenced pew allocations. Elderly parishioners sat downstairs not far

George Griswold commissioned this imposing neoclassical-style marble bust by sculptor John Frazee in 1842. A *New York Times* obituary later described the grandson of Rev. George Griswold as one of "the last of the race of mercantile magnates who laid the foundations of the commercial greatness of this city."

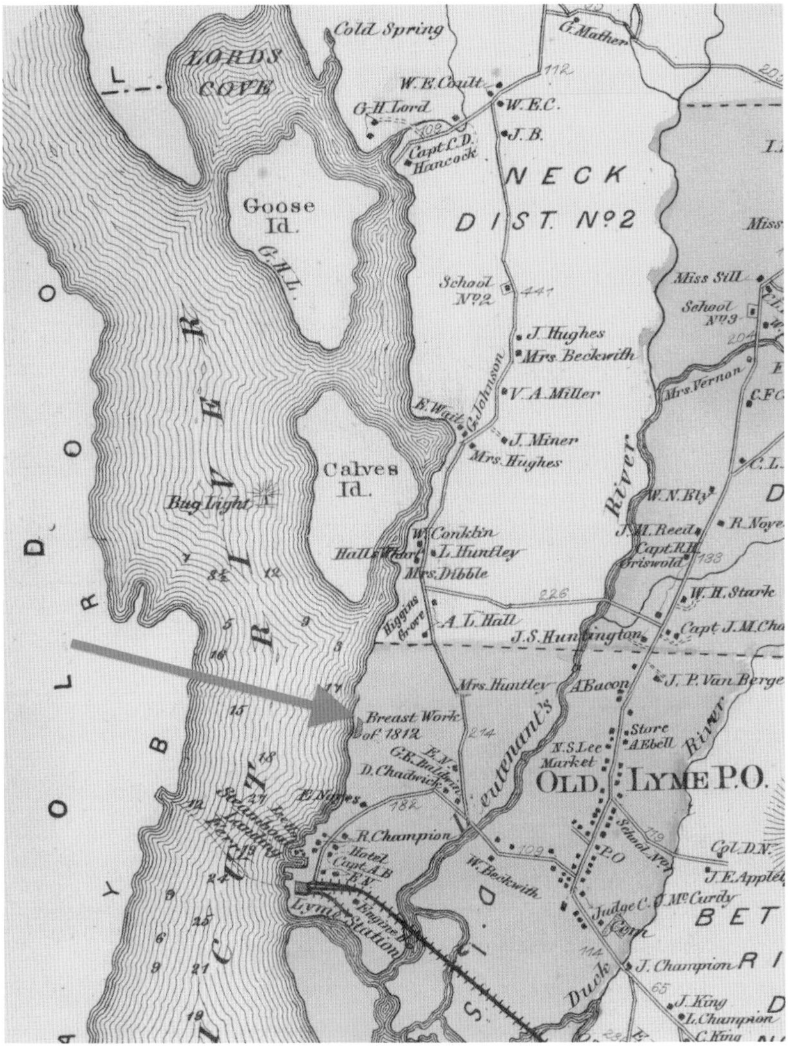

A map of Old Lyme in 1868 locates the breastworks built on a hill above the mouth of the Connecticut River to defend against possible British attack during the War of 1812.

from the pulpit. Women sat upstairs, according to a vote "that the east gallery extending to the center of the front gallery be appropriated to the use of the females." The status of "black people" had not changed as slavery declined in Connecticut, and "recently free blacks" still sat in the gallery's rear corners. In 1814 the Society specified that pew reservations would "be made for white persons only." It also voted "to raise the seats for the black people in the gallery in such a manner to enable them to see the minister."

The congregation & others to assemble at ...
n's inn at 1 o'clk P.M and a procession to ...
d by the Marshall in the following or...

Young Men to form in front by pairs.

Young Ladies

Elderly Ladies

Elderly Men

Singers with Psalm-Books

Masons with the implements of their profe...

Carpenters with - do -

Building Committee

Clergyman & Deacons on each side

...on to march up street to a proper distan...
...nd return back - and when the front of th...

CHAPTER TWENTY

Architecture and Adornment

When the meetinghouse in Lyme's first parish moved from its hilltop site to a more accessible location beside the town's two highways, the contract specifying the terms of its construction set ambitious architectural goals.

To perform the work in the best manner and point of style, materials and workmanship to make said house equal to any Meeting House in the State of Connecticut east of Connecticut River.

In July 1815, six months after a peace treaty formally ended the War of 1812, fire ignited by a lightning strike engulfed Lyme's recently renovated third meetinghouse. A week later the Ecclesiastical Society agreed "to sell such effects as were recovered from the old meeting house as cannot be wanted and store such as may be wanted for a new one." Only the Bible, a hymn book, and some pew doors were said to be saved. The Ecclesiastical Society announced that Sabbath services would be held in the district schoolhouses "until a permanent house of public worship shall be erected."

A month later the county court approved a request to relocate the meetinghouse a mile west of its hilltop site, which Yale president Timothy Dwight (1752–1817) had recently described as a "bleak and solitary spot." The Society then purchased for $300 a field adjoining the former parsonage of Rev. Jonathan Parsons where Lois Parsons (1766–1844), Marshfield Parsons's widow, operated a coaching inn and tavern. An appeal to Governor John Cotton Smith (1765–1845), who succeeded Roger Griswold, brought a recommendation that other Connecticut congregations "help defray the costs of rebuilding" in Lyme.

The construction of the town's earlier meetinghouses had been guided by thrift and practicality, but a growing concern with architecture and adornment led a fifteen-member building committee to announce in December 1815 that the new structure would equal in design, quality, and elegance "any Meeting House in the State of Connecticut east of Connecticut River." The committee chose Samuel Belcher (1779–1849), age thirty-six, as the builder. A decade earlier he

Among the drawings of Connecticut towns that engraver John Warner Barber made in 1834 was a western view of Ellington showing the meetinghouse designed by Samuel Belcher.

had designed a stately white meetinghouse sixty miles away in Ellington, where Rev. Diodate Brockway (1776–1849), at a dedication service in 1806, commended Belcher for discovering "an excellent taste, and superior skill in architecture." Brockway also remarked that Ellington's new house of worship "equals, and perhaps exceeds, in point of elegance, any of the kind in Connecticut."

The detailed contract for Lyme's fourth meetinghouse specified not just dimensions and materials but architectural elements and ornamental details. It stipulated a portico supported by four Ionic columns, a belfry with an Ionic cornice, forty-four windows containing forty squares each with glass "equal to the English Crown glass," a circular gallery with columns, and an oval arched ceiling "with a handsome cornice at the springing of the arch around the same." Sketches in an unsigned hand-stitched notebook show a cross-section of the gallery, a floor plan for the pulpit, a banister for the communion table, and a frame for the bell.

Elaborate "religious ceremonies" in June 1816 accompanied the laying of the cornerstone. A procession included "people of both sexes" who assembled at one o'clock at Mrs. Parsons's inn. Young men in pairs took the lead, followed by young ladies, elderly ladies, elderly men, singers with Psalm books, masons and carpenters carrying tools, and finally the building committee flanked

The congregation & others to assemble at M[r.]
on's inn at 10 Clo P.M and a procession to b[e]
ed by the Marshall in the following orde[r]

— Young Men to form in front by pairs,
Young Ladies
Elderly Ladies
Elderly Men
Singers with Psalm-Books
Masons with the implements of their professi[on]
Carpenters with – do –
Building Committee
Clergyman & Deacons on each side
sion to march up street to a proper distanc[e]
and return back – and when the front of the
reaches the corner of the house, to halt –
sion then to open to the right and left and th[e]
al to pass through to the Clergyman & escort
own to the corner – the procession closing in
llowing in order. — — — — —

The last of sixteen steps described in a handwritten "Order of the Ceremony to be used at the laying of the cornerstone" for Lyme's meetinghouse in June 1816 instructs: "Procession to return & take a glass of cold water to close the Ball."

A costly communion service purchased for Lyme's new meetinghouse included six cylindrical beakers and a decorated flagon marked by silversmiths J. and A. Simmons, New York.

by deacons and clergymen. Participants marched "a distance" up the main street, then "wheeled" and turned back. The program included hymns sung "at proper intervals" and prayers delivered by "several clergymen from the neighboring societies." Rev. Lathrop Rockwell read aloud the cornerstone's inscription, then deposited the commemorative copper plate in a cavity prepared by the masons and offered a "short address."

The *Middlesex Gazette* reported a week later that Lyme's meetinghouse when completed would "be one of the finest and best religious Edifices in this State" with its "elegant, lofty steeple, and a rich portico in front." The columnist, likely borrowing words from the minister's address, described the new structure as "none other than the House of God, and the gate of Heaven." To cover the $8,000 cost of the meetinghouse, a subscription collected contributions from church members, while pew sales provided additional revenues. Squire Richard McCurdy, John McCurdy's youngest son and a grandson of Rev. Stephen Johnson, contributed an eighth of the building's cost.

Robert H. Griswold purchased in 1841 for his bride Helen Powers the house built for William Noyes Jr. by Samuel Belcher, today the Florence Griswold House. Powers considered it the most elegant dwelling in Lyme.

As the meetinghouse neared completion, church members met "to devise measures for procuring such Plate as will be found necessary for the Communion Table." They authorized the purchase of a new silver tankard and two silver cups, along with "two dishes & a baptismal basin, for the use of the church." Five months later, in August 1817, the Ecclesiastical Society gathered for the first time in the finished building and voted "that the Society do accept and approve of the new Meeting House lately built in this society by Samuel Belcher." A decision in November that "no town meeting be in any wise held in the Meeting House" confirmed that not only its style and setting but also its function had changed.

The removal of civic gatherings from Lyme's meetinghouse preceded by more than a year Connecticut's adoption in October 1818 of a constitution that officially separated church and state. The constitution's preamble affirmed that "the exercise and enjoyment of religious profession and worship, without discrimination, shall forever be free to all persons in this State" and

A piece of hand-carved scrollwork that fell undamaged to the Florence Griswold House porch in 2017 allowed a close look at the workmanship of Samuel Belcher's skilled carpenters.

specified that "no preference shall be given by law to any Christian sect or mode of worship." The resulting removal of religious instruction from the public schools led Rockwell in 1819 to establish a Sabbath school for parish youth. A church manual states that "a negro girl" won first prize for the recitation of Bible verses.

While constructing the meetinghouse, Samuel Belcher also designed two stately homes along the main highway through Lyme for William Noyes Jr., a member of the building committee. Today those houses, built for his son William Noyes 3rd (1792–1873) and his son-in-law John Sill (1787–1852), serve as the Florence Griswold Museum and the Lyme Academy College of Art. The identity of the skilled artisans who completed three distinguished structures in Lyme in as many years is not known, but they were likely ship's carpenters experienced at joinery and cabinetmaking. Some may have worked at the Samuel Hill shipyard, which in 1813 had produced its largest schooner, the 290-ton *Meteor*, intended to serve as a privateer during the second war with Britain.

The mercantile success of the two former minister's grandsons contributed to Lyme's changing architectural landscape. As the Griswold shipping houses in New York expanded beyond the West Indies trade into the profitable transport of southern cotton, the lucrative China trade, and the growing transatlantic packet ship service, Griswold family members and other aspiring mariners from Lyme found work as ship captains, shipping agents, cabin boys, and crew. Those who prospered returned home influenced by foreign travel to build and furnish homes that reflected cosmopolitan tastes. Social practice in Lyme changed more slowly. The whipping post and stocks moved from the hillside to stand near the elegant new meetinghouse, and behind its columned façade Lewis Lewia (1770–1852), formerly the enslaved servant of Marshfield Parsons, sat with other "free blacks" in triangular boxes that Samuel Belcher's carpenters built in the gallery's rear corners.

Mrs. Beckwith
G. Johnson
V. A. Miller
E. Wait
Mrs. Ve
J. Miner
Mrs. Hughes
Calves Id.
River
W. N. Bly
W. Conklin
J. M. Reed
Hall's Wharf
L. Huntley
Capt. R. H. Griswold
Mrs. Dibble
226
Higgins Grove
A. L. Hall
J. S. Huntington
Mrs. Huntley
A. Bacon
J. P. V
Breast Work of 1812
214
Lieutenant's
Store A. Ebell
N. S. Lee Market
E. N.
G. R. Baldwin
D. Chadwick
OLD LYME
182
R. Champion
Hotel Capt. A. B.
E. N.
109
P. O.
School
W. Beckwith
Lyme Station
Engine H.
Judge C. J. McCurdy
Cem.
114
J. Champion
Duck
65

CHAPTER TWENTY-ONE

Women Gathering

A hand-stitched notebook preserves records of Lyme's first women's organization, which after the War of 1812 gave wives and daughters of prominent parishioners a charitable role outside the meetinghouse.

The first quarterly meeting of the Female Reading Society was held at Mrs. Phebe Lord's on Monday the 2nd of December 1816 and was opened with an appropriate prayer by the Rev. Mr. Rockwell.

For more than a century, women played no publicly acknowledged role in the affairs of Lyme's first church. They were admitted as members, their names appeared on marriage and baptismal lists, they responded to the emotional appeal of revival sermons, they confessed sinful behavior, but they did not participate in discussions or decisions in the meetinghouse. The earliest women's organization convened in 1816, six months after Lathrop Rockwell laid the cornerstone for the new house of God, when the minister welcomed a Female Reading Society that scheduled weekly gatherings for prayer, inspirational reading, and charitable projects.

The formation of women's benevolent groups in Connecticut followed the establishment in 1798 of a state Missionary Society pledged "to Christianize the heathen in North America, and to support and promote Christian knowledge." By 1810, ten women's auxiliary groups had followed the lead of the Charitable Female Association of Litchfield, whose members each donated fifty cents a year for mission work starting in 1804. The Female Reading Society in Lyme had benevolent but also devotional and educational goals.

At the initial meeting held in the parlor of Rockwell's neighbor Phoebe Griffin Lord (1768–1841), the minister offered the "prayer of a brother" and presented his "dear sisters in Christ" with a letter of guidance. "I trust you have been moved by the Spirit to associate together for the pious & commendable purpose of reading the scriptures," he wrote. While urging the women's attention to individual piety, he also encouraged their "collective capacity as a Society." He then asked them to pray earnestly for the church

When Phoebe Griffin Lord sat for the miniature portrait painted by her daughter Phoebe Griffin Noyes ca. 1820, she chose a ribboned cap with ruffled edges and a black dress with ruffled lace collar, which her granddaughter Katharine Ludington described as the formal attire of an elderly lady of the day.

at a time when "the things of Religion are low and circumstances discouraging," so "that God would water it from on high, that it be no longer a place of desolation."

The Female Reading Society's ten founding members, all wives and daughters of prominent Lyme families, chose a slate of officers and adopted a constitution. Mrs. Mary Ann Noyes (1768–1819), the widowed daughter-in-law of Judge William Noyes, served as president, and Mrs. Phoebe Lord, also widowed and Mrs. Noyes's relative by marriage, managed the Society's affairs as vice president. Instructed in her youth by the tutors who prepared her two brothers for Yale, and trained by her accomplished mother Eve Dorr Griffin (1733–1814) in the art of embroidery, Mrs. Lord had acquired a level of education unusual among Lyme's women.

The sudden death of her husband Joseph Lord (1757–1812) in 1812 when she was pregnant

A photograph of the Lord family home on Lyme Street ca. 1890, not long before it was demolished to create space for a town library, shows children from the district school next door playing beside the white fence.

with their eighth child led Mrs. Lord to a profession of faith. "I am happy to hear that you have been enabled to make a public profession of religion & hope you . . . will persevere in the habit of not only closet, but also family prayer," her brother George Griffin (1778–1860), a New York attorney, wrote in 1813. "The pious women in this city, who are widows, are, I believe, universally in that habit." Despite the hazards of travel during the War of 1812, Mrs. Lord sent her second child and namesake Phoebe Griffin Lord (1797–1875) to live with her brother in New York. There the young Phoebe studied miniature portrait painting, an artistic pursuit that allowed women like the talented miniaturist Mary Way (1769–1833) from New London to earn an independent income in the commercially expanding city.

To support seven daughters at home during the economic disruption of wartime, Mrs. Lord prepared homespun fabric that her brother placed unsuccessfully with a New York merchant. She attempted to rent her farm with its dwelling house and two barns through an advertisement in the *Connecticut Gazette*. She also offered private instruction during the winter months for day and boarding students, following the example of Lathrop Rockwell, who prepared young men for college in his parsonage nearby. His students sometimes boarded at Mrs. Lord's home, like David Huntington (1810–1870), grandson of a former North Lyme minister, who cared for her livestock in exchange for lodging.

At the initial meeting of the Female Reading Society in Mrs. Lord's parlor, the founding members adopted a constitution that defined the organization's religious and charitable purposes. "Sensible of our obligation to God and desirous of increasing our knowledge and love of him; and of our duty to our fellow creatures," the constitution stated, "we the undersigned form ourselves into a society with the name of the Reading Society." Any woman "who bears a good moral character and pays 12½ cents" was eligible for membership, and half of the Society's annual income "would be given in charity to the poor of this parish, the other half to the missionary cause." Two years later the Reading Society presented Rockwell with $40 "for the purpose of constituting him a Member of the Connecticut Bible Society," established in 1809 to circulate "God's written word among the indigent and careless."

Weekly Reading Society meetings held initially on Sabbath evenings allowed Lyme women to gather apart from their husbands and households. Both Abigail Noyes Sill (1786–1883), the group's secretary, and her sister-in-law Hannah Townsend Noyes (1789–1856), a director, hosted meetings in their gracious new homes constructed by Samuel Belcher and his builders. An inventory of John L. Sill's (1787–1852) personal property offers a glimpse of the surroundings in which women read together when his wife Abigail, age thirty-one, hosted them in 1817. Among her household possessions were four gilt-framed mirrors, one sideboard, one tea table, one dining table with ends, twenty-three chairs, one case of drawers, two globes, one carpet, one china dining set, one tea set, one set of china jars, one clock, one trunk of linens, plus her monogrammed silver marked ALN. The rear barn held a horse cart and a sleigh.

When Reading Society membership increased to twenty-two women in 1828, a revised constitution stated that the group would thereafter meet "at the house of some member of this Society every Wednesday between the hours of 2 & 4 PM." Specifying an educational as well as a religious purpose, it noted that they would "read a portion of the holy scriptures and any other book whose tendency is to elevate the mind and improve the heart, and our meeting to begin and end with prayer." Local family libraries with their varied collections of histories, biographies, and

Abigail Noyes, captured in her youth by itinerant artist James Martin ca. 1798, lived only briefly with her husband John Sill and their two sons in the elegant house built for them in Lyme by Samuel Belcher. Jailed in New Haven for failing to pay customs duties, Sill sold their home and its contents in 1820.

works of "popular devotion" likely supplemented the group's reading of holy scriptures.

The notebook documenting the Reading Society's meetings concludes in 1841 after the death of Phoebe Lord, who by then had served as president for more than twenty years. As her successor the group chose Maria Selden Wait (1791–1866), whose son Morrison Remick Wait (1816–1888), a Yale-educated attorney practicing law in Ohio, would later be appointed chief justice of the United States Supreme Court. Another forty years passed before women participated directly in meetinghouse affairs, but during Rev. Rockwell's ministry their voices could be heard.

Phoebe Griffin Lord's cousin Eunice Noyes became skilled in needlework at Lydia Royse's school in Hartford, where she embroidered a mourning scene on silk in 1810. Eunice embellished the local landscape when depicting her grieving family gathered in the Duck River Cemetery beside a monument commemorating two younger siblings. Paul foundation, Essex, Connecticut.

Rev. Diod. Johnson

Millington

...v. Mr Rawson

III.d Par.

Rev. Mr Beckwith

Mr Miner

Sep.a

...t River

Chapter twenty-two

Revivals

Family letters provide firsthand accounts of the Second Great Awakening in Lyme when some fifty people in the first parish, most of them women, expressed the hope of conversion.

Mr. Colton is unremitting in his exertions, & looks almost worn out with anxiety, & labor. The same course is adopted here as in other revivals, but perhaps not with as good success, about fifty I believe are among the hopeful, & hoping—More are serious, there are but few men.

In the months that followed the ailing Lathrop Rockwell's death in March 1828 after a thirty-four-year ministry, Lyme's Ecclesiastical Society procured "ornamental trees to be set about the meetinghouse" and built a fence around the Duck River burying ground. Later that year as a spirit of social reform and religious revival swept through New England, the Society invited Rev. Chester Colton (1783–1850), age forty-five and a Yale graduate raised in West Hartford, "to settle with them as their Gospel minister."

Already a seasoned pastor, Colton had left, because of an eye affliction, a congregation in New Hampshire where he enjoyed "the warmest attachment of his people." The invitation to settle in Lyme made him consider "diligently and seriously" on the subject and weigh "the reasons for and against the acceptance of the call." Ordained in February 1829, he awakened renewed religious commitment in the parish and drew urgent social issues into the meetinghouse.

During Lathrop Rockwell's illness Mrs. Lord had lamented the "deplorably low" state of religion in Lyme. "Even the Bible class is given up," she wrote to her daughter Julia Lord (1803–1865) in December 1826, "but I hope it will be resumed in the spring and that the holy spirit in powerful influences will attend it." With others from Lyme, she crossed the river the following summer to observe a revivalist camp meeting held under

In *West View of Lyme* drawn in 1834, John Warner Barber placed the meetinghouse at the center of the village and included the distinctive gambrel roof of Samuel Mather Jr.'s house nearby.

multiple tents in Saybrook. The outpouring of religious enthusiasm attracted large crowds. "Many thousands of people of every color & every description were there," her eldest daughter Harriet Lord (1795–1882) reported. "The good people here, high & low, rich & poor all went—& among the rest I elbowed my way through the mixed multitude."

Never before had Harriet witnessed such confusion as when she observed "a praying circle in which every person went who desired to be converted, & from that, & the surrounding tents issued such shrieks for mercy, such shouts of 'victory, victory,' & supplications for 'power, power.'" The thundering preachers made it sound "as if no person can form an idea of conversion who has not been to a camp-meeting," she wrote, noting that Mrs. Lord remained unmoved by the "stentorian" preachers. "Ma aptly compared their distortions, & extravagances to the mummeries practiced by Baal's priests, when they called their God to come in his power but he was deaf to their prayers," Harriet reported to her sister.

Four years later as the movement called the Second Great Awakening unfolded in Lyme, a church account book with marbled cover listed

Soon after Phoebe Lord's brother Dr. Edward Dorr Griffin became president of Williams College in 1821, he sat for New York portrait artists Samuel Lovett Waldo and William Jewett. Raised in Lyme, Jewett was Dr. Griffin's nephew.

an expense of $3.00 in cash "paid to Samuel Miner for ringing bell at protracted meetings in summer of 1831." Like Mrs. Lord's younger brother Rev. Edward Dorr Griffin (1770–1837), president of Williams College and a leading New England evangelist and theologian, Chester Colton rejected the zealous emotionalism that had divided the church almost a century earlier and quietly stirred the spiritual longings of potential believers. About fifty of his parishioners were considering "giv[ing] themselves up to Christ," noted Daniel R. Noyes (1795–1877). A descendant of Rev. James Noyes, he had married in 1827 Harriet Lord's younger sister Phoebe.

Daniel Noyes sent a lengthy account of Lyme's revival to his wife's sister Catherine Lord (1807–1844), then teaching private tuition students in Litchfield. He mentioned with regret

Harriet Lord, the eldest of Phoebe Lord's eight daughters, lived unmarried in the family home at the head of Lyme's main street until her death at age sixty-seven.

that two of her sisters had been "so taken up" with the wedding in Lyme that week of Captain William Griswold and Sarah Noyes (1815–1903) that "they could not think of anything else," but he knew Catherine's heart would "gladden to think that so many of her friends & acquaintances are seeking an interest in Christ at the same time when she herself is begging at the same fountain of mercy." His letter also described extended services in June in the meetinghouse. "They commenced on Tuesday last," he wrote. "Afternoon & evening service well attended. Wednesday morning prayer meeting at sunrise; morning, afternoon & evening service all well attended."

After several visiting clergymen delivered moving sermons, among them Hadlyme's long-serving minister Rev. Joseph Vail (1751–1838), Colton requested that "all who felt any anxiety about their souls or with an interest in Christ" should remain in the meetinghouse. Those who had previously professed their faith adjourned to the district schoolhouse nearby to pray for those "anxious souls," while the forty or fifty who remained "hopeful" in the meetinghouse were "very affectionately & feelingly addressed by the different clergy."

In a letter to her sister Julia about the "progress of the revival," Harriet Lord wrote in September that Mr. Colton looked "worn out with anxiety & labor." She reported that the minister's efforts had brought results but noted that there were few men "among the hopeful, & hoping." Several of the visiting preachers, she observed, were eligible and attractive. "Mr. Jones, the same who was in the revival in the North Quarter early in the season, has been here three weeks," she said, describing him as "an intelligent, zealous young man, besides being uncommonly good looking, & agreeable in his manners & address." By November 1831, Daniel and Phoebe Noyes, along with twenty others, all but two of them women, had been admitted to Lyme's first church.

In an affectionate letter to Julia Lord, Rev. Edward Dorr Griffin emphasized in 1837 "how infinitely important" it was "for revivals of religion to prevail in Lyme." Voicing concern about those in the family who remained unconverted, he worried what would become of her dear sisters. Only three of his eight nieces had professed their faith, and he especially feared for the state of Harriet's soul. She had lived with him in Williamstown for a year in 1828, and Griffin warned that the likelihood of conversion decreased with age. "Surely no more time ought to be lost," he wrote. "Every hour that is lost increases the danger."

Alms House
Auction
This House & the
premises will be
Sold to the
st bidder on
without Reserve
Sheriff

Chapter twenty-three

Entire Abstinence

Connecticut's temperance movement gathered momentum after Rev. Lyman Beecher preached four sermons in Litchfield in 1826 exposing the social and spiritual hazards of consuming alcohol. A vote four years later in Lyme's meetinghouse decided that entire abstinence would be required of all church members.

Resolved, That it is the peculiar and solemn duty of this Church of Christ, by the force and purity of its example and precept, to regulate and enlighten public opinion and manners, and moreover to take the lead in every plan formed for promoting the present and everlasting welfare of our fellow beings . . . and therefore . . . that we as a church, feel ourselves required . . . to abstain entirely, from the use of ardent spirits.

Three months before Chester Colton's installation, leading members of Lyme's first church had gathered in a district schoolhouse in December 1828 to organize a local Society for the Promotion of Temperance. A surviving notebook documents their agreement to "unite their exertions with others in promoting the cause of Temperance in our land." Adopting a constitution that described intemperance as "a most extensive, alarming & deadly evil," they pledged to abstain entirely from drinking "distilled spirituous liquors." A year later a church meeting applied abstinence principles to all members.

"This Church of Christ," members resolved in January 1830, has a solemn duty "to regulate and enlighten public opinion and manners" and "to take the lead in every plan formed for promoting the present and everlasting welfare of our fellow beings." They declared that "ardent spirit is opposed to the spirit of the gospel we profess . . . and when practiced by the professed Christian . . . brings reproach and injury on the church." Pledging to abstain entirely from the use of ardent spirits "except in case of bodily hurt or sickness," they voted to make abstinence "an invariable condition of membership." The next month on a Sunday

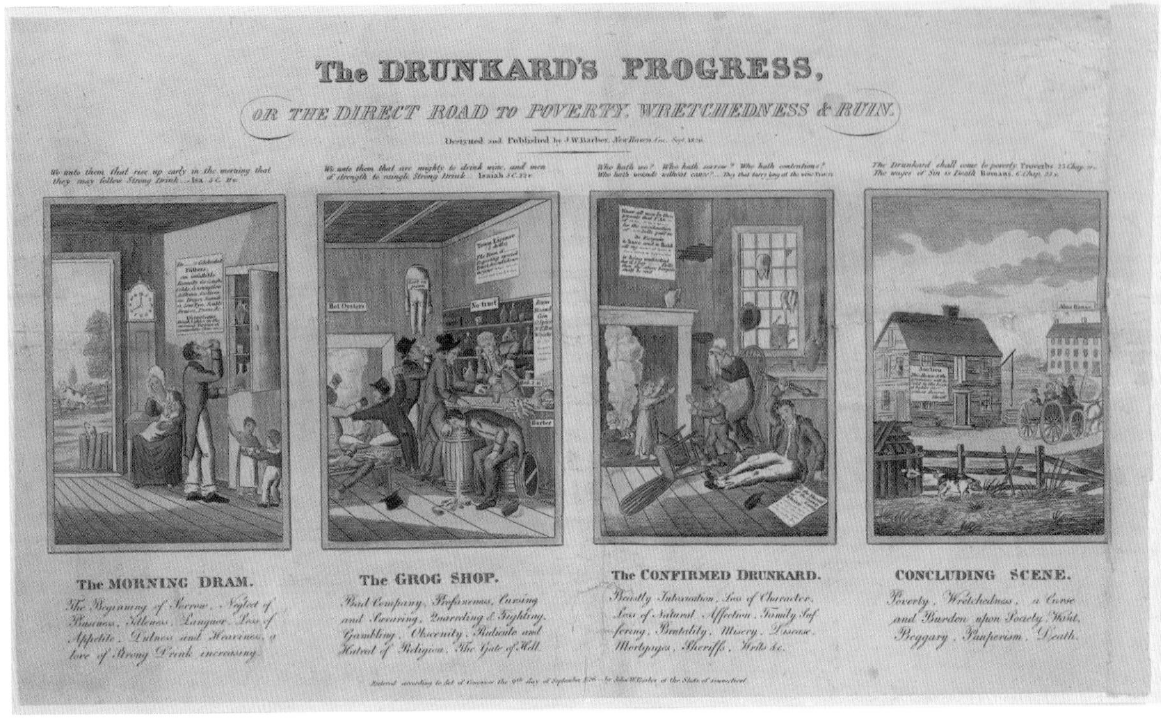

In a series of panels displaying a drunkard's inevitable progress toward wretchedness and ruin, New Haven engraver John Warner Barber conveyed his support for the temperance movement in 1826.

evening a visiting temperance speaker warned in the meetinghouse that at least fifty persons in the parish were "generally acknowledged to be hard drinkers."

Among them was Nancy Freeman (1771–1853), a servant of Mrs. Mary Ann Noyes, born into hereditary slavery in the household of Mrs. Noyes's father-in-law, Judge William Noyes. The date of Freeman's emancipation is not known, but the census in 1820, which for the first time listed no enslaved persons in Lyme, counted ten "free colored persons" in Noyes households. Freeman had joined the church in 1817 at age forty-six, and two years later Mrs. Noyes specified in her will that both Nancy and her brother Prince Freeman (1774–1826) would receive, as compensation for services rendered in her household, "the sum of one thousand dollars each, for their use and maintenance."

When Prince Freeman died in 1826, his remaining legacy passed, by terms of the will, to Nancy. Three years later Lyme's selectmen decided that the bequest from Mrs. Noyes was in jeopardy. Because of Nancy's "intemperance and mismanagement," they expected that this "woman of color" was likely "to spend her estate & be returned to want & become chargeable to said town." To prevent Nancy from becoming a public burden, they appointed William Noyes Jr., a youth of eleven when Nancy was born in his household, to oversee her affairs.

When Dr. Richard Noyes practiced medicine in the house built by his father ca. 1814, close to the site of Rev. Moses Noyes's parsonage, he retained as a household servant at least one of his family's former slaves.

Nancy Freeman and her three younger brothers followed different paths through slavery. Prince, the eldest, continued beyond his years of bondage to serve Judge Noyes's grandson Dr. Richard Noyes (1787–1864). "Prince has been a very faithful servant & my dear Brother & Sister will feel his loss very much," Daniel Noyes wrote in a letter informing Rev. Matthew Noyes of Prince's death at age fifty-two. A decade earlier Nancy's brother Pompey (1776–1822) had run away from Richard Noyes's father, Captain Joseph Noyes (1758–1820), who advertised for his return. The *Connecticut Gazette* posted the notice on December 15, 1816: "Negro man Pomp, age ca. 40, has run away from Joseph Noyes of Lyme. Pomp is blind in one eye and has poor vision in the other." Nancy's youngest brother, Harry

(1790–1823), born when their mother Jenny (1748–1832) was forty-two, followed Prince's example and served Rev. Matthew Noyes, minister in Northford, later North Branford, beyond his years of enslavement. When Harry Freeman died in Northford at age thirty-three, Matthew Noyes paid his burial costs. A surviving receipt itemizes expenses of $2.45 for a sheet and handkerchief, $2.00 for digging a grave, $3.50 for a coffin, and $12.00 for a gravestone.

After Nancy married Jordan Freeman, she lived for an interval apart from the Noyes families. The marriage date is not known, but town records list the birth of their son Isaac Plato in 1812. Five years later Jordan Freeman posted

Mary Ann Williams Noyes, shown at about age thirty in a pastel portrait by James Martin, served as the first president of Lyme's Female Reading Society. She later provided in her will a substantial bequest to a formerly enslaved household servant.

a notice in the *Connecticut Gazette* announcing that Nancy had left his house, which released him of obligation for her support. Despite the substantial bequest from Mary Ann Noyes in 1819, Nancy Freeman's life as a free black in Lyme remained troubled. At a church meeting in May 1830, Richard Noyes denounced her intemperance in a complaint read in the meetinghouse. He charged Nancy, age fifty-nine and "a woman of color, member of said church," with "great neglect of Christian duties, and gross violation of covenant vows," describing her conduct as "contrary to the rules and regulations of the Gospel of Christ . . . and a great dishonor to that religion which she professes."

Dr. Noyes charged that Nancy was "in the frequent habit of being intoxicated with spiritous liquors" and had "neglected Sabbath worship and the Lord's table." While he had "frequently told her of her faults, and invited and entreated her to turn from her evil habits," she had "paid little or no attention to his entreaties." After church members found Nancy guilty, Rev. Colton wrote a compassionate admonition urging her to respond to the charges in the meetinghouse: "I call upon you with feelings of kindness, and a desire for your absolution, that you would immediately turn from your evil ways." Lewis Lewia, also formerly enslaved, read the minister's letter aloud to Nancy. When she "persevere[d] in her ungodly course, unhumbled & incorrigible," having been "intoxicated since the time she was publicly admonished," church members resolved that "she be cut off from all communion and connection."

Similar judgments denounced the intemperance of other church members. Dan Tinker was accused of "the unlawful practice of using intoxicating liquor to excess," failing "to abandon his ruinous habits," and "becoming frequently intoxicated." George W. Mather was found guilty of frequently "drinking distilled liquors . . . and other intoxicating fluids to excess." After extended deliberation both were excommunicated, but church records refer only to Nancy Freeman as a "wicked person."

An assessment of temperance efforts in Middlesex County in 1832, two years after Nancy Freeman's excommunication, reported that the cause was advancing in Lyme. A total of 175 males and 247 females had joined the local temperance organization, six drunkards had reformed, and forty-nine farms along with twenty-four factories and mechanics' shops and nine stores were conducted without ardent spirits. Only one tavern sold "liquid poison."

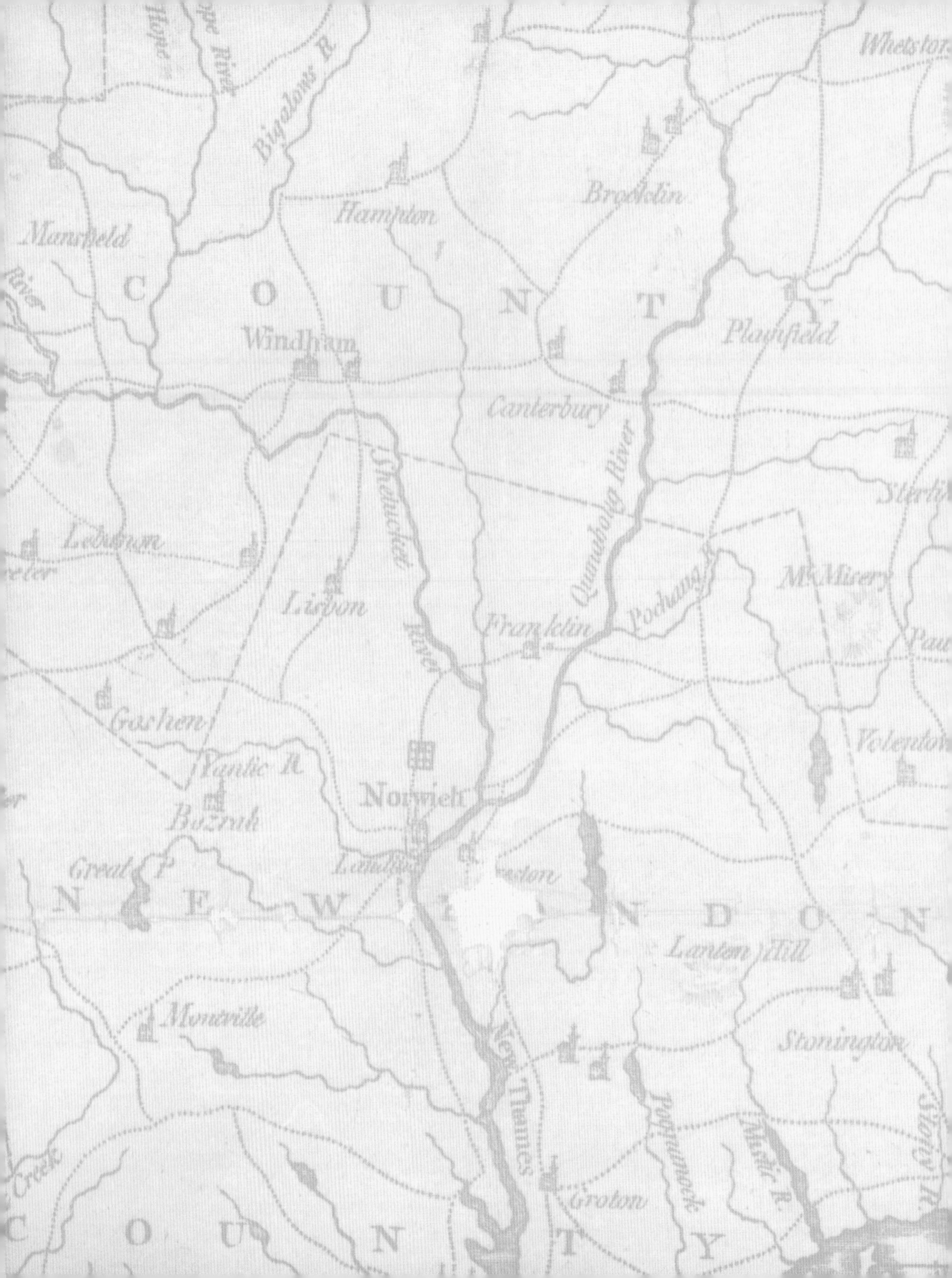

Hope

Hope River

Bigalows R.

Whetston

Mansfield

River

C O U N T

Hampton

Brooklin

Windham

Plainfield

Canterbury

Shetucket River

Quinabaug River

Sterli

Lebanon

Lisbon

Franklin

Pochaug R.

M^t. Misery

Goshen

Yantic R.

Volentow

Norwich

Bozrah

Great P

Landing

reston

N E W L O N D O N

Lantern Hill

Montville

Stonington

New Thames

Poquatnock

Mystic R.

Stony R.

Creek

Groton

C O U N T Y

Chapter twenty-four

Erasing the Records

A decision to erase Ecclesiastical Society records obscured the difficulties existing in Lyme's first church in 1840 and the reasons for the minister's sudden dismissal.

Whereas the report of the committee appointed to ascertain the difficulties existing in the Society ought not in the opinion of the Meeting to have been recorded, now therefore resolved that the Vote of the Society, directing the same to be recorded, be reconsidered, and that Said report be now erased and the clerk be directed to remove the same from the records of the Society and destroy the original report.

The first indication of problems with Lyme's minister came in December 1839 with the appointment of a committee to consider "the difficulties now existing in the Society, ascertain whether they could be settled and report to an adjourned meeting their opinion about what should be done." A vote two weeks later decided that "this Society by reason of the inability under existing circumstances to pay the Rev. Chester Colton his salary of five hundred dollars are disposed to dissolve the connection." Despite the committee's claim of insufficient funds, a surviving account book shows no decline in the Society's finances. The sale of pews raised the usual $550 dollars to cover annual expenses in 1838, the Society's cash on hand increased in 1839, and a subscription covered the additional cost of painting the inside of the meetinghouse in 1840.

As required by contract, the Ecclesiastical Society provided written notice to the minister six months in advance of his dismissal. As the date approached, Rev. Colton sent a formal reply in mid-June objecting to the dissolution procedure. "I presume the Society do not expect that the connection between us is to be dissolved, except in the regular way of calling an Ecclesiastical Council for the purpose," he wrote. Otherwise "it will be injurious to both parties, as you cannot resettle a Pastor, neither can I become a Pastor, if I desire it, of another Church." Only then did the Society call an Ecclesiastical Council "in

In Lyme's stately new meetinghouse, free blacks sat in "so-called 'nigger pews'" constructed in the gallery's rear corners.

relation to the difficulties existing." One day before the neighboring ministers convened, the Society decided that an earlier meeting held to "ascertain the difficulties existing in the Society" should not have been recorded. It then took the unprecedented step of directing clerk Stephen J. Lord (1707–1851) to erase the report from the records and "destroy the original report."

The destruction of Society records in 1840 and the departure from regular procedure suggest the sensitivity of Rev. Colton's dismissal. During the Council's hearing in the meetinghouse, a question "respecting the grounds of procedure in this case" led to "some inquiry and discussion." The Council nevertheless proceeded, "in view of all the circumstances in the case," to confirm "the necessity of the dismission of Reverend Mr. Colton." It also stated that he remained "in regular and good ministerial standing," and it "affectionately recommended [him] to the Ministers and Church of Christ for employment wherever in the providence of God he may be called to labor."

While the missing record obscures the reasons for Rev. Colton's dismissal, no ambiguity surrounds the departure in 1842 of Rev. Aaron Dutton (1780–1849), minister for 36 years of the first church in Guilford twenty miles away. The question of slavery had so divided his congregation that Rev. Dutton, a fellow of Yale College and long an abolition advocate, resigned his position in an attempt to preserve harmony in his parish. A year later when the conflict had not resolved, 123 members of Rev. Dutton's congregation separated to establish Guilford's Third Congregational Church, known at the time as the Abolition Church.

Connecticut ministers took opposing sides on the issue of slavery. The New England Anti-Slavery Society had argued since its founding in Boston in 1832 that slavery was contrary to the principles of Christianity, but some churches dismissed the arguments for abolition. Defining it as a political rather than a religious issue, they insisted that the slavery question did not belong in the meetinghouse. Abolition supporters in Guilford accused

Guilford's "Abolition Church," built on the west side of the town green, became the Third Congregational Church when Rev. David Root settled as minister in 1845. A gravestone in the local cemetery describes him as a "pioneer and untiring laborer in the anti-slavery cause."

their church brethren of "gagging pulpit and pew alike" and keeping "the mouth of the church shut and sealed upon the question which their neighbors were most anxious to discuss, both as citizens and as Christians." No mention of slavery or abolition appears in Lyme's church records, but Rev. Colton had made his stance clear in 1833.

That spring Quaker educator Prudence Crandall (1803–1890) opened her boarding school in Canterbury to colored girls despite fierce local opposition. When Canterbury's Congregational church refused to allow her "Negro" students to attend services, Rev. Samuel J. May (1797–1871), Unitarian minister in neighboring Brooklyn, became Miss Crandall's most outspoken supporter. Amid that bitter contention the Congregational General Association gathered in 1833 at the Brooklyn meetinghouse. Rev. Dutton from Guilford served as moderator at the Association's annual meeting, Rev. Porter from Farmington offered the prayer, and Rev. Colton from Lyme delivered the sermon. He chose brotherly love as his topic and used as his text the Biblical commandment: "These things I command you, that ye love one another."

The next day the Association recommended that Congregational ministers on the July 4th observance address their congregations "on the objects and operations of the American Colonization Society." Advocates for colonization, among them Rev. Leonard Bacon (1802–1861) from New Haven, supported the creation of a country in Africa to resettle freed American slaves. But although the Colonization Society's treasurer in 1833 paid dues of two dollars on behalf of Rev. Colton, he did not renew his membership. A meeting in Lyme convened the previous year "by the colored citizens of this place" had voiced the "sincere opinion" that the Colonization Society was "one of the wildest projects ever patronized by a body of enlightened men." The meeting of free blacks in Lyme, chaired by Yale tutor Rev. Luther Wright (1796–1870) and recorded by secretary Daniel R. Condol (1791–1875), resolved "that we will resist every attempt to banish us from this our native land."

A letter that attorney Charles Griswold, Governor Roger Griswold's son and a church deacon, received in March 1838 likely heightened concern about the violence provoked by spreading abolition support. Farmington's minister Rev.

Above the book-strewn desk in his parsonage study, Rev. William Cary, Old Lyme's post–Civil War minister, hung a portrait of Rev. Leonard Bacon.

Noah Porter had introduced a petition to the United States Senate in January "praying [for] the immediate abolition by law of slavery and the slave trade in the Territories of the United states." Two months later Charles Griswold's friend in Philadelphia described his relief that abolitionist activities in that city had quieted following an outburst of violence. "Our Abolitionists here are quite quiet since the burning of their Hall," John Wilson wrote. "This was mainly brought about by the shock they gave to the feelings of our Citizens by exhibiting themselves publicly arm in arm with their Colored 'brothers & sisters.'"

Widespread publicity about African captives taken from the ship *Amistad* in New London and held in New Haven's jail in December 1839 intensified the abolition controversy in Connecticut. While Rev. Bacon promoted education for the *Amistad* captives and Rev. Porter welcomed them to his Farmington church, a church committee in Lyme that same month recommended Rev. Colton's termination. Whether he had preached to his own congregation on brotherly love or spoken out in the parish supporting abolition is not known, but the context of his dismissal suggests that the "circumstances of the case" involved his convictions about slavery.

In June 1840 when the Ecclesiastical Council convened in Lyme's meetinghouse to confirm Rev. Colton's dismissal, the Congregational General Association met at the New Haven home of Rev. Leonard Bacon. It resolved: "That the system of American slavery is, in the opinion of this Body, inconsistent with the principles of the Gospel; and its immediate abolition, by those who have the legal power, is a duty, in the discharge of which the blessing of heaven may be expected." The group recommended that Congregational churches conduct "a prayerful consideration of this important subject" and exert "their appropriate influence for the emancipation of all the enslaved in this land and throughout the world."

Today Rev. Colton has been largely forgotten, but the succeeding pastor's daughter Martha Brainerd Farwell (1864–1946) voiced admiration for the dismissed minister in notes she compiled on Lyme's church history. Rev. Colton had baptized her mother Anna Chadwick Brainerd (1821–1890) in 1834, and she described her mother's pastor as an instructive and interesting preacher with a sense of humor. He was highly esteemed among his brethren in the ministry, Mrs. Farwell wrote, and "tenacious in his convictions and firm for what he esteemed to be right." She also noted that he was dismissed from his people "with the sincere regret of a large portion of his parishioners."

Chapter twenty-five

Separations

As Lyme's religious landscape diversified, the town's first church denounced the faithlessness of anyone who joined newly established Baptist, Methodist, or Catholic congregations.

Amanda Robbins has . . . been rebaptized by immersion, by one who does not acknowledge our mode of administering the ordinance of Baptism to be scriptural and valid . . . [and] we do most solemnly advise and warn the members of this Church, to avoid all unnecessary intercourse with this, and all other covenant-breakers, that she may be shamed, and humbled and brought to repentance for her faithlessness.

A year after Chester Colton's dismissal, members of Lyme's first parish chose Rev. Davis Brainerd (1812–1875), a scholarly Yale graduate from a prominent East Haddam family, to settle as their Gospel minister. Brainerd, age twenty-nine, had completed theological studies at Princeton and Andover, and he accepted the offer of an annual salary of $550. Ordained in June 1841, the eligible young bachelor within a year married Anna Maria Chadwick and settled into a house on Lyme's main street provided as a wedding gift by her father Daniel Chadwick (1795–1855), captain of the elegantly appointed New York packet ship *Wellington*. One of the first challenges Brainerd faced was the outflow of church members.

Before the completion of the Conference House, Rev. Davis Brainerd hosted church socials and community concerts in his parsonage next door to his father-in-law Captain Daniel Chadwick's stately home.

The number of parishioners leaving Lyme to seek land and livelihood elsewhere had accelerated, and the census count of 4,092 residents in 1830 dropped to 2,896 a decade later. Some had left their native place after the opening of the Erie Canal in 1825 to launch commercial ventures in the newly opening West. Some sought opportunity in the cotton-rich South and along the Mississippi River. Others left for the busy port of New York, where flourishing shipping companies, among them John Griswold's Black X line, carried cabin-class passengers in comfortable staterooms to London and Liverpool, and mail along with cargo like cotton and turpentine. By the mid-1840s, immigrants, mostly from Germany and Ireland, filled the holds of the sleek sailing vessels on their return crossings.

Competition from other religious groups heightened Brainerd's efforts to sustain church membership. A year after his arrival, the First Ecclesiastical Society, acknowledging the town's altered religious landscape, changed its name to the First Congregational Society of Lyme, but church members met requests for dismissal from the congregation with condemnation. Charging that Amanda Robbins had pledged "to walk with this church" and shown herself "utterly faithless" by publicly associating with Baptists and being "rebaptized by immersion," Brainerd pronounced her excommunication. Twice the pastor had "kindly, affectionately and solemnly advised and warned against her disorderly conduct," but she could not be "reclaimed."

When he severed Amanda Robbins's connection with Lyme's first church, Brainerd issued a warning that members should "avoid all unnecessary intercourse with this, and all other covenant-breakers, that she may be shamed, and humbled and brought to repentance for her faithlessness." Similar circumstances prompted the excommunication of Daniel Caulkins, who had "connected himself with the Baptist Church in this place" and had been rebaptized despite continuing efforts to convince him "of his sin and error." The "case of Mrs. Mary Outel" presented church members with a different defection.

Because of her "solemn determination" to join the Roman Catholics and adhere to doctrines that "we deem unscriptural and heretical and dangerous to the soul," Brainerd pronounced Mrs. Outel's excommunication in 1842. She had "deliberately violated her covenant" and connected herself with a church that was "now so degenerate and corrupt as to be unworthy of the name of a Christian Church," he wrote. He also warned his congregation to "avoid the false and dangerous doctrines into which this offending sister has fallen." Church records do not mention where Mrs. Outel connected with Roman Catholics, but a small group of believers in New London had celebrated a first Mass in 1840. A decade later "ten families plus forty single persons" professed the Catholic faith across the Connecticut River in Chester as manufacturing developed.

Departures from Lyme's first church had a long history. The earliest separations occurred when residents in the east and north quarters established independent parishes during the final decade of Moses Noyes's ministry. Thirty years later dissenting brethren and sisters loyal to Rev. Jonathan Parsons publicly withdrew from any connection with the established church. A decade after he settled in Newbury, they organized a separatist church led by pastor Daniel Miner (1737–1799). Later calling themselves "strict Congregationalists," the separatists built a meetinghouse on Grassy Hill where Elder Seth Lee (1777–1826) began preaching in 1812 when it had "only temporary seats and a workbench for the public."

Steve Rosenthal captured the timeless grace and beauty of New England's white churches in a photographic series that included this image of the Grassy Hill meetinghouse in 2012.

Baptists had gathered intermittently in Lyme for half a century by the time Rev. Ezra Stiles observed in 1768, "We are breaking to pieces very fast in our churches in Connecticut." He counted some forty-five families attending two small Baptist churches in Lyme's north parish that year, but Baptists in the first parish, according to a history of New London County, remained "destitute of a place of worship" until 1843. That year in May they held services "in the dooryard of Stephen L. Peck, Esq." (1791–1857) because the Congregational meetinghouse had been "refused for the occasion." By year's end a Baptist meetinghouse on land donated by Stephen Peck opened its doors almost opposite Davis Brainerd's parsonage. Forty of its seventy members were said to be "received by baptism and thirty by letter."

Methodist believers had assembled in Lyme in growing numbers during the 1820s when itinerant preachers attracted crowds of followers at camp meetings. Methodist records describe a gathering in Lyme's Mile Creek schoolhouse in 1830 when "the power of God came down upon the people and many were converted." The construction of a Methodist church nearby on Mile Creek Road in 1841, soon after Brainerd's ordination, expanded

A Baptist Church opened in 1843 on Lyme's main street beside the recently established Lyme Academy, which offered private instruction to area students until fire consumed the building in 1885.

Soon after the Methodist Church celebrated its one hundredth anniversary in 1943 with special music and commemorative speeches, a shrinking congregation closed its doors. The abandoned church deteriorated with age and lack of use, but today it has been repurposed as a private home.

the denomination's membership. By the time Mrs. Mary Ann Mather applied in 1848 for dismissal from the first church and recommendation "to the Methodist Church in the Mile Creek neighborhood," Brainerd's stern warnings about separation had moderated. Her request received favorable consideration, and two years later first church members approved a similar request from her husband. Although they "unanimously regard[ed] him as erroneous in his impressions," they also noted that Elisha Mather "appears to entertain towards this Church, the kindest feelings." He had based his request for dismissal, they decided, "solely on a sense of duty, believing that he could be more useful in the Communion of the Methodist Church than in this."

When Brainerd looked back at his ministry after twenty-five years, he applauded the continuing growth of the church "amid some strong adverse influences." Lyme's population had declined substantially, he noted, and two other churches had been organized "within the limits of this town." Those institutions, with "entirely distinct religious communities and interests," had "necessarily caused a considerable diminution of the number of persons who would otherwise have sought the privilege of religious worship in this original church." Despite those influences, 65 names had still been added to the list of 106 church members at the start of his ministry, and he concluded his anniversary sermon with words of confidence. "That this church has been able to hold its own, as to members and strength under this ceaseless drain upon its vitality, is, I think, a fact in its history quite remarkable."

NL&GG
HYSON
KINCUNE
No. 234

Chapter twenty-six

Improvements

Contentious political issues remained outside the Congregational meetinghouse during the antebellum decades when prominent members improved church property, enhanced their residences, and secured the establishment of the first parish as a separate town.

The history of this church, for the period under review, presents no very great changes, either in its external or internal estate; no events having occurred to disturb the steady and uniform course which it has pursued.

The enhancement of meetinghouse property began in 1845 when Charles C. Griswold, after retiring as a partner in his family's New York shipping firm, purchased a strip of land behind the meetinghouse to provide ten horse sheds "for the comfort and convenience of the dignitaries." The deed required the horse sheds and stalls to "be kept clean and neat and painted" and stipulated that the property could never be "appropriated to any other purpose than that of a shelter of horses and carriages."

Improvements continued two years later when his cousin Richard S. Griswold (1809–1849) funded a Conference House beside the horse sheds to fill a pressing need. Church social events had crowded Brainerd's parsonage, Sabbath school students met in the meetinghouse basement, and town meetings rotated among the district schoolhouses. The deed conveying the Conference House and its land from Richard Griswold to trustees of the Congregational Society in 1848 specified that when not needed for church affairs, the new facility could be used "for such other public meetings as might be useful and profitable to the inhabitants of said Society." The deed also noted that the Ladies Society, which had contributed funding, would have full access to the Conference House for meetings and fairs.

The Griswold family's wealth and influence contributed importantly to Lyme's ongoing improvements. Charles C. Griswold had accumulated "a handsome fortune" from the transatlantic

The horse sheds behind the meetinghouse were still in active use when this photograph was taken ca. 1905. Four years later the local *Deep River New Era* reported that there was "only one car in town, a red Maxwell owned by someone up the Neck Road."

shipping trade when he retired at age fifty-two, a year after Davis Brainerd's installation, and built a spacious new dwelling in 1843 on the site of Governor Matthew Griswold's home in Black Hall. He continued adding furniture and refinements. "The improvements will add greatly to the looks of the house, inside and out," Helen Griswold (1820–1899) wrote in 1848 to her husband Robert H. Griswold (1806–1882), Charles Griswold's cousin and a Black X shipping line captain. Robert Griswold had purchased in 1841 the stately home designed by Samuel Belcher for William Noyes Jr., and he regularly improved his own residence with carpets, draperies, lamps, and a handsome harp purchased in England.

Richard S. Griswold remained a partner in his father's N. L. & G. shipping firm in New York when he built an imposing brick house on Lyme's main street in 1841. The house would be "much more elegant than any thing that has, or ever will be built in Lyme," Helen Griswold reported to her husband. It was "to be of brick and completed in December, all the workmen are from N York," she wrote, noting that Richard was "in Lyme most of the time, attending to and overseeing his workmen" and that the materials were already on the ground. "His house is to be fifty feet square, to be set high for rooms in the basement, a verandah all round it . . . to be built after the English cottage style only he has made some improvements." Helen gave her husband "some

The Conference House on Ferry Road became the regular venue for town meetings, community concerts, church social activities, and festive fund-raising fairs.

little idea of it" so he "might not be too much astonished" when he returned from his voyage.

After graduating from Yale in 1829, Richard Griswold represented his father's mercantile house in Canton, where he negotiated the purchase and shipment of porcelain, silk, and tea. Heavy crates of "china" glazed in the imperial kilns at Jingdezhen served as ballast on N. L. & G. clipper ships like the *Panama*, providing a platform on which perishable silks and teas avoided damage from bilgewater. Among the furnishings in his gracious new home in Lyme was a dinner service of Fitzhugh-patterned porcelain decorated in Canton with an intricate green-and-white border and the initial *G* painted in gold in a center medallion.

Other improvements altered the landscape of Lyme's main street during Brainerd's early ministry. Deacon Daniel Noyes renovated the coaching inn that Marshfield Parsons and his wife Lois had operated beside the meetinghouse, adapting its rear ballroom to provide a schoolroom where Phoebe Griffin Noyes taught tuition-paying students. Captain Daniel Chadwick built a stately new home on land just south of his earlier residence, which then became the new minister's parsonage. Dr. Shubael Bartlett (1811–1849), a Yale graduate who settled as the town's physician and married Charles C. Griswold's daughter Fanny Griswold (1822–1906), built a house based on a cottage design in a recently published book of architectural plans by Alexander J.

Stereograph images capture the elegance of the home on Lyme's main street built by Richard S. Griswold on land acquired from his father-in-law James Mather, who had inherited the Samuel Mather Jr. house next door.

This N. L. & G. tea box traveled from Canton to New York ca. 1844 on the ship *Cohota*, designed and built for the China trade the previous year by the William H. Webb Company.

Downing (1815–1852). Set back from the road with a sweeping front lawn, broad veranda, and upper balcony, it contrasted boldly in 1844 with residences nearby and at the time seemed startlingly modern.

Monthly musical programs in the new Conference House began in 1848, along with a series of talks on anatomy and hygiene that attracted a large audience. A movement to improve public health had spread from England, where sanitary reformers urged cleanliness as a path to health and moral improvement. "Dr. Cutcheon has been lecturing in the Conference Room upon Anatomy and the laws of health, exhibiting some mannikins and a skeleton," Evelyn McCurdy (1823–1917), Richard McCurdy's granddaughter and a devoted Sunday school teacher, noted in her diary that year, when she was twenty-five. "The

Named for Thomas Fitzhugh, an East India Company agent who helped open Chinese ports to foreign trade, the Fitzhugh pattern decorated Chinese export ware from the 1780s through the 1820s. Skilled enamelers in busy Canton workshops decorated sets of Fitzhugh porcelain with monograms for wealthy buyers in the West.

lectures were excellent and very well attended, and will I think be beneficial, for the community sorely needs light upon these subjects. He spoke much of the necessity of daily thorough bathing."

Two years later, in 1850, Sabbath worship moved to the Conference House after a committee completed "a plan for altering the pews and slips in the meetinghouse," along with other improvements. It took almost a year for carpenters to remove the large west window, remodel the high-backed square pews, and strip ornamentation from the pulpit. When Brainerd preached again in the meetinghouse in April 1851, he delivered a "discourse deemed appropriate to the occasion." Six months later "an organ was set up in the House of God," and the congregation "for the first time enjoyed the pleasure of its music."

After tracks were laid across wetlands south of the meetinghouse, wooden carriages operated by the New Haven & New London Railroad Company crossed the Connecticut River in 1853 on a new steam-powered train ferry. "From the twenty-second of July to the twentieth of August, two trains daily were run from New Haven to Brown's Wharf in New London," noted a report prepared for the company's board of directors, on which Charles C. Griswold served. The infrastructure improvements prompted his effort to establish

Changes to the meetinghouse interior in 1850, which included removal of the west-facing Palladian window, stripped away many of the decorative elements in Samuel Belcher's original design.

the southern part of Lyme as a town separate from the less prosperous and more agricultural north society. When the General Assembly in 1854 approved his petition "praying for the incorporation of a new town," it specified that the twenty-seven-square mile area, which approximated the boundaries of the first parish, would have "all the rights, privileges, and immunities . . . of other towns in this state." It also confirmed that the newly separated town would retain ownership of the ferry house, wharf, and other property "used in connection therewith." On July 2, 1855, Deacon Daniel Noyes moderated in the Conference House the first town meeting for the independent town of South Lyme, which changed its name to Old Lyme two years later.

When Davis Brainerd looked back on the course of his ministry after the Civil War's end, he assured his congregation that no events had occurred "to disturb the steady and uniform course" the church had pursued. Outspoken ministers like Rev. Leonard Bacon in New Haven had continued to denounce slavery publicly as an "atrocious abomination in the sight of God," and Brainerd had become a lifetime member of the American Colonization Society in 1853, but his sermons remained focused on sustaining the life of the church, while church meetings attended to matters of internal discipline. Brainerd's successor would later describe him as "given to the work of quiet upbuilding and strengthening the kingdom of God."

Phoebe Griffin Noyes, an active member of the church Ladies Society, conducted a private tuition school emphasizing literature and the arts in her home beside the meetinghouse.

Outside the meetinghouse political arguments divided the community. The decision in 1854 to separate Lyme into two towns coincided with passage of the Kansas-Nebraska Act allowing western territories to choose whether as states they would permit slavery. James A. Bill (1817–1880), a prosperous sheep farmer and outspoken Democrat in the north parish who had been elected to several terms as a state representative, promoted the act so vigorously that he named a son born in Lyme in 1855 Kansas Nebraska Bill. The next year the Republican presidential candidate John C. Frémont won a majority of votes in Connecticut, but Democrat James Buchanan, who supported the right of southern states to allow slaves, was elected president on November 4, 1856. Two days after Buchanan's inauguration, the Dred Scott decision opened all American territories to slavery.

"The Evil Omen," a lengthy ballad written that year by students at Mrs. Noyes's school, declared the upcoming presidential election the "all-absorbing subject." The poem described one group of her students supporting a candidate "for fancy," without "reflect[ing] upon the sufferings / Of the poor unhappy slaves," while others "think of bleeding Kansas" and "mourn their country's shame." Two final stanzas conveyed Mrs. Noyes's convictions even more directly. "Silent and aghast" to see Buchanan's name displayed on the wall "when all thought his name had perished," the teacher cast the poster into the stove, calling his supporters "traitors." But then a puff of wind "snatched him from out the grate."

The Omen is a bad one—
"Alas," the lady cries;
For Freedom and for Kansas
My only hope now dies!

UNION

Chapter twenty-seven

This Dreadful Rebellion

After South Carolina seceded from the Union in December 1860, Deacon Daniel Noyes conveyed in a family letter his alarm at "all this commotion" and his uncertainty about the outcome of "the present crisis."

God only knows what is to be the result of all this commotion—he rules the nations of the Earth, and I trust will in time subdue the angry passions of men, that they may do what is right & just, our Liberty & Union be still preserved.

After the secession of seven slave states and the attack on Fort Sumter in April 1861, some 115 men from Old Lyme served in what Union supporters in the North referred to as the War of the Rebellion. Spurred primarily by a sense of duty but also by the promise of enlistment bounties and the lure of adventure, local volunteers fought and died to preserve the Union. As casualties mounted in 1862, a series of town meetings in the Conference House approved financial incentives to meet local enlistment quotas. In August the town raised "the Bounty to be paid to volunteers from Old Lyme" from $75 to $200. A year later voters approved payment of the same bounty to those who furnished a substitute rather than personally serving.

John Griswold (1837–1862), attorney Charles Griswold's son and a Yale graduate whom Rev. Chester Colton had baptized, volunteered in December 1861 after a year at sea engaged in the Sandwich Island guano trade. Gravely wounded the following September at Antietam, where he led a company of the Eleventh Connecticut Infantry into enemy fire, the courageous young officer, age twenty-five, died in a nearby farmhouse. After his body was returned home, an elaborate marker erected in the Griswold family cemetery commemorated his heroism and preserved a parting message: "Tell my mother I died at the head of my company."

A year later, in February 1863, the body of Corporal James Peckham was returned to Old

Rev. Davis Brainerd, admired for his learning and refinement, kept political controversy outside the meetinghouse in the years leading up to the Civil War.

Captain John Griswold, age twenty-five, died leading his company into enemy fire at Antietam in September 1862.

Lyme's rail depot. Peckham (1841–1862), who served in the Sixteenth Regiment of Infantry soon after his marriage, had died in Virginia from yellow jaundice at age twenty-one. His grieving widow described his return in a letter to his brother serving in Alexandria. "Our father and mine watched the cars day and night until Saturday afternoon when poor Jamie's body arrived," she wrote. "They then took it to the Conference House and it was left until Monday at 11 o'clock when the funeral was attended in the Congregational Church by Mr. Brainerd." She "had the bell tolled for him," she wrote, and she also noted that two other bodies had reached Old Lyme that week. Private Ebenezer Clark, who went "with the 26th Regiment Boys to New Orleans," had died there of typhoid fever.

That spring Captain Enoch Noyes Jr. (1830–1897), a descendant of Lyme's first minister, commanded at Camp Parapet outside New Orleans some seventy-seven volunteers from Old Lyme and East Lyme in Connecticut's

Twenty-Sixth Regiment, Company C. From his nephew Charles Noyes Chadwick (1849–1920), age fourteen, he learned in April about activities in the meetinghouse to support the war effort at home. "We are having grand times now," Charlie wrote. "The folks here have built a staging around the pulpit in the church and hung up a dozen flags or so, and got a piano for a concert." A second fund-raiser followed. "They had one last Wednesday and are going to have another one next Wednesday with refreshments," Charlie noted. "It is for the benefit of the soldiers, they made 48 dollars last time. Admission is 15 cents." Captain Noyes's sister Martha Noyes (1833–1874) had played the piano in the meetinghouse, and his wife, Laura Banning Noyes (1841–1918), "beat them all singing."

Captain Noyes had recently recovered from a severe attack of "swamp fever" and was preparing his company for an assault on Port Hudson to establish Union control of the Mississippi River. In a letter to Charlie's mother, he remarked on the meetinghouse concert. "You must have had a nice time of it," he wrote to his sister Ellen Noyes Chadwick (1824–1900). "I would [have] liked very much to have been there but I have something else to do about these times." Since he was writing on a Sunday, he included "a few words about Sunday matters." A new chaplain, "recently from Connecticut and a splendid preacher," had that morning "spoke to the point and stirred up the fighting qualities of the boys."

Captain Noyes's letters describing life at Camp Parapet mentioned finding rattlesnakes in the privy and killing moccasin snakes and alligators in the swamps. They also remarked on his changing attitudes about the "colored troops" training for the attack on Port Hudson. "We are well blessed with niggers and I think sometimes that they are quite useful," he wrote. "I got down

Captain Enoch Noyes served for nine months with the Twenty-Sixth Regiment Connecticut Volunteer Infantry outside New Orleans during intense fighting to secure Port Hudson, the last Confederate bastion on the Mississippi River.

on them when I was in the hospital but since I have seen them uniformed and drilled as soldiers I think different." By then he had heard stories about the brutal whipping of southern slaves, and he assured his sister, "I don't consider the Union in any great danger, as the nig, only arm them, will take care of this part of the world, they mean [to] fight and will." During the ensuing siege of Port Hudson, Captain Noyes entered brief notes in a pocket diary. He described a night in June spent lying in a rifle pit with shells bursting nearby and his position "pretty well exposed." Three days later in a letter to his wife, he wrote, "I am thankful I am well and able to do something for my name and my Country." If he lived to get back, he added, he would "be proud of the part [he] took in the Bombardment of Port Hudson."

At home sharp opposition between staunch Republicans who embraced the Union cause and local Democrats who condoned secession and opposed the war had played out at the ballot box when Connecticut voters in April 1863 narrowly returned Republican governor William A. Buckingham (1804–1875) to office. After the election Charlie Noyes wrote to his Uncle Enoch at Camp Parapet that "the Democrats alias Copperheads, beat us by ten Majority on the state ticket," but "we beat them 2 on the Representative." Mrs. Noyes's description of Election Day was more explicit. "The election reports today make every one feel very triumphant," she wrote to her daughter Josephine Noyes Ludington (1839–1908) in New York. She added that "the Copperheads got so drunk . . . there were three or four pitched battles & several wounded." One of the most "hateful" had boasted, "You see how the Democratic party has grown since last year."

As Davis Brainerd's parishioners waited anxiously for war updates and news of family members, Mrs. Noyes reflected somberly in a letter to her son serving in Harrisburg on the lives being sacrificed. Union forces had prevailed in July 1863 when General Robert E. Lee pulled his Confederate

A cartoon in *Harper's Weekly* in February 1863 caricatured northerners who opposed the war as dangerous copperhead snakes threatening the Union.

144 HARPER'S WEEKLY.

THE COPPERHEAD PARTY.—IN FAVOR OF *A VIGOROUS PROSECUTION OF PEACE!*

Harper's Weekly reported on February 28, 1863, that Louisiana's free colored troops were "ready and anxious for a brush with the enemy."

troops back from their objective of Harrisburg to fight instead at Gettysburg, but "I do not like to dwell on it," she wrote. "Our victory has been bought by the lives & sufferings of so many brave men, dear to somebody, who have been cut off in the midst of their days, that the country may rejoice in hope that this dreadful rebellion may soon come to an end." With so many boys being killed off, she added, soon "there will be nothing but womankind left—They will be able to get all their rights then & soon get the upper hand."

The entertainment provided at a festive church fair the next year drew attention to the controversial issue of women's rights. The fair filled the Conference House and raised $125 for the U.S. Sanitary Commission, which distributed bandages and medicines to Union army field hospitals. Mrs. Noyes, then sixty-seven, contributed baskets of apples from her orchard behind the meetinghouse for homemade ice cream and spent weeks helping assemble lavish costumes for elaborately staged tableaux. Those scenes showed "pictures" of colorful gypsies, the pirate Blue

Beard, and the Indian maid Pocahontas, which had been popular at previous fairs. The program also included a new tableau called "Women's Rights, or the Union as It Will Be." On one side of the stage, ladies sat around a table "reading & smoking & their legs crossed, dressed as much in the womens rights fashion as possible," while on the other side one man trotted a baby on his knee, another carried dishes, and a third sat knitting. Mrs. Noyes thought the caricature of women's equality was "very good."

Soon after the war a dispute within the church strengthened the influence of women members. When a committee of brethren asked the Ladies Society in 1867 to contribute funds to paint the meetinghouse, the women requested a voice in

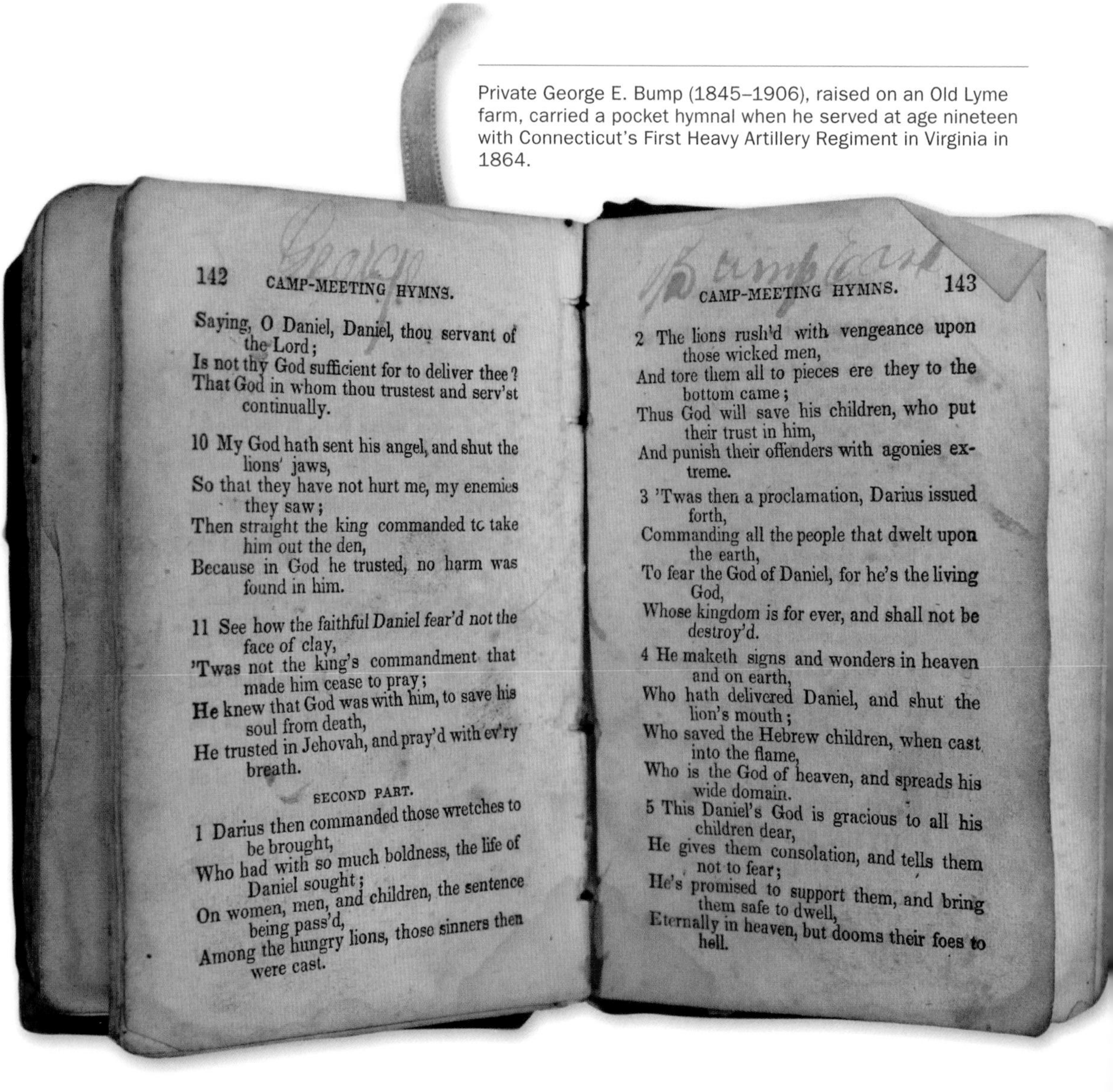

Private George E. Bump (1845–1906), raised on an Old Lyme farm, carried a pocket hymnal when he served at age nineteen with Connecticut's First Heavy Artillery Regiment in Virginia in 1864.

142 CAMP-MEETING HYMNS.

Saying, O Daniel, Daniel, thou servant of the Lord;
Is not thy God sufficient for to deliver thee?
That God in whom thou trustest and serv'st continually.

10 My God hath sent his angel, and shut the lions' jaws,
So that they have not hurt me, my enemies they saw;
Then straight the king commanded to take him out the den,
Because in God he trusted, no harm was found in him.

11 See how the faithful Daniel fear'd not the face of clay,
'Twas not the king's commandment that made him cease to pray;
He knew that God was with him, to save his soul from death,
He trusted in Jehovah, and pray'd with ev'ry breath.

SECOND PART.

1 Darius then commanded those wretches to be brought,
Who had with so much boldness, the life of Daniel sought;
On women, men, and children, the sentence being pass'd,
Among the hungry lions, those sinners then were cast.

CAMP-MEETING HYMNS. 143

2 The lions rush'd with vengeance upon those wicked men,
And tore them all to pieces ere they to the bottom came;
Thus God will save his children, who put their trust in him,
And punish their offenders with agonies extreme.

3 'Twas then a proclamation, Darius issued forth,
Commanding all the people that dwelt upon the earth,
To fear the God of Daniel, for he's the living God,
Whose kingdom is for ever, and shall not be destroy'd.

4 He maketh signs and wonders in heaven and on earth,
Who hath delivered Daniel, and shut the lion's mouth;
Who saved the Hebrew children, when cast into the flame,
Who is the God of heaven, and spreads his wide domain.

5 This Daniel's God is gracious to all his children dear,
He gives them consolation, and tells them not to fear;
He's promised to support them, and bring them safe to dwell,
Eternally in heaven, but dooms their foes to hell.

deciding the paint color. The resulting controversy prompted sardonic newspaper comments as far away as Springfield and New York. Closer to home the weekly *East Lyme Star* reported with mock concern on the local dispute: "Many of our readers will remember that our sister town of Lyme has been shaken from 'centre to circumference' for some time past, and all because its excellent citizens could not agree upon what color their church should be painted."

Mrs. Noyes explained in a family letter what she wryly termed "the great trouble of the day." The difficulties began, she wrote, when the ladies agreed to pay for the work "on condition they painted the trimmings white & the rest of the church one shade darker or some light color to throw out the beautiful work about the cornishes." But the men, who had "not the least thought of leaving it to the ladies," voted that "white is to be the color." The men prevailed and the meetinghouse remained white, but the ladies' voices brought change. In 1869, half a year before the Connecticut Woman Suffrage Association was organized in Hartford, "a motion was orderly made and seconded, that the female members of the church, be requested to cast their votes, with the male members of it, in the election of another deacon." The motion allowing women limited voting rights "passed unanimously."

How beau

Chapter twenty-eight

A Wealth of History

When Old Lyme's postwar minister, a former cavalry officer in the Union army, delivered a historical address in the meetinghouse in 1876 to commemorate the nation's centennial, he presented the town's "wealth of history" as a call to action and urged that the "lesson of the past" not be lost.

And here let me urge those who are just entering upon manhood's duties to heed the lives of these men of old, these giants of worth and of work, whose deeds beautify history's page; let me urge you to emulate them. The lesson of the past will be lost to us, and our rehearsal of its worthy deeds will be vain parade, except we profit by it in shaping our lives according to the pattern displayed. Oh! Let not the story of the past be fruitless.

Not everyone favored the selection of a Civil War cavalry officer without a college degree to succeed the learned Rev. Davis Brainerd after his death in 1875. Prominent parishioners like Evelyn McCurdy Salisbury, accustomed to "men of culture and refinement" as their ministers, raised doubts about William B. Cary (1841–1923), age thirty-four, who had "presented himself for our church" but "isn't polished, and never will be." The candidate won approval after demonstrating his respect for church tradition and his thoughtful understanding of its "wealth of history" in a *Memorial Discourse* delivered in the meetinghouse on July 4, 1876, to commemorate the nation's centennial. An all-day celebration on Meetinghouse Hill with an elaborate picnic and afternoon races and games followed the minister's formal address.

A centennial exhibition in the new Pierpont Hotel a month later displayed objects and documents reflecting the "earliest records of our history." Ellen Noyes Chadwick had read in the meetinghouse a request for the loan of "particularly those things which show taste, ingenuity and skill in construction such as carvings in wood, drawings,

Rev. William B. Cary brought to Old Lyme's meetinghouse the war-wise perspective of a battle-tested Civil War cavalry officer.

paintings, embroidery, needlework & &." In September the *Hartford Courant* reported that "the beautiful and quiet little town of Lyme has been recently seized with a violent fit of Centennial fever, and opened its archives for three days and evenings to the public eye." The article praised the "artistic and decorated pottery" as "the most notable feature of the occasion," and the columnist singled out pieces described as exquisitely decorated porcelain, along with a "modest teapot" that had belonged to Jenny Freeman, for many years an enslaved servant of the Noyes family. The teapot of "Old Black Jenny, a good Christian woman," the columnist observed, served as a useful reminder "to keep us from losing sight of the fact that the early settlers of Connecticut were, many of them, slaveholders."

Two months after the centennial celebration, following an extended "time of trial," church members in September 1876 invited the acting minister to settle as pastor. His claim of descent from a prominent Lyme family eased his acceptance. Tracing his Lyme ancestry to Richard Ely, Cary had referred to himself in his *Memorial Discourse* as "a stranger to Lyme two months ago" but by descent "a rightful participant in all that pertains to her history." The Society offered an annual salary of $1,200 plus a rent allowance of $150 for a "suitable parsonage," and an ordination service in November opened and closed with prayer and singing.

William Cary, a lawyer's son, had been raised on a farm in New Jersey in a family of Democrats and wrote in an unpublished memoir that he had "imbibed a dislike and a hatred for the party branded 'Black Republicans' by its opponents." As a youth he had considered Abraham Lincoln "entirely unfit to hold an office of trust," but reading the Lincoln-Douglas debates changed his views. In those speeches delivered in 1858 he discovered "a giant intellect, a clear and discerning mind." Lincoln, he wrote, "won me, heart and soul."

At age twenty in 1861, William Cary enlisted in the Fifth New York Cavalry. He took part in the punishing second battle at Bull Run and later in the protracted Wilderness campaign, but in the summer of 1863 he was detached to the

Ellen Noyes Chadwick, a descendant of Lyme's first minister, preserved the family's papers, photographs, and traditions.

headquarters of General Samuel Heintzleman (1805–1880) in Washington. There he served several times as a mounted escort for President Lincoln, whom he described as "a great soul" and "the most wonderful man in the world." From his conversations with the embattled nation's weary leader, the young officer, by then "somewhat war-wise," learned lessons in kindness, humility, and purpose that would later, he wrote, "come home to me forcibly and irresistibly."

The war led Captain Cary to Union Theological Seminary, and after graduating in 1871, he devoted four years to mission work in Kansas. With a seminary classmate he established small churches near frontier towns like Abilene, famed for its cattle pens, marauding cowboys, and raucous saloons. Looking for a quiet place to settle with his wife and two young sons in 1875, he felt "providentially directed to Lyme," where the pulpit was vacant and he had distant Ely family relatives.

The town remained small when Cary arrived, with a population in 1870 of 1,363, but its acclaim had grown in the post–Civil War decade as its historic character and scenic landscape attracted tourists, artists, and journalists. A railroad bridge that spanned the lower Connecticut River in 1871 eliminated the steam ferry, which author Charles Dickens (1812–1870) had deplored on a reading tour four years earlier. "The steamer rises and falls with the river," Dickens wrote on his second American tour in 1867 as he crossed from Old Lyme to Saybrook, "and the train is banged uphill or banged downhill." A broken rope had caused his train to rush back "with a run downhill into the boat again," and he had "whisked out" of his carriage, but noted that few others seemed alarmed.

Completion of the rail bridge led a local business syndicate in 1872 to open the Pierpont House, a handsome summer hotel built on land that a century and a half earlier had been given as a settlement to Rev. Samuel Pierpont. "Artists are beginning to find the picturesque attractions of the neighborhood," Ellen Noyes Chadwick, who had studied painting with Mrs. Phoebe Noyes, wrote in 1874 to historian Martha Lamb. "Miss Fidelia Bridges [1834–1923], after spending last summer near the lakes in the center of the town, came again this year, and expects to make it a special summer resort for the prosecution of her beautiful art." Mrs. Lamb's illustrated account of "this ancient and interesting town" that appeared

A new summer hotel, the Pierpont House, opened in 1872 on Ferry Road, which connected the railroad depot with the town's main street.

in the centennial issue of *Harper's New Monthly Magazine* two years later described Old Lyme's meetinghouse as "strikingly ornate." It also urged readers to stop at Lyme station and discover the charming town where the meetinghouse "towers above you, like an anciently bound and well-preserved chapter of ecclesiastical history." Noting that the town was "exceptionally rich in family reminiscences," she called it "one of the loveliest nooks on the New England coast." A New York newspaper reported, "Mrs. Lamb's article called up so much interest as to nearly fill the Pierpont House for several summers."

Newspaper columnists repeatedly featured Old Lyme as a place of social prominence and refined entertainment. One event that captured admiring press notice in New York was a steeplechase in September 1877. Among the carriages gathered near two stately mansions, the journalist noted, "stood that of Chief Justice Waite, and to the right, seated in another carriage, I saw Rev. Mr. and Mrs. Cary and friends." Morrison Remick Waite had been chosen in 1874 as chief justice of the Supreme Court and continued to summer in Old Lyme. The article also described Captain Robert Griswold's youngest daughter Florence Griswold (1850–1937), age twenty-seven, as a "graceful rider who might surprise our English cousins should we ever put our national equestrian skill to the test." An archery shoot at a festive lawn party in 1880 also drew a large crowd. "There must have been about two hundred people there, both from Lyme and Saybrook, all in their fine clothes and war paint," one participant reported.

Over three summers New York watercolorist Fidelia Bridges created lyrical studies of birds, wildflowers, and field grasses in Old Lyme. She painted *Wild Roses among Rye*, held today by the Florence Griswold Museum, in 1874.

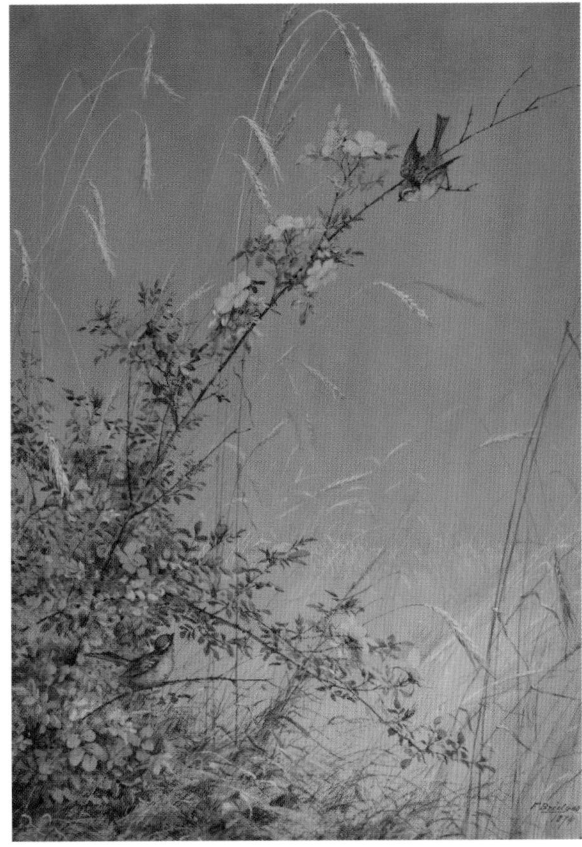

"They had a good many games besides Tennis and Archer, a nice band, and delicious supper."

As Old Lyme's reputation spread, the town became known for providing educational opportunities in a refined setting. The Black Hall School for Boys began offering "preparatory studies" in 1875 in the former estate of Captain George Moore (1792–1848), a packet ship commander on John Griswold's New York–London line, and three years later Florence Griswold with her mother and two sisters opened a private home school for girls. "Mrs. Robert H. Griswold and her daughters, in their healthy and very pleasant home at Lyme, Conn., will receive a few young ladies," a New York newspaper announced. The school would "thoroughly teach piano, harp, guitar, singing by the Italian method, and drawing, sketching and painting in water and oil colors." Earlier that year Florence and her sisters had provided graceful sketches for William Cary's autograph book, and she chose as her subject the elegant harp, purchased by her father in London, that adorned their parlor.

The minister's ease with narrative engaged eager listeners. A cousin recalled Cary's moving account at a family gathering of setting out reluctantly one evening to locate a Union soldier left behind on the battlefield, only to discover that the wounded man was his younger brother. The boys in his Sunday school class waited to hear his war stories, and Harriet Lord wrote that on Christmas Day in 1877, when "the church was profusely & beautifully decorated with ferns & greens & flowers, & the children sang & spoke," the minister "made a good address about Santa Claus." That evening the congregation adjourned to the new town hall, "where they had a bounteous feast & Magic Lantern & pictures in the evening."

Cary's experience as a cavalry officer and a clergyman on the frontier informed a series of articles written for New York newspapers. His sermons have not been discovered, but his columns call attention with quiet urgency to pressing social issues. He described the emotional burdens borne by overworked farmers' wives, the dangerous availability of pistols that made local boys feel like western gunslingers, and the availability of cheap alcohol that led to a winter fire in Old Lyme and the tragic death of a child.

Charles Parsons, a lithographer, watercolorist, and art editor of *Harper's Monthly*, likely drew the updated version of John Warner Barber's *West View of Lyme* that illustrated Martha Lamb's article. In addition to the Congregational meetinghouse, the later view included the Baptist Church, the Pierpont Hotel, and the Gothic revival home of Ellen Noyes Chadwick on the road from the railroad depot.

Cary also pursued his interest in church history and in 1883 published a detailed account of Rev. Jonathan Parsons's revivalism in Lyme during the Great Awakening. That same year he arranged for a Parsons family member living in Ohio to give the church a "crayon" of the celebrated preacher. The portrait, described as "a life size bust, in black gown, white wig, lawn neck tie," hung in the Conference House until fire consumed the building along with the meetinghouse in 1907.

Cary had already secured for the church a more lasting gift, having arranged with his widowed neighbor Mrs. Edwardanna Chadwick (1809–1882) the bequest of her historic home, built almost a century earlier by Samuel Mather Jr., to serve as a permanent parsonage. There Rev. Lathrop Rockwell had answered questions about his theological beliefs on the eve of his installation as pastor almost a century earlier, and Cary moved into the new parsonage with his wife and six children in the spring of 1883. His resignation the following August was "most unexpected." The minister had secured wide "respect and esteem," and the Congregational Society adopted a unanimous resolution stating "that we are unwilling to part with him without expressing our

A national audience viewed the sketch of Old Lyme's meetinghouse, attributed to Charles Parsons, that appeared in America's centennial year in *Harper's Monthly*.

confidence in his Christian character [and] our appreciation of his services in the ministry here."

Cary's resignation letter sounded a wistful tone. "Perhaps another may be able to do somewhat for you that I have not been able to do," he wrote. His departure meant parting from "loved friends and hallowed association," but it would also "spare myself where my utmost endeavors have failed to realize my eager wishes." After his announcement that he would "seek another field of usefulness," a council assembled in the meetinghouse to confirm the dissolution. It rejoiced "that this separation involves no want of harmony between the pastor and the people."

Cary accepted a call to serve in the less affluent and largely agricultural community of North Stonington, where he remained as minister for sixteen years. While there he ventured into politics

Florence Griswold drew a finely detailed pen-and-ink sketch of the harp in her family home on a page in William Cary's leather-bound autograph book, purchased in 1876 when he attended a reunion of his cavalry unit near the Gettysburg battlefield.

and as a representative to Connecticut's General Assembly in 1889 drafted legislation mandating indeterminate sentences rather than fixed terms for the state's prison inmates. His final ministry began in 1914 when, at age seventy-three, he accepted a position as Protestant chaplain at the state prison in Wethersfield. There he conducted chapel services, oversaw the print shop, built a library, and directed the night school. "Some sincere and hopeful professions of penitence and reform have been made to me," he wrote in a report to the state prison directors. After his death in 1923, a newspaper obituary noted that William Cary became known as the "Fighting Parson" not only for his Civil War service but also for his social reform initiatives and his recruitment efforts during World War I.

Forty years earlier, in his centennial address in Old Lyme's meetinghouse, Cary had urged church members to follow the example of their eminent predecessors so that "the lesson of the past will not be lost to us." The war-wise pastor closed his historical discourse with a question that shaped his own direction: "Shall we not reproduce to the world, by the help of God, what was noble and true in them, and give to future history a record as unimpeachable as that of the past?"

An unknown artist contributed to William Cary's autograph book a sketch of the meetinghouse surrounded by copies of *Harper's Magazine* illustrations of Lyme's scenic places.

"Heaven from all creatures hides the book of Fate."—*Pope*.

For sale for benefit of the Chu[rch]

25

A Simple Story now told in Rhyme Concerning a darkened window in Lyme.

By M. G. POND.

CHAPTER TWENTY-NINE

A Story Told in Rhyme

Forty years after improvements altered the meetinghouse interior, changing architectural tastes brought an elegant restoration of Samuel Belcher's original design.

Forty years pass away. The people awake
To the fact that the architect made no mistake.
"The church is quite ugly," the new pastor said.
"Those galleries now are down on one's head.
"We are tired of that ice box, 'tis nothing but pine;
For the House of the Lord there is nothing too fine."
Respond his adherents. " 'Tis time it be changed,
We will see if this matter can be rearranged."

The restoration of Old Lyme's meetinghouse that New York architect Henry Rutgers Marshall (1852–1927) completed in 1887 received dazzling acclaim. The *New York Tribune* commended "the exceeding beauty of the interior" and noted that "the people of Old Lyme have in their possession one of the choicest gems of old New-England, a unique and beautiful relic of the past, only with added graces." The *New Haven Register* called the changes and redecorations an "unqualified success" that demonstrated "great taste, together with high educational accomplishments and a warm love for the venerable and beautiful." A student of the renowned architect Henry Hobson Richardson (1838–1886), Marshall would later serve as president of the American Institute of Architects.

A ballad written in 1895 by a neighbor on Ferry Road praised the meetinghouse improvements in lighthearted verse. Martha Gillette Pond

Studio space was scarce when artists clustered in Old Lyme at the turn of the twentieth century, and Abraham L. Laiblin, a painting instructor at the Boxwood School, worked in an outbuilding beside the home on Ferry Road of Martha G. Pond, whose portrait he painted ca. 1904.

In *A Simple Story Now Told in Rhyme*, printed as a pamphlet and "sold for benefit of the church, 25 cents," Martha Pond documented changes made to the meetinghouse interior in 1850.

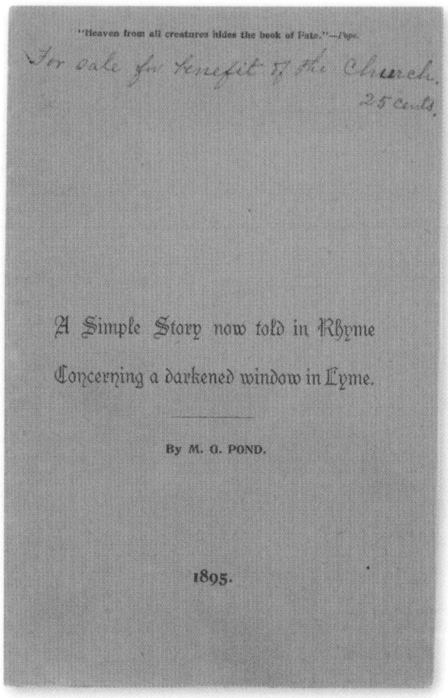

"Heaven from all creatures hides the book of Fate."—Pope.
For sale for benefit of the Church.
25 cents.
A Simple Story now told in Rhyme
Concerning a darkened window in Lyme.
By M. G. POND.
1895.

(1838–1916), then age forty-nine, commented on changing architectural tastes while narrating the discoveries of two young lovers who roamed through the meetinghouse during the renovation, "when it looked so forlorn." Attracted by the outline of "the old pulpit window" still visible on the exterior wall, they climbed "over rubbish and plaster and dirt" and found a love letter deposited long ago in a chink in the wall. With her "Simple Story" Miss Pond, who could see the meetinghouse from the stately home built by her uncle Horace Lynde Sill (1794–1874) after his retirement from the N. L. & G. shipping firm, eloquently mocked a prior lapse in aesthetic judgment. While lamenting the loss of the original Palladian window and mahogany pulpit, she explored shifting ideas about embellishment and austerity.

After forty years people awoke, she wrote, and recognized belatedly that the original builder had "made no mistake." They regretted the

When Rev. Benjamin Bacon urged restoration of the meetinghouse interior, he stressed the costly project's contribution to "the spirit and the enterprise of the town."

destruction of the west window that "gave the preacher some light" and the installation of a high desk, "cold-looking and bare," that served after 1850 as the pulpit. When the "new pastor" agreed that the church was "quite ugly," the congregation moved forward with plans for restoration. "'Tis time it be changed," they agreed. "We will see if this matter can be rearranged."

Old Lyme's new pastor, Rev. Benjamin Wisner Bacon (1860–1932), had brought to the meetinghouse both cultural refinement and an illustrious heritage. After completing Yale's graduate program in divinity in 1884, the accomplished young scholar supplied the pulpit left empty by William Cary's departure. The stature of his father, Rev. Leonard Woolsey Bacon (1830–1907) from Norwich, and his grandfather Rev. Leonard Bacon from New Haven, heightened his appeal, as did the impressive family connections of his bride Eliza Buckingham Aiken (1862–1933), whose grandfather William A. Buckingham had served as Connecticut's Civil War governor. Benjamin Bacon and his wife were "received by the town with much enthusiasm," and the *New London Telegram* praised the "singular beauty and great power" of his initial sermon.

Those who attended Bacon's ordination on July 1, 1884, partook of "an elegant collation . . . served by ladies of the parish, in the lecture-room of the church," where "the benignant countenance of the Rev. Jonathan Parsons . . . looked upon the scene from a portrait on the wall." Inside the meetinghouse they heard Rev. Leonard W. Bacon's "weighty and affectionate charge to his son." Although the new minister's grandfather had not lived to attend the ceremony, Rev. Leonard Bacon's reflections on the role of the meetinghouse influenced his grandson's views. In a sermon delivered in Hartford in 1879, the elder Bacon had praised the contribution to local communities of Connecticut's early meetinghouses.

Benjamin Bacon's community involvement began soon after his ordination when he organized a Reading Club in Old Lyme and helped establish a Music and Literary Association that had ambitious

Charles Ludington donated a gracefully carved mahogany communion table and two high-backed chairs upholstered in burgundy velvet to furnish Old Lyme's newly renovated meetinghouse in 1887.

plans for a new meeting place. The proposed building would provide shelving for the three thousand books in the town's lending library and rehearsal space for its concert band. In a plea for funding, Attorney James Griswold (1828–1892), the Congregational Society's treasurer, emphasized the band's importance for young men in the community. They rarely missed a rehearsal, he wrote, and participation in the band had the surprising effect of "enlarging and heightening their ideas" while also ridding them of their "rustic sullenness." Charles Ludington (1835–1910), a New York businessman who in 1862 had married Josephine Noyes and who summered in the Noyes family home beside the meetinghouse, sent a check for half the estimated cost.

Plans to renovate the meetinghouse coincided with construction of the Band Room, and in 1886 Bacon delivered an inspirational sermon urging generous contributions for "beautifying the House of the Lord." The effort would serve not only the interests of the church, the minister noted, but also "the spirit and the enterprise of the town." Mr. Ludington, who had also recently funded a new consolidated schoolhouse on the main street, provided a major gift to support the meetinghouse alterations.

Where the west window had "been walled in by new plaster," Marshall created a gracious elliptical apse. He also lowered the meetinghouse floor, softened the contours of the seating, added curving mahogany stairs leading to an ornately carved pulpit, and removed the triangular pews where "black people" had sat in the gallery's rear corners. Gold-leaf tracery outlined the dome, and harmonious tones of cream and ivory highlighted the intricate details, much as Mrs. Noyes and others in the Ladies Society had proposed for the exterior of the meetinghouse two decades earlier. Graceful new pulpit furniture and a mahogany communion table donated by Mr. Ludington adorned the sanctuary. Mrs. Charles C. Griswold contributed a handsome new organ, and the "untiring efforts" of Mrs. Richard S. Griswold Jr. obtained sufficient subscriptions to place a clock in the belfry.

Soon after rededicating the restored meetinghouse in 1887, Benjamin Bacon resigned. Mrs. Salisbury explained his "wish for a wider field in a more active business community," but his letter of resignation hinted at other factors. "The mistakes, the inexperience and the discouragement, which have clogged our progress here, will be lifted from the path of the wiser and better successor," he wrote. Bacon served next as pastor in Oswego, New York, then returned to New Haven at age thirty-six to teach New Testament exegesis at Yale. In Old Lyme's parsonage he had started working on his first scholarly book, after Mrs. Salisbury's husband donated a substantial library for his use. In a preface to *The Genesis of Genesis*, dedicated to Edward E. Salisbury, Bacon urged the intersection of meetinghouse and community. The Bible was "something not to be left merely to the pulpit and the Sunday-school teacher," he wrote, "but to be eagerly welcomed into the domain of school, college and university training." He would later be described as "one of the finest Biblical scholars in the United States."

The Ecclesiastical Council that convened in the meetinghouse in December 1888 to approve his resignation expressed regret at "the early termination of a pastorate so pleasant and hopeful" and hope that the church "may be speedily and wisely guided to the choice of a successor." A week later Charles Griswold Bartlett (1848–1912), Dr. Shubael Bartlett's son and headmaster of the Black Hall School for Boys, wrote a personal letter to Charles Ludington suggesting the qualities to be sought in the next minister. Bartlett agreed that the Society should "secur[e] the services of a gentleman [and] of a reverent and cultivated preacher," but he argued that "the parish generally needs a pastor, one who will call upon his congregation in their homes and, while preserving his own dignity and refinement, will consider it no small part of his duty and make it a pleasure to be on terms of confidence with anyone who needs his advice or sympathy." The task ahead would be difficult, Bartlett observed, as "any young man of real ability would stay in Lyme no more than four or five years." The notice of the pulpit vacancy that appeared in the *Christian Union* in 1889 stressed the appeal of the place: "There is a large, commodious parsonage, partially furnished, the society of the town is good, and the place is a healthful and agreeable one for residence."

During his four-year ministry, Benjamin Bacon ensured lasting recognition of the iconic beauty of Old Lyme's meetinghouse, but its former austerity was not the only matter to be "rearranged." An Ecclesiastical Society meeting in 1885 that considered whether female members should "vote on matters pertaining to the interest of the church" brought a unanimous vote allowing the women "liberty to express their opinions." It specified that their votes would be "of equal consideration in right with them of other members."

Old Lyme's concert band, which offered entertainment for the community and educational enrichment for its local members, performed on the meetinghouse steps.

THE CONGREGATIONAL CHURCH

IN OLD LYME

WILL

Celebrate the 200th Anniversary

OF ITS ORGANIZATION

Thursday P. M., Aug. 31, 1893.

At 3:30 there will be a Roll call of members, and every member is earnestly desired to report in person or by letter.

AT 4:15 AN HISTORICAL ADDRESS.

AT 5 A SOCIAL TEA.

ARTHUR SHIRLEY,

Pastor.

Chapter thirty

Progress and Philanthropy

The sermon that celebrated the two hundredth anniversary of Lyme's first church in 1893 traced its progress, praised its influence, and affirmed its essential role as "a leader of the community in morality and philanthropy."

There is a natural and proper satisfaction in being connected with an institution which took root in this virgin soil in the day of origins, and in reviewing the beginning and the progress of its life and influence.

The concerns of the church spilled out from the meetinghouse in the 1890s as Progressive Era social reforms sought to relieve poverty, strengthen families, and expand education. After his installation in April 1890, Rev. Arthur Shirley (1845–1927), age forty-five and the son of a Maine temperance worker, devoted his efforts during a seven-year ministry to community improvement. Formerly the pastor in Conway, Massachusetts, Shirley had been valedictorian of his class at Yale in 1869, and Old Lyme's influential church members responded favorably when he supplied the pulpit. "His sermon on Sunday was delivered in a pleasant, un-oratorical voice, and was a plain practical one, everyone seems to like him," observed Charles Ludington's daughter Katharine Ludington (1869–1953) in 1889. "Everyone would like to see him settled here."

To commemorate the two hundredth anniversary of the church in August 1893, Shirley reviewed its progress. "The address was given at 4:15," music was "furnished by an orchestra in connection with the organ and choir," and a "social tea" followed. The sermon acknowledged that "the history of this Old Lyme Congregational Church has already been given us in outline" and that Rev. William Cary had provided "the essential items concerning this edifice." Shirley's own address relied on works of "contemporaneous history," like "the narratives of John Mason . . . and the testimony of other contemporaneous witnesses," and he hoped to "set forth a few supplementary facts in regard to the present situation."

THE CONGREGATIONAL CHURCH
IN OLD LYME
WILL
Celebrate the 200th Anniversary
OF ITS ORGANIZATION
Thursday P. M., Aug. 31, 1893.

At 3:30 there will be a Roll call of members, and every member is earnestly desired to report in person or by letter.

AT 4:15 AN HISTORICAL ADDRESS.

AT 5 A SOCIAL TEA.

ARTHUR SHIRLEY,
Pastor.

Rev. Arthur Shirley delivered a historical address in 1893 commending the progress of Old Lyme's church over two centuries and revising mistaken assumptions about its past.

To "elucidate some points which have been left in obscurity," Shirley began by examining the belief that Lyme's early settlers had found themselves "in the midst of fierce and treacherous and bloodthirsty tribes." Although colonists along the lower Connecticut River had judged it necessary in 1637 to burn alive the inhabitants of a nearby Pequot encampment in order to save themselves, Shirley said with regret, thereafter the "intercourse of the first settlers with the Indians in Lyme was wholly of a peaceful nature." Another early marker of progress was the decision to call the first minister to office. Although Moses Noyes had waited twenty-seven years for a church to be gathered, most likely spending his time overseeing the slaves tending his fields and performing whatever ministerial duties were allowed, after 1693 "the full tide of church-life [began] to flow." As a more recent sign of progress, Shirley described the meetinghouse renovation in 1887 that had removed the "so-called 'nigger pews,'" after which the substantial architecture of the old church acquired "a delicate new spirit."

Shirley's concern with the welfare of African Americans and Native Americans had already influenced mission projects undertaken by the Ladies Benevolent Society, which in 1891, soon after his arrival, replaced three earlier women's groups. Members that year used their dues of fifty cents, together with $68 collected from an "ice cream & apron sale," to send a barrel filled with yard goods and hand-stitched garments to the Warner Institute in Jonesboro, Tennessee, established in 1876 "to educate colored people and train colored teachers." They sent a second barrel of clothing to a needy parish serving primarily native people in Custer County, South Dakota.

Shirley's ongoing concern with social progress prompted an effort in 1894 to revitalize the local temperance movement. Earlier church attempts to promote abstinence had faded after the mid-1840s, and prohibition had recently suffered electoral defeats in Connecticut. The *Sound Breeze* had reported in 1889 that a "prohibitory amendment" to prevent the manufacture or sale of intoxicating liquors had passed in only twenty-two towns, with 22,805 votes supporting the amendment and a majority of 27,561 opposed. The minister's endeavors to revive temperance support in Old Lyme drew ecumenical support, and monthly meetings of a newly organized Temperance Union convened alternately in the

Students in the graduating class of 1902 posed on the porch steps of the Boxwood School for Girls, established by Mrs. Richard S. Griswold Jr. in 1890.

Congregational meetinghouse and the Baptist church. Together with Baptist minister Rev. J. C. Gavin, Shirley organized in 1894 a weeklong mass temperance gathering, and the *Sound Breeze* provided extensive coverage of the "Gospel meetings" that recruited a local "cold-water army" pledged to abstain from alcohol.

Every evening in the town hall, temperance evangelist William H. Spear, who had recently spoken in New Haven, the *Sound Breeze* reported, drew an attentive crowd. The speaker's remarkably fine voice "ringing throughout the hall, seem[ed] to have a magnetic influence on his audience" so that "even the hoodlums quieted." Choirs from both churches provided music, and young ladies from the Boxwood School for Girls that Mrs. Richard S. Griswold Jr. had recently established in her home on the main street occupied several rows of reserved seats. On the first Sunday night, about eighty signed the pledge, and the newspaper predicted the number would rise "to a hundred and twenty-five or even more." At the annual business meeting of the Congregational Church in January 1895, Shirley reported that "the Old Lyme Temperance Union, which has drawn a large proportion of our young men into its membership, seems to be doing useful & permanent work."

Concern with educational improvement prompted the minister's encouragement of philanthropic contributions from wealthy church members, and that same year he agreed to serve as secretary for the Old Lyme High School Association, which Evelyn McCurdy Salisbury had established to fund the town's first public high school. Mrs. Salisbury envisioned a "broad avenue" providing access to land she owned across from the Duck River cemetery, but her insistence that a wood-frame building recently moved to her property must also house a new town library brought objections from other church women. Such an important public facility, Josephine Ludington wrote in a family letter, should not be located on a back road in Mrs. Salisbury's field where "no one would go through the winter's snows to the spring mud." When Congregational women divided sharply over competing philanthropic initiatives, Shirley became tangled in the controversy.

The Ladies Library Association, of which Mrs. Ludington was a founding member, preferred to erect a fireproof brick building in a more accessible location. To provide land for a centrally located town library, her husband Charles Ludington proposed demolishing the aging Lord homestead where his wife's grandmother Phoebe Lord had founded the Female Reading Society in 1816. When he also offered generous financial backing, the escalating dispute played out in the pages of the *Sound Breeze.* The newspaper printed a letter to Shirley from a Princeton University librarian supporting Mrs. Salisbury's plan, but when influential church members still did not favor her proposal, she indignantly withdrew all support. The rupture within the congregation brought the minister's departure.

Announcing in the meetinghouse his decision to resign, Shirley in January 1897 voiced the hope "of promoting the unity and welfare of the congregation." Church members, stating that they "heartily regret the condition of the church causing this action," reluctantly accepted his resignation. Expressing gratitude for his "hearty goodwill toward all," they described his ministry as "a blessing to the church and the community." Three months later an Ecclesiastical Council that convened in the meetinghouse to dissolve the pastoral relation voiced "deep regret that this should take place." Its resolution described Shirley as "an eminent scholar, a superior preacher of the Gospel, and a pastor of unusual faithfulness and tenderness."

Arthur Shirley's endeavors to make the influence of the church "directly felt in the family life of the

Evelyn McCurdy Salisbury's proposal to expand public education in Old Lyme with a combined high school and public library on property across from the Duck River Cemetery drew resistance from other philanthropic churchwomen.

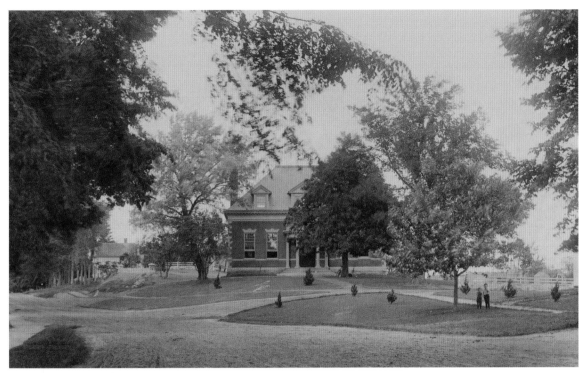

Old Lyme's handsomely furnished public library, which opened on the main street with elaborate ceremonies in 1898, replaced the aging house occupied until recently by Phoebe Lord's daughters.

community" brought ongoing tributes. "Probably no one of the ministers of this church gave more of his time and means to work in the parish than he," Martha Farwell observed. "With his wife they were often seen driving in different parts of town on their way to some house where there was sickness or need." Nor were the home visits "confined alone to their parishioners," she wrote, "but included any in town who were in trouble or distress."

A year after Shirley's departure, a handsomely furnished brick library designed by New York architect Ernest Greene (1864–1936) and dedicated to Mrs. Ludington's mother Phoebe Griffin Noyes opened with extended ceremonies. Mrs. Noyes, who had been born in the house that stood for two centuries at the head of "the Street," had educated young women in the town over four decades. Guests arriving for the celebration in June 1898 were met at the train depot, then taken to the Conference House for refreshments. The succeeding minister Rev. J. Charles Villiers (1858–1928) opened the dedication proceedings with prayer.

A Public Meeting

Of the

ople of Old Ly

Will be held on

Sunday, July 7, 1907

Upon the

n near the burned C

At

Four o'clock in the Afternoon

For the reverent expression of sorrow,
And the strengthening of hearts.

Chapter thirty-one

Nostalgia amid the Elms

When an image of Old Lyme's historic church appeared on the cover of the *Ladies' Home Journal* in 1906, an editorial note stressed the nostalgic recollections inspired by the stately New England meetinghouse.

It is seldom that we have the good fortune to present so typical a picture of the olden times in this country as that on this month's cover. The artist, Mr. A. I. Keller, has caught with the most sympathetic art the spirit of a sunny old-time Sabbath morning immediately after service. The scene is laid in front of a stately old New England meetinghouse, which is still actually standing amid its venerable elms.

For visitors and local families alike, the meetinghouse at the foot of elm-fringed Lyme Street captured a timeless sense of New England's historic charm and rural sophistication. At the turn of the twentieth century when Rev. J. Charles Villiers served as acting minister, the town became an increasingly popular destination for summer residents and tourists, art students and landscape painters. Church members took pride in the socially prominent visitors who attended Sunday morning services.

Villiers, the most traveled of Old Lyme's ministers, was born in Edinburgh and educated in London. While affiliated with Yale as a resident licentiate, he preached his first sermon in the meetinghouse in October 1897 amid a flurry of headlines declaring the town's religious extremism. The *Sound Breeze* had reported in April the lease of a piece of land in the Black Hall section of town by an evangelical group called the Holiness League, which planned to "put up a large tent thereon and hold services there during the summer." In the fall the group's activities drew national attention. "Since the days when witches were hanged in Salem, no more atrocious form of religious fanaticism has shocked a civilized community than

"Mr. Hassam [Childe Hassam] is standing out on the green at this moment, painting the church," Katharine Ludington wrote to a cousin in November 1903. "Isn't it curious that the leader of the Impressionist school in this country should have found his way into this coterie of artists!"

The graceful simplicity of Old Lyme's meetinghouse drew the attention of an unknown photographer ca. 1905.

Arthur Keller relied on a striking photograph of the meetinghouse taken by John Baynes to create his illustration for a magazine cover.

THE LADIES' HOME JOURNAL

Painted by Arthur I. Keller, after a Photograph by John R. Baynes

NOVEMBER 1906 THE CURTIS PUBLISHING COMPANY, PHILADELPHIA FIFTEEN CENTS

New York illustrator Arthur I. Keller imagined a congregation from an earlier era in a nostalgic view of Old Lyme's meetinghouse that appeared on the cover of the popular women's magazine *Ladies' Home Journal*.

Sunday school students and teachers in their best attire gathered with Rev. Charles Villiers for a photograph on the meetinghouse steps.

that which was flashed over the wires from the little Connecticut town of Old Lyme last week," the *Sacramento Daily Union* reported.

The California newspaper's story, headlined "The Holy Ghosters: A Sensational Hearing in Old Lyme," described a seven-hour hearing in the town hall at which six members of the Holiness Band were charged with "assault and battery and breach of the peace upon Mrs. Albina Mather, an aged cripple whom they sought to cure from rheumatism by faith and treatment altogether rigorous." The next month, the *Freethinker*, a British monthly magazine, picked up the story and reported that the Holy Ghosters had "recently nearly knocked a poor old woman to death" as they tried "to drive the Devil out of her." Connecticut newspapers like the *Plainville News* and the *Meriden Morning Record* also carried the sensational story.

Among those arrested for assault were Old Lyme's postmaster Herbert F. Caulkins (1856–1920) and Holiness preacher Wilbur F. Anderson, a graduate of nearby Wesleyan University who was said to be "a firm believer." According to the *Morning Record*, the evangelical group had quickly disbanded, and Mr. Anderson had left town abruptly, announcing plans to go to Jerusalem. A year later, when he tried to claim the pulpit at Old Lyme's Methodist Church, the congregation sharply rejected his effort. "There was an exciting scene for a time, and Anderson was in danger of being regarded as the incarnation of Satan and of being subjected to violence," the *New York Times* reported in November 1898.

Old Lyme's churchwomen lavishly decorated the meetinghouse in celebration of the harvest season, ca. 1888.

Far more favorable publicity during Villiers's early ministry surrounded the arrival of the country's most accomplished landscape artists, many of whom boarded at the gracious but aging family home where Florence Griswold had directed a school for girls. "Lyme is particularly beloved of artists, because of its beautiful surroundings," the *New-York Daily Tribune* reported in August 1902, "and men and women of brush and palette congregate there in great numbers for their summer vacations." Remarking on the popularity of the meetinghouse as an artistic subject, a *New York Times* columnist claimed that "its portrait was taken oftener than any other church in New England—at dawn, at noon, at sunset when the katydids jar the trees with a million rattles, at night when the moon singles it out from the surrounding groves."

Although the artists viewed the historic white church primarily as a source of beauty and not as a place to worship, distinguished summer visitors like future president Woodrow Wilson (1856–1924) regularly joined the congregation on summer Sundays. After one service in July 1906, Mr. Wilson's sister-in-law, commenting on others who attended, remarked that Katharine Ludington "was looking exquisitely lovely in a gown all cream and violet, with an amethyst collar about her breast." Four months later, in November, the *Ladies' Home Journal*, owned by the Curtis Publishing Company, where Katharine's brother Charles Ludington Jr. (1866–1927) served as an officer, featured Old Lyme's meetinghouse on its cover.

The widely circulating ladies' magazine had commissioned Arthur I. Keller (1866–1925), president of the New York Society of Illustrators, to convey "the spirit of a sunny old-time Sabbath morning immediately after service." To capture the nostalgic aura of the meetinghouse surrounded by majestic elms, Mr. Keller relied on a recent photograph taken by John Baynes (1873–1952), then imagined a congregation from an earlier era elegantly attired in top hats and hoop skirts. The magazine made a special edition mail-order copy of the popular cover illustration available for separate purchase, and Louisa Perkins Griswold (1872–1968), Mrs. Richard S. Griswold's daughter-in-law, used her copy to create a jigsaw puzzle.

Amid widespread celebration of the beauty of the meetinghouse, Charles Villiers announced his resignation. He had held special services "for the quickening of the spiritual life of the Church" in February 1906, but six months later at the close of a Sunday morning service he explained his decision to leave. Expressing gratitude for the congregation's friendship, forbearance, and financial generosity, he reminded them that from the pulpit, in a spirit of love, he had often "pressed home the sterner side of truth." He then reflected on treating the meetinghouse as a work of art. "We are all lovers of this church fabric," he observed. "We admire it for what it is, and I trust also, for the ideals for which it stands, ideals not only of art, but also of religion, thinking of it not only as an ornate building, but as indeed the house of God, the place of progress and worship."

When Villiers accepted a position as Congregational pastor in Kingston, Ontario, Katharine Ludington drafted a resolution commending his faithful and sympathetic service in Old Lyme and noting "the harmonious relations that have always existed between himself and the church." In 1913 Villiers accepted a pastorate in Maui, far from the nostalgic setting of Old Lyme. Four years later in Honolulu he delivered a "most interesting sermon . . . to a large and appreciative audience" at a memorial service for Hawaii's last queen.

World War I prompted Katharine Ludington to set aside work as a professional portrait artist and assume leadership of Connecticut's suffrage movement.

Chapter thirty-two

Flames at Midnight

The flames that consumed Old Lyme's meetinghouse on a summer night in 1907 prompted an outpouring of grief, reflection, and anger, along with a determined search for the fire bugs responsible for destroying a sacred landmark.

Perhaps we loved it too much and thought more of the shell of our religion than we did of the kernel, but it was the symbol of everything that was best and had been best in the history of the town.

Cinders rained down in the early hours of Wednesday, July 3, 1907, as fire devoured Old Lyme's beloved fourth meetinghouse. The steeple bell tolled the midnight hour, then fell silent as flames ravaged the church, blackened the surrounding elms, and layered the town's green with ash. Liveryman John Sterling discovered the blaze shortly before midnight when he returned to his stables behind the Old Lyme Inn after an evening trip to the ferry dock. At a furious pace he rode through the street to alert the sleeping community. "Soon after twelve was roused by cry of fire," the recently installed minister Rev. Edward M. Chapman (1863–1952) noted in his journal on July 3. "Looked out & saw light on north Church windows which I hoped was caused by some exterior fire. It was the Church itself however, as a voice from the street soon assured me."

Sociable and scholarly, a descendant of one of the Saybrook Colony's founding families and a Yale graduate, Chapman had spent summers in Old Lyme and made many local friends. His decision in December 1906 to accept a unanimous invitation to settle as pastor was met "with rejoicing." The minister and his wife had moved into the newly renovated parsonage on June 1, a month before the fire.

Rev. Edward Chapman, newly settled as Old Lyme's minister, moved into the parsonage one month before an arsonist's fire consumed the historic meetinghouse.

Old Lyme Inn proprietor Herbert Caulkins arrived at the church within minutes of Sterling's shouted warning. Hoisting himself up to a window, he could see fire already leaping through two gaping holes in the roof. "It was but a short space of time before nearly the entire population of the town was at the scene," reported the *Deep River New Era*. Townspeople fought through the night to contain the blaze, pumping water from an eight-thousand-gallon tank at Charles Ludington's house next door to fill waiting buckets. Long before daybreak, the meetinghouse, the newly renovated Conference House, and the horse sheds behind had been lost to the flames.

"The Church could not be saved," Katharine Ludington wrote the next day to her brother. "It was a mass of flame five minutes after I first saw the fire." Their own house fifty yards to the south had been saved "only by the most heroic efforts I have ever seen," she wrote. "The entire town turned out and worked in a way which stirs me to think of, risking their lives in a rain of falling, burning wood, on the roof, in heat which broke all the glass on that side of the house & charred much of the wood. No one thought at first that the house could stand." She later recalled in a family memoir how "the old spire with its heavy bell . . . fell with an awful crash. A semicircle of silent people stood on the green watching the familiar and sacred landmark go. Many were sobbing, and all were still, as if at service."

Arson seemed certain. Just two weeks earlier the Ludingtons' stables had burned suspiciously after midnight. On the afternoon before the fire, no trace of smoke had been detected inside the meetinghouse when Katharine Ludington sang beside the piano with other church women. Not only did the blaze break out on the pulpit platform where no lamp had been lit since the previous Sunday's service, but the church burned precisely on the anniversary of the lightning fire that had consumed the third meetinghouse in 1815. "If such a thing is possible the fire that destroyed the Congregational Church at Old Lyme is going to be ascertained," the *New Era* declared. "The leading citizens of the town are determined in this and steps have already been taken toward a solution of the mystery."

Childe Hassam (1859–1935), the most prominent of the landscape artists who summered in Old Lyme, had painted three views of the historic church and expressed outrage to Florence

The gracious neocolonial home that New York architect Henry Rutgers Marshall completed for Charles Ludington in 1903 was several times "given up for lost" when fire destroyed the meetinghouse next door in 1907.

Griswold after the fire. "Who is the devil who did it?" he asked. "I don't need to say that I always had a real and pagan delight in the many and beautiful aspects of the old church. They cannot rebuild it—never! And the fine and immemorial elms—Oh! It is a pity." For almost a century the church beside the green had seemed to define the character of the village, and people struggled for explanation. "Perhaps we loved it too much and thought more of the shell of our religion than we did of the kernel," Katharine Ludington wrote to a cousin ten days later.

Judge Walter C. Noyes (1865–1926), a grandson of Dr. Richard Noyes appointed to the U.S. Circuit Court of Appeals for New York by President Theodore Roosevelt, addressed the significance of the meetinghouse at a solemn public gathering beside the ruins: "It was not as a fine building that the old church was most dear to us. It entered into our innermost lives." Following his remarks, Frank Vincent Du Mond (1865–1961), a leading member of the Lyme art colony, "voiced the sorrow of the artists for the loss of so much beauty." Katharine Ludington described how "the whole town mourns, & is drawn together in a wonderful way—no Fourth of July celebrations were allowed, & the whole talk is of rebuilding the Church—& of probing the cause of the fire, for no one doubts that it was of incendiary origin."

To calm fears about "firebugs" who might strike again, detectives from Hartford searched the ruins for evidence, and a security guard kept the charred Ludington home under surveillance. Worry mingled with grief as concern spread about the identity of the firebugs. "The matter will not be allowed to drop," the *New Era* reported on July 19, but by summer's end the arson investigation had stalled. Hopes of an indictment revived in November when two arrests followed an unsuccessful attempt to burn the town's consolidated school. An unemployed town resident claimed in court that his codefendant had "told him on the night of the burning of the schoolhouse that he had burned the Lyme church." The allegation brought a flurry of headlines but could not be substantiated.

A Public Meeting

Of the

People of Old Lyme

Will be held on

Sunday, July 7, 1907,

Upon the

Green near the burned Church

At

Four o'clock in the Afternoon.

For the reverent expression of sorrow,
And the strengthening of hearts.

On the Sunday after the meetinghouse fire, Rev. Benjamin Bacon, Judge Walter C. Noyes, and artist Frank Du Mond voiced the community's profound sense of loss at a subdued gathering on the town green.

Suspicions persisted that one or both of the defendants in the school fire had started the meetinghouse blaze, but the mystery was never solved. An anonymous observer who reflected sadly on the ruined church and its imperishable memories remarked, "High Heaven somewhere looks down upon a guilty man with a scar upon his heart as red as the flame that his hand kindled."

Ideal New England Church at Old Lyme Dedicated Today

Chapter thirty-three

Restoring the Country Church

When Woodrow Wilson spoke at the dedication service for Old Lyme's restored meetinghouse in 1910, he recalled the historic importance of New England's country churches and anticipated the important role that the congregation's new home would play in the continuing life of the community.

There was a time, as I need not tell you, when the life of every community of New England centered in the church; not merely the religion, but the life represented in its business, every kind and part of the life of the community had its residence and place of operation in the church.

At the dedication ceremony for Old Lyme's fifth meetinghouse in June 1910, Princeton University's president Woodrow Wilson recalled the once encompassing role of New England's churches. Three days earlier he had telegraphed a letter from his summer residence in town indicating his willingness to accept the Democratic nomination for governor of New Jersey, and in 1912 he would be elected president of the United States. From the pulpit of the restored meetinghouse, where he said he felt "not quite a stranger," he spoke about the declining vitality of rural areas depleted by the lure of rapidly growing cities and urged the restoration of country churches across America to create wellsprings of local renewal.

Woodrow Wilson's affection for Old Lyme, where he summered with his family at Boxwood and at Florence Griswold's boardinghouse, brought speculation that the town would become the site of the president's summer White House.

On that pleasant June evening, the *New Era* reported, "the church was filled to its capacity with those from miles around who were eager to hear the famous educator." Disregarding the slow pace of the church restoration, Wilson opened his remarks with praise for the "rapid completion of this beautiful structure." The fire-swept corner at the foot of Lyme Street had remained desolate for more than a year when Rev. Edward Chapman delivered a sermon in November 1908 to dedicate a new parish house and lay the cornerstone for the new meetinghouse. "The time was long," the minister repeated almost as a refrain.

A debate over design had brought the initial delay. A *New Haven Register* editorial declared soon after the fire that the next meetinghouse "must be as nearly the same as modern ingenuity, guided by tradition, painting and photograph can make it," but that assumption proved premature. A communitywide controversy erupted when

The painstaking replication of Old Lyme's celebrated meetinghouse progressed slowly in 1909 on the fire-swept corner of the main street.

Sorrow and solemnity infused the sermon that Rev. Edward Chapman delivered when laying the cornerstone for a new meetinghouse in 1908.

building committee member Ernest Chadwick (1868–1916), a respected lawyer and nephew of the former minister Davis Brainerd, advised: "Unless sentiment insists upon a reproduction of the old work, a much better building (from the standpoint of pure art) may be erected out of stone." Chapman then recommended replacing the white clapboard structure with an "up-to-date" redbrick church. A brick building, he advised, would improve facilities, contain costs, and provide fireproofing. When New London architect Louis R. Hazeltine (1861–1931) submitted drawings to the building committee, he also stated a preference for "Harvard brick," suggesting terra cotta only "if a white exterior was essential."

Ideal New England Church at Old Lyme Dedicated Today

FIRST CONGREGATIONAL CHURCH IN OLD LYME TO BE DEDICATED TODAY.

(Special to The Register.)

Influential church members raised their voices in protest, and Evelyn McCurdy Salisbury, an early and generous contributor to the rebuilding fund, attempted to terminate the debate. "No doubt your wish as well as mine is that the church shall be restored on the old foundations, and on the same plan," she wrote to Judge Walter Noyes. "So many of us will give our contributions for this purpose that it will save much contention if it is accepted." By mid-July a majority of the building committee wanted "something new." Katharine Ludington noted with alarm the growing support for "a fireproof brick building of generally colonial character." Some people, she wrote, wanted "a nondescript institutional church such as you might find in any second rate suburban town, instead of the distinguished, reserved, & perfect thing which we had before." In a letter to the *New Era*, Charles Vezin (1858–1942) voiced sharp concern on behalf of Old Lyme's artists: "There is talk of building an 'up-to-date structure,' or of 'improving' on the old one. . . . It will surely [be a] breach of good taste and would be a constant sorrow to all."

Three months after the fire the building committee engaged in a final "animated discussion of the material to be used in rebuilding the church," then brought the matter to a vote. Two

The New Haven Register headlined its report on the dedication of a new meetinghouse, "Ideal New England Church at Old Lyme."

Photographer Steve Rosenthal in 2011 departed from traditional views of Old Lyme's meetinghouse with this asymmetrical image of the front steps that includes a sliver of landscape.

members, including Ernest Chadwick, refused to be swayed, but the majority supported a resolution to erect a new structure "upon the lines of the old one." When an extended search could not locate Samuel Belcher's original plans, the committee spent weeks studying paintings and photographs to document the building's architectural details. In May 1908 it chose New York architect Ernest Greene, who had designed the town's public library a decade earlier, to undertake the meetinghouse reconstruction.

Three hundred people gathered when Rev. Edward Chapman laid the cornerstone in 1908 and expressed hope "this winter to see the framework of our Church go up, and in a year or so to enter upon a new church home that will be like the old home renovated and refreshed." In January 1909 the walls were in place, the slate roofing had arrived, and erection of the steeple had begun. In October the spire had been completed above the belfry and a new bell installed, but there were setbacks. In December when the clock first struck the hour, several of the new elms "of an unusually large size" that Katharine Ludington had donated "showed scant signs of life, possibly due to two seasons of prolonged drouth."

With replacement elm trees set out and interior work progressing, the *New Era* reported "a keen struggle to get everything in readiness" as the dedication ceremony approached. The large organ had yet to be installed and "furnishings of many descriptions to be placed," but it was clear that Greene had reproduced the old church "with pleasing exactitude." He had also achieved almost complete fireproofing by using steel girders and trusses to frame the structure and steel laths encased in cement for the walls. Reserving wood for the clapboard exterior and the interior pulpit, he had pioneered a building process said to be "unique in the annals of church construction." One observer who compared the hollow porch columns to the original pillars fashioned from huge trees floated down the Connecticut River from Vermont said that the fireproof replacements could not be detected by the untrained eye. Ernest Greene described his approach as "an adaptation of old forms to new methods of construction, or perhaps, rather, the expression of a past historical style in new materials."

When Edward Chapman laid the cornerstone in 1908, he acknowledged that "the backward look is one of mingled sadness and thanksgiving." Mindful of the community's lingering sense of loss two years later, Woodrow Wilson looked ahead while offering words of reassurance: "You must almost feel at home in the old church again." The dedication ceremonies marked the end of an era, Katharine Ludington observed. "The burning of the old church seems to date the passing of a period" and "the closing of one volume of Lyme's story."

Notes

Abbreviations

CCHS Collections of the Connecticut Historical Society.

CH Thomas Prince, ed. *The Christian History, Containing Accounts of the Revival and Propagation of Religion in Great-Britain, America &c. For the Year 1744.* Boston, 1745; reprinted Shropshire, England, 2016.

CSLMC Connecticut State Library Manuscript Collections.

EPP Susan Hollingsworth Ely and Elizabeth Plimpton Papers at the Florence Griswold Museum.

ESR Records of Lyme's First Ecclesiastical Society, 1721–1876. Photocopy 1930, FCCOL.

FCCOL First Congregational Church of Old Lyme Archives.

FCR Records of Lyme's First Church.

LHSA Lyme Historical Society Archives at the Florence Griswold Museum.

LLR Lyme Land Records.

LR Jean Chandler Burr, ed. *Lyme Records, 1667–1730.* Stonington, CT, 1968.

PR J. H. Trumbull and Charles J. Hoadly, eds. *The Public Records of the Colony of Connecticut.* Hartford, 1850–1890.

VR Verne M. Hall and Elizebeth B. Plimpton. *Vital Records of Lyme, Connecticut, to the End of the Year 1850.* Lyme, 1976.

Preface

vii *public buildings* For the role of colonial meetinghouses and the adoption "only in modern times" of the designation "church" as a physical edifice rather than an organized body of believers see J. Frederick Kelly, "The Ecclesiastical Society and the Function of the Meetinghouse," in *Early Connecticut Meetinghouses: Being an Account of the Church Edifices Built before 1830 Based Chiefly upon Town and Parish Records* (New York, 1948), 1:xxiv.

vii *local Pequots* For an overview of colonial assumptions about New England wilderness areas as "vacant" and about colonists' "natural right to the use of this land that God had provided for his people" see John Lazuk, "Cultural Perception in Early New England: Europeans, Indians, and the Origins of the Pequot War of 1637" (MA thesis, University of Montana, 1983), 55–59.

vii *Captain John Mason* See Mason, *A Brief History of the Pequot War: Especially of the memorable taking of their fort at Mystic in Connecticut in 1637* (Boston, 1736). For a detailed historiography of early colonial military conflicts see Andrew Lipman, "'A meanes to knit them together': The Exchange of Body Parts in the Pequot War," in *William and Mary Quarterly* 65, no. 1 (January 2008): 3–5.

vii *settler colonists* For settler colonialism and the construction of new colonial societies on expropriated native land see Patrick Wolfe, "Settler Colonialism and the Elimination of the Native," *Journal of Genocide Research* 8, no. 4 (December 2006): 387–89.

vii *described as* *New Haven Register*, June 14, 1910; *Country Life*, April 1914, 44.

vii *Lorado Taft* Cited in Julia B. Rosenbaum, *Visions of Belonging: New England Art and the Making of American Identity* (Ithaca, NY, 2006), 114.

Meeting Together

1 *This Court, apprehending a necessity* Court of Assistants, New London (May 31, 1664). Cited in Frances Manwaring Caulkins, *History of New London, Connecticut; From the First Survey of the Coast in 1612 to 1860* (New London, CT, 1895), 175.

1 *General Court* For the Connecticut colony's early court system see Scott Douglas Gerber, *A Distinct Judicial Power: The Origins of an Independent Judiciary, 1606–1787* (Oxford, 2011), 150–51; Bruce P. Stark, "The Upper House in Early Connecticut History," in *A Lyme Miscellany, 1776–1976*, ed. George J. Willauer Jr. (Middletown, CT, 1977), 137–41.

1 *permission in 1663* *PR*, 1:419 (March 10, 1663).

1 *constable* Caulkins, 174, notes: "When a town is to be organized, the preliminary step is the choice of a constable. It is the first act of self-government—an unfurling of the banner of independence by a subordinate district."

1 *servants* The General Court ordered in 1660 "that neither Indian nor negro servants shall be required to train, watch or ward in this Colony." *PR*, 1:349 (May 17, 1660).

1 *more comfortable subsistence* *Ancient Records of Saybrook*, vol. 1, *East Side Lyme (1648–1773)*, typescript, 1960, p. 93 (January 4, 1648/9).

1 *contested* See *PR*, 1:354 (October 4, 1660); *PR*, 1:404 (May 14, 1663); John Adams Comstock, *A History and Genealogy of the Comstock Family in America* (Los Angeles, 1949), 2.

1 *suspicions about witchery* *PR*, 1:338 (June 15, 1659).

1 *east quarter* *Ancient Records of Saybrook*, 1:10, 13.

1 *capital crime* "If any man or woman be a witch (that is) hath or consulteth with a familiar spirit, they shall be put to death." *PR*, 1:77 (December 1, 1642). See R. G. Tomlinson, *Witchcraft Prosecution: Chasing the Devil in Connecticut* (Rockland, ME, 2012), 58; Donald Perreault, *Saybrook's Witchraft Trial of 1661* (Old Saybrook, CT, 2013).

2 *two deaths* Cited in Tomlinson, 76–79. The indictment mentioned "in particular the wife of Reynold Marvin [1634–1676] and the child of Balthazar de Wolfe" (1620–1695).

2 *deservest to die* Cited in R. G. Tomlinson, *Witchcraft Trials of Connecticut* (Hartford, 1978), 24.

3 *questioned the evidence* *PR*, 1:397 (March 11, 1662/3).

3 *Articles of Agreement* *Ancient Records of Saybrook*, 1:39.

4 *established a committee* *PR*, 2:48 (October 11, 1666).

4 *intendment* *Book of Grants*, LLR, 1a:4 (October 12, 1666).

4 *already served* Richard Anson Wheeler, *History of the First Congregational Church, Stonington, Conn., 1674–1874* (Norwich, CT, 1875), 39–40. In Stonington, James Noyes lodged with Thomas Stanton (1616–1677), a successful merchant and accomplished Indian translator. It may have been

Stanton's brother-in-law William Lord (1618–1678), an early and influential landowner in Saybrook, who conveyed to Moses Noyes the need for a minister in the east side settlement. The town originally named Southerton became Mystic in 1664 and Stonington in 1666.

4 *opportunities for trade* Greenfield Larrabee (1620–1666), one of the first to acquire land on Saybrook's east side, voyaged to Barbados in 1650 in the ship *Tryall*, built in Wethersfield, with a cargo of barrel staves. The construction of sawmills in the east side settlement and the arrival of coopers like Wolston Brockway (1638–1717) in 1659 and John Huntley (1624–1676) in 1661 supported a growing export of barrel staves to the profitable sugar plantations in the West Indies. See Thomas A. Stevens, *Old Lyme, a Maritime History* (Essex, CT, 1959), 7; *Ancient Records of Saybrook*, 1:93; David William Patterson, ed., *The Brockway Family: Some Records of Wolston Brockway and His Descendants* (Oswego, NY, 1890), 3; Virgil W. Huntley, *John Huntley, Immigrant* (Mystic, CT, 1978), 1:2; Richard S. Dunn, *Sugar and Slaves: The Rise of the Planter Class in the English West Indies, 1624–1713* (Durham, NC, 1972).

4 *followed his cousins* David Dudley Field, *A History of the Towns of Haddam and East-Haddam* (Middletown, CT, 1814), 25.

4 *heard a complaint* Cited in Glenn E. Griswold, ed., *The Griswold Family, England-America* (Rutland, VT, 1943), 190.

4 *large tract* The size of Matthew Griswold's tract is not known, but the General Court decided in 1649 that "in their division of land on the east side of the River," Saybrook's boundaries would extend "from the River eastward, five miles; and northward up the River, on the east side, six miles." *PR*, 1:185. For speculation about the name "Black Hall" see Adeline Bartlett Allyn, *Black Hall: Traditions and Reminiscences* (Hartford, 1908), 7–9.

5 *on two sides* *Ancient Records of Saybrook*, 1:60.

5 *court judged* Griswold, 190.

5 *formally established* *PR*, 2:60 (May 9, 1667). The name Lyme was already in use the previous year. See *PR*, 2:48 (October 11, 1666).

6 *minister's rate* "Voted and consented to that William [Waller] and John Tillotson shall make a list of the Town for the meeting of the minister's rate for this year ensuing." *LR*, 1 (August 29, 1667). Tillotson is likely the "neighbor" who had raised witchcraft suspicions about Mrs. Griswold.

6 *parsonage lot* *LR*, 3 (May 4, 1669).

6 *status as a freeman* *PR*, 2:131 (May 12, 1670). For a discussion of inhabitants and freemen in Lyme see May Hall James, *The Educational History of Old Lyme, Connecticut, 1635–1935* (New Haven, CT, 1939), 80.

6 *sixty acres* *LR*, 7 (September 30, 1672).

6 *younger brothers* *LR*, 10 (February 9, 1673/4), 11 (October 29, 1674).

6 *make search* *PR*, 2:88 (May 14, 1668).

6 *complaint of the constable* New London County Court records, 3:21. Transcription, Clipping File, LHSA.

6 *ye Negro servant* The court summons in 1670 is the earliest document known to establish the presence of black slaves in Lyme. Whether Richard Ely named his slave "Moses" after Lyme's minister is not known. The General Court reported that in 1680 "there are but few servants among us, and less slaves, not above 30, as we judge, in the Colony." The Court noted: "And for Blacks, there comes sometimes 3 or 4 in a year from Barbados; and they are sold usually at the rate of 22 pounds

a piece, sometimes more and sometimes less, according as men can agree with the master of vessels, or merchants that bring them hither." Although the Court had "no account of the perfect number," it stated that few blacks were born in the colony, and "but two blacks christened, as we know of." *PR*, 3:298.

7 *wealthiest inhabitant* For Richard Ely's arrival in Lyme and his ongoing property disputes see Moses S. Beach and William Ely, eds., *The Ely Ancestry* (New York, 1902), 31–33.

7 *townsman* *LR*, 2 (January 6, 1667/8).

7 *extensive property* LLR, 1:37 (March 1, 1673).

7 *almost certainly* See Caulkins, *History of New London*, 177; Bruce P. Stark, *Lyme, Connecticut: From Founding to Independence* (1976), 7. However, Susan Hollingsworth Ely et al., *History of the First Congregational Church of Old Lyme, Connecticut, 1665–1993* (Old Lyme, CT, 1995), 9, speculates that the first meetinghouse "was most likely built in 1665/6."

7 *remake the highway* *LR*, 8 (March 1, 1673/4).

7 *sum of 60 pounds* *LR*, 9 (March 1, 1673/4).

Debate and Delay

9 *And concerning* *LR*, 49 (February 8, 1685/6).

9 *had doubled* The tax list prepared in 1688 for Edmund Andros (1637–1714), appointed governor of New England two years earlier, reported seventy-one taxable families in Lyme. Photocopy, Noyes-Ely Collection, LHSA. See also Richard Henry Graves et al., *New York Genealogical and Biographical Record* (New York, 1921), 52:94.

9 *provide and saw* *LR*, 41 (February 1, 1680/1).

9 *dimensions* *LR*, 46 (January 22, 1683/4). The dimensions approximated those of Stonington's first meetinghouse, erected in 1673, which measured forty feet by twenty-two feet, with fourteen feet between joints. The second meetinghouse in New London, completed in 1682, measured forty feet square, with the studs twenty feet high. It had two galleries, four gables, a turret, and three doors. See Charles Phelps Noyes and Emily H. (Gilman) Noyes, *Noyes-Gilman Ancestry* (New York, 1907), 21; Leroy S. Blake, *The Early History of the First Church of New London* (New London, CT, 1897), 1:123–25, 135.

9 *providing boards* *LR*, 48 (June 25, 1685).

9 *agreed to resolve* *LR*, 49 (February 8, 1685/6); *PR*, 3:196–7 (May 13, 1686).

9 *Before Lyme meeting house* Connecticut Archives, Ecclesiastical Affairs, 1:2 (May 10, 1686). Cited in James, *Educational History*, 48.

10 *what will be needful* *LR*, 61 (November 22, 1687).

10 *salt and Barbados goods* *LR*, 66 (May 21, 1688).

10 *supply the town* *LR*, 18 (November 12, 1686).

10 *transport of the same* *LR*, 44 (April 17, 1683).

11 *in repair* *LR*, 47 (December 25, 1684).

11 *dame schools* *LR*, 40 (February 1, 1680/1).

11 *pair of stocks* *LR*, 47 (May 25, 1685).

11 *take care* *LR*, 63 (December 6, 1687).

11 *seating and the sealing* *LR*, 68 (July 11, 1689).

12 *raise the pulpit* *LR*, 71 (November 29, 1690).

12 *pay for seats* *LR*, 72 (December 16, 1690), 73 (November 23, 1691), 73 (December 7, 1691).

12 *all bachelors* *LR*, 20 (April 18, 1692).

12 *all maids* Cited in William Hall, "Old Lyme, Connecticut," *New York Observer*, n.d. Scrapbook, LHSA. See also James, *Educational History*, 49. The second volume of town meeting records has been missing for more than half a century.

Gathering a Church

15 *At a town meeting* *LR*, 21 (March 27, 1693).

15 *wild and jealous tribes* "The unsettled state of society at that time, when the fathers were attempting a settlement among wild and jealous tribes of Indians, may account for it." William B. Cary, *Memorial Discourse* (Hartford, 1876), 4.

15 *left for Norwich* Shirley found "the inference obvious" that the Saybrook church had desired ongoing "help and support" from inhabitants across the river. Saybrook's church historian argued instead that the Articles of Agreement signed in 1665, five years after Rev. James Fitch (1622–1702) left for Norwich, had included a tax abatement allowing the east side to settle its own minister, proving "that the old Church interposed no obstacles" to the formation of a new church across the river. Arthur Shirley, *Discourse Delivered at the Two Hundredth Anniversary of the Organization of the Old Lyme Congregational Church, 1693–1893* (Lyme, CT, 1893), 10–11; Amos Chesebrough, "History of the First Church, Old Saybrook," in *The First Church of Christ (Congregational), Old Saybrook, Conn.* (Middletown, CT, 1896), 20.

16 *Harvard schoolmate* Rev. Simon Bradstreet, son of Massachusetts governor Simon Bradstreet (1602–1697) and poet Anne Bradstreet (1612–1672), graduated from Harvard in 1660, a year after the Noyes brothers, and settled in New London in 1666, the same year that Moses Noyes acquired land in Lyme.

16 *formally inducted* Blake, *Early History of the First Church*, 1:125–27; Caulkins, *History of New London*, 193. A diary kept by the early Stonington settler Thomas Minor (1608–1690) notes that "15 January [1670/1] was the first sacrament of the lord's supper administered by Mr. Bradstreet." Cited in Blake, 1:127.

16 *In Stonington* Wheeler, *History of the First Congregational Church, Stonington*, 39.

16 *there may be a church* *LR*, 26 (February 13, 1675/6).

17 *subjected to the necessity* Chesebrough, 20.

17 *baptized in 1670* Blake, 2:446.

17 *sufficient highway* *LR*, 4 (July 7, 1670).

17 *in behalf* *PR*, 3:18 (October 10, 1678).

17 *substantial estate* Mr. Pickett's estate, appraised at 1,140 pounds, ranked him "as one of the wealthiest merchants of the place." Ruth's brothers John Pickett and William Pickett also died on voyages to Barbados. Caulkins, 286.

17 *going to and from* James Savage, *A Genealogical Dictionary of the First Settlers of New England* (Boston, 1860–1862), 2:415; Caulkins, 307–8.

17 *Mr. Pickett's children* Blake, 2:445.

17 *negro servant* Caulkins, 25.

17 *accidental discharge* *PR*, 2:254 (May 13, 1675). The General Court had previously examined "a matter concerning Mr. Hill" in 1670 when it investigated his possession of a "Spaniard." If the said Spaniard had been legally purchased, the Court would order his freedom and transportation home, with Mr. Hill reimbursing the public treasury. *PR*, 2:128 (May 12, 1670).

17 *second offense* Caulkins, 251.

17 *wharves and warehouse* Christophers later received permission to build a warehouse in Lyme for salt and Barbados goods. Caulkins, 308; *LR*, 18 (November 12, 1686), 66 (May 21, 1668).

17 *enlistment* The list of volunteers, recorded in order of enlistment, includes Moses Noyes's name near the end, number 180 out of 185. He apparently served from June to December 1675. See George M. Bodge, *Soldiers in King Philip's War* (Boston, 1906), 442; Noyes and Noyes, *Noyes-Gilman Ancestry*, 17. For recent interpretations of King Philip's War see Lisa Brooks, *Our Beloved Kin: A New History of King Philip's War* (New Haven, CT, 2018); Jill Lepore, *The Name of War: King Philip's War and the Origins of American Identity* (New York, 1998).

17 *first child* LLR, 1:33 (August 2, 1678).

17 *three scores of upland* LLR, 2:42 (May 8, 1688). For evidence supporting an earlier date see Ely et al., *History of the First Congregational Church*, 24.

18 *gather all* *LR*, 33 (May 28, 1679).

18 *all lawful means* *LR*, 45 (January 8, 1683/4).

18 *as full power* *LR*, 48 (November 26, 1685).

18 *desired and agreed* *LR*, 21 (March 27, 1693).

19 *General Court invited* The Court expressed thanks "to the Reverend Mr. Moses Noyes for his great pains in preaching the election sermon." *PR*, 4:121 (May 10, 1694).

19 *four children* For life dates of Noyes's children see LLR, "Inscriptions at Old Lyme, Conn.," *The New England Historical and Genealogical Register*, vol. 76–77, 206, 208.

19 *bequeathed by will* In a will sealed on August 19, 1719, Noyes, age seventy-six, gave "the negro maid Arabella" to Sarah Noyes, who had married a decade earlier, in 1709, Captain Timothy Mather (1681–1755). Photocopy, EPP, box 6.

19 *I heard but now* James Noyes to Samuel Sewall, March 12, 1693/4, cited in Noyes and Noyes, 18–19.

Opinion on Blasphemy

21 *The opinions of four ministers* Cited in Anna B. Williams, *History of the Rogerenes* (Boston, 1904), 184.

21 *propertied New London merchant* Caulkins, *History of New London*, 90, 95; Blake, *Early History of the First Church*, 1:176; Allegra di Bonaventura, *For Adam's Sake: A Family Saga in Colonial New England* (New York, 2013), 16.

21 *Baptist sect* David Benedict, *A General History of the Baptist Denomination in America* (Boston, 1813), 422.

21 *conjugal bond* *PR*, 2:292 (October 12, 1676).

22 *under so great distress* Testimony to Court of Assistants (1675), cited in George Elliot Howard, *A History of Matrimonial Institutions* (London, 1904), 2:357.

22 *utterly renounce[d]* *PR*, 2:326 (October 11, 1677).

22 *known as Rogerenes* di Bonaventura, 30–32.

22 *compel his submission* For accusations and punishments of John Rogers see Williams, 179–81; di Bonaventura, 50; Blake, 1:138, 181–87.

22 *spanned two decades* Bradstreet's diary notes on May 25, 1675, that "John Rogers of N. London, aged about 26 (not many months before turned a proud Anabaptist) was arraigned at Hartford, at the Court of Assistants up[on] trial of his life. The testimony against him was his own wife (a prudent, sober young woman), to whom he told it with his own mouth." Cited in Blake, 1:137.

22 *blasphemous nature* Williams, 183–84. See also Caulkins (214): "Doubtless a sober mind would not now give so harsh a name, to expressions which our ancestors deemed blasphemous."

22 *devil is now making* Cotton Mather, *The Wonders of the Invisible World: Being an Account of the Trials of Several Witches Lately Executed in New England* [. . .] (Boston, 1693), xii.

23 *brother-in-law* Playwright Arthur Miller (1915–2005) made Hale a central character in *The Crucible*, published in New York in 1953.

23 *wealthy Boston merchant* Wendy Warren, *New England Bound: Slavery and Colonization in Early America* (New York, 2016), 221, 227–28; Richard Archer, *As If an Enemy's Country: The British Occupation of Boston and the Origins of Revolution* (Oxford, 2010), 17.

23 *kept the Sabbath* Samuel Sewall, *Diary of Samuel Sewall, 1674–1729*, Collections of the Massachusetts Historical Society (Boston, 1878), 5:153 (October 2, 1686).

23 *one of the nine* See John R. Vile, "Samuel Sewall as Defender of the Law?," in *Noble Purposes: Nine Champions of the Rule of Law*, ed. Norman Gross (Athens, OH, 2007), 5–6.

23 *five unfortunates* Sewall, 363 (August 19, 1692); Vile, 7. For the close ties of family and friendship linking those who conducted the Salem witchcraft persecutions see Stacy Schiff, *The Witches: Suspicion, Betrayal, and Hysteria in 1692 Salem* (New York, 2015), 312.

23 *encountered* Mary Herrick, age seventeen, claimed before Hale that "on the 5th of the 9th [November 5] she appeared again with the ghost of Goody Easty, & that Mrs. Hale did sorely afflict her by pinching pricking & choking her." Cited in "Witchcraft Papers," *Proceedings of the New England Historical Society* (1873), 55.

23 *doubts about the reliability* Massachusetts governor Sir William Phipps (1651–1695) appointed nine judges to the special Court of Oyer and Terminer that tried witchcraft cases in May 1692. Judge Nathaniel Saltonstall (1639–1707), father of New London's minister, questioned the evidence in June and resigned from the court, which the governor dissolved in October. Noyes and Noyes, *Noyes-Gilman Ancestry*, 261–65.

23 *hastened by the excitement* Noyes and Noyes, 264.

23 *public apology* "Petition Put Up by Mr. Sewall on the Fast Day," Sewall, 445 (January 15, 1697/8); Judith S. Graham, "Samuel Sewall," in *Puritans and Puritanism in Europe and America: A Comprehensive Encyclopedia*, ed. Francis J. Bremer and Tom Webster (Santa Barbara, CA, 2006), 1:231.

On Elderly Childbearing

25 *Hence we learn* Moses Noyes, *A Sermon, Delivered by the Rev. Mr. NOYES, and taken down in Short hand, by one of the Tutors of Yale College* (Vermont, 1785), 4. Photocopy, FCCOL.

25 *Only one* A newspaper clipping preserved in a Griswold family scrapbook and datelined Pierrepont House, Lyme, Conn., August 24, 1876, notes that Ellen Noyes Chadwick (1824–1900), a descendant of the first minister, loaned for Lyme's centennial exhibition "a volume of manuscript sermons by Rev. Moses Noyes (one of her ancestors)." The location of the manuscript sermons is not known.

25 *trustee* Rev. Moses Noyes became the twelfth trustee of the Collegiate School in 1703.

25 *for public employment* *PR*, 1:363 (October 9, 1701). For the formation of the Collegiate School, and for letters requesting advice from Cotton Mather, Samuel Sewall, Increase Mather (1639–1723), and Isaac Addington (1645–1719) see Edwin Oviatt, *The Beginnings of Yale, 1701–1726* (New Haven, CT, 1916), 163–67. Oviatt, 285ff., provides details about the school's early years in Saybrook, where "two or three scholars were graduated annually." See also Franklin Bowditch Dexter, *Biographical Sketches of the Graduates of Yale College, with Annals of the College History, October, 1701–May, 1745* (New York, 1885), 1–6.

26 *sheet to discourage* Judge Sewall opposed the enslavement of Africans but expressed doubt whether a place for freed blacks could be found in white society. See Patricia Bradley, *Slavery, Propaganda, and the American Revolution* (Jackson, MS, 1998), 7. For Sewall's antislavery views and his relationship to Cotton Mather see Warren, *New England Boun*d, 222–32; Vile, "Samuel Sewall," 10–12.

27 *Demographic data* Birth, marriage, and death dates for Connecticut inhabitants before 1700 are imprecise and approximate, and demographic information remains scattered and incomplete. For the relatively high marriage age for men and low age at first marriage for women in the first decades of New England settlement see Daniel Scott Smith, "The Demographic History of Colonial New England," *Journal of Economic History* 32, no. 1 (March 1972): 176. Smith also notes that regional variation makes demographic patterns "probably unverifiable above the local level." In a now classic study of Plymouth, Massachusetts, historian John Demos calculated a mean marriage age between 1600 and 1625 of 27.0 years for men and 20.6 for women. See Demos, *A Little Commonwealth: Family Life in Plymouth Colony* (New York, 1970), 193. Di Bonaventura notes in *For Adam's Sake* (86) that it was unusual for a man to marry before his late twenties but that Joshua Hempstead married at age eighteen when his wife Abigail Bailey (1677–1716) was in about her twentieth year. For the difficulty of calculating early infant and maternal mortality rates see Nancy Schrom Dye, "History of Childbirth in America," *Signs* 6, no. 1 (Autumn 1980): 100.

27 *grandfather* James Wadsworth (d. 1777), son of Moses Noyes's daughter Ruth Noyes Wadsworth (1681–1774) and Colonel James Wadsworth (1677–1756), was born ca. 1700.

27 *age five weeks* Noyes and Noyes, *Noyes-Gilman Ancestry*, 24.

27 *senior tutor* Dexter, 64, 80; Oviatt, 252.

27 *founding minister* Ellen Douglas Larned, *History of Windham County, Connecticut, 1600–1760* (Worcester, MA, 1874), 1:219–20. See also Williston Walker, *The Creeds and Platforms of Congregationalism* (New York, 1893), 497.

Lessons from a Wayward Son

29 *In this time* Matthew Griswold to Cotton Mather, November 8, 1712, typescript copy, Wolcott Griswold Lane Papers, LHSA. Cited in Edward Eldridge Salisbury and Evelyn McCurdy Salisbury, *Family Histories and Genealogies: A Series of Genealogical and Biographical Monographs* [. . .] (New Haven, CT, 1892), 2:29–33; see also Noyes and Noyes, *Noyes-Gilman Ancestry*, 182.

29 *prayed with the Griswold family* George Griswold (1692–1761), Matthew Griswold's third son, who was fifteen when his oldest brother escaped from home, likely joined the family's prayers. A decade later he gave the salutatory address in Latin at the Collegiate School's first graduation in 1717. See Dexter, *Biographical Sketches of the Graduates*, 168–69.

29 *had succeeded* Dexter, 80, 89.

29 *I have a Kinsman* *Diary of Cotton Mather* (Boston, 1812), 2:59. For othert refgerences to Cotton Mather's kinsman see also 66, 160, 207.

32 *shorter account* *History of the Ely Reunion Held at Lyme, Conn.* (July 10, 1878), 139–40. See also Beach and Ely, *Ely Ancestry*, 35. Whether the man of war, galleon, or privateer mentioned in the Griswold and Ely narratives would also havbe transported enslaved persons across the Atlantic or from the West Indies cannot be known.

32 *close ties* *VR*, 251, 231.

32 *urgently called for* Cited in Cotton Mather, "Extracts from the Diary of Cotton Mather," *Panoplist, and Missionary Herald* 15 (1819): 56 (October 7, 1712), 57 (October 14, 1712). See also Abijah Perkins Marvin, *The Life and Times of Cotton Mather* (Boston, 1892), 379.

Finding a Successor

35 *It was an awful stroke* Moses Noyes to Samuel Sewall, September 3, 1723, photocopy, FCCOL.

35 *stretched back* Rev. Thomas Parker (1595–1677), who voyaged from England with his cousin Rev. James Noyes (1608–1656), Moses Noyes's father, in 1634, lived unmarried in the Noyes home in Newbury where he prepared for college an ongoing group of twelve or fourteen pupils. When Judge Sewall learned of Parker's death, he referred to him as "my dear Master." Noyes and Noyes, *Noyes-Gilman Ancestry*, 9–12; Sewall, *Diary*, 41 (April 28, 1677).

35 *"Arminian" notions* A letter in May 1722 alerted Cotton Mather to the alarming theological shifts at Yale College: "I hear some in Connecticut complain that Arminian books are cried up in Yale College for eloquence and learning, and Calvinists despised for the contrary: and none have the courage to see it redressed." Cited in Dexter, *Biographical Sketches of the Graduates*, 260. For Arminianism see E. Brooks Hilifield, *Theology in America: Christian Thought from the Age of the Puritans to the Civil War* (New Haven, CT, 2003), 83–85; Robert L. Geiger, *The History of American Higher Education: Learning and Culture from the Founding to World War II* (Princeton, NJ, 2015), 23.

35 *this contentious* Will of Rev. Moses Noyes (August 1719), photocopy, EPP, box 6, LHSA.

35 *initial choice* For the town's extended efforts to bring Samuel Russell to Lyme see *LR*, 142 (February 25, 1717/8), 143 (February 24, 1717/8), 143–44 (April 28, 1718), 150 (October 6, 1719), 153 (January 4, 1719/20). Also see Stark, *Lyme, Connecticut*, 8–9.

37 *another minister* *LR*, 155 (January 2, 1720/1).

37 *majority vote* *LR*, 153–54 (January 18, 1719/20).

37 *Mr. Samuel Pierpont* LR, 156 (January 23, 1720/1), 161 (March 13, 1720/1), 163 (November 12, 1722).

37 *now assisting minister* LR, 166 (June 26, 1722).

37 *ongoing dispute* LR, 141–42 (February 25, 1717/8), 162 (February 12, 1720/1).

37 *ordination* The *Boston News-Letter* (April 4, 1723) states that Pierpont "was ordained a minister December last."

37 *to the great satisfaction* Rev. Jonathan Parsons to Rev. Thomas Prince, *CH*, 67:120 (June 9, 1744). Cited in Dexter, 191.

37 *after courting* Rev. William B. Cary later wrote that Samuel Pierpont "crossed the Connecticut River to Pettipaug, now Essex, to visit his ladylove living in Middletown. The ferriage was made by the Indians, in canoes, from near Higgins' wood to Ferry-point." Cary, *Memorial Discourse*, 9.

37 *printed an elegy* *Boston News-Letter*, May 16, 1723.

38 *leave Saybrook* Noyes had attended in 1716 a weeklong gathering of Collegiate School trustees in Saybrook at which they formally voted to remove the school to New Haven. As moderator he did not vote but voiced a preference that the school remain in Saybrook. Only if a move could not be avoided would he agree with the choice of New Haven. Dexter, 160.

38 *choosing Timothy Cutler* See Robert E. Daggy, "Education, Church, and State: Timothy Cutler and the Yale Apostasy of 1722," *Journal of Church and State* (Winter 1971): 46; Dexter, 271.

39 *Saybrook Platform* See *The Cambridge and Saybrook Platforms of Church Discipline: With the Confession of Faith of New England Churches* (Boston, 1829), 117ff.; Paul R. Lucas, *Valley of Discord: Church and Society along the Connecticut River, 1636–1725* (Hanover, NH, 1976), 184–87; Lewellyn Pratt, "The Saybrook Platform," in *Saybrook's Quadrimillenial: Commemoration of the 250th Anniversary of the Settlement of Saybrook* (Hartford, 1886), 27–45.

39 *shrinking* The town had voted "that there be 100 acres of land reserved to accommodate the north part of the town and 100 acres of land reserved to accommodate the east part of the town . . . better to enable each of these parts of the town to settle the ministry amongst themselves when they come to be societies by themselves." LR, 145 (December 1, 1718). See also James, *Educational History*, 70–72.

39 *often lamented* *CH*, 67:120 (June 7, 1744).

Oxford and Temperance

41 *After 1694* PR, 4 (October 11, 1694), 136. See also Noyes and Noyes, *Noyes-Gilman Ancestry*, 22. While Joshua Hempstead's diary notes that Moses Noyes performed the marriage in November 1717 of Deborah Ely (1697–1760) and Ebenezer Dennis (1682–1726), he likely refers to Moses Noyes Jr., a justice of the peace for New London County who was Deborah Ely's brother-in-law. After attending the marriage, Hempstead "went at night to Richard Lord's & lodged there." Joshua Hempstead, *The Diary of Joshua Hempstead: A Daily Record of Life in New London, Connecticut, 1711–1758*, New London County Historical Society (New London, CT, 1999), 70.

41 *Oxford negro man* LLR, 4:170 (January 21, 1725/6).

41 *unprecedented* Although Judge Samuel Sewell conducted "slave marriages" in Boston after publishing his antislavery tract *The Selling of Joseph* in 1700, no prior formalized unions of enslaved couples have been discovered in Lyme records. For Sewall's role in the Massachusetts legislature's legalization of slave marriages in 1705 see Bradley, *Slavery*, 18; Jared Ross Hardesty, *Unfreedom:*

Slavery and Dependence in Eighteenth-Century Boston (New York, 2016), 153; Catherine Adams and Elizabeth Pleck, *Love of Freedom: Black Women in Colonial and Revolutionary New England* (New York, 2010), 111–12. Also see Darlene C. Goring, "The History of Slave Marriage in the United States," *John Marshall Law Review* 39, no. 2 (2006): 310; di Bonaventura, *For Adam's Sake*, 270–71.

41 *genial man* Salisbury and Salisbury, *Family Histories*, 1:293.

41 *large household* William Lord (1623–1678), an early Saybrook proprietor and Rev. James Noyes's uncle by marriage, had acquired extensive acreage along the river in 1669 from his "very loving friend" Chapeto, a kinsman of the Mohegan sachem Uncas (1598–1682/3). At William Lord's death, the land passed to his two sons, and a Lyme town meeting in 1707 confirmed that Richard and Thomas Lord (1645–1730) had received their land, including their home lots, "upon the account of a purchase of lands of Chapeto, an Indian." *PR*, 2.93–4 (October 13, 1681); *LR*, 94 (April 8, 1707). See also John W. De Forest, *History of the Indians of Connecticut from the Earliest Known Period to 1850* (Hartford, 1851), 266; Salisbury and Salisbury, 1:267–68, 286–7. For alternative views of Uncas see Emma W. Sternlof, "History, Language, and Power: James Hammond Trumbull's Native American Scholarship" (senior thesis, Trinity College, Hartford, 2013), 28–29, 38–41.

41 *later baptized* The baptism and admission to the church of Oxford and Arabella together on February 3, 1733/4, suggests but does not confirm a relationship between the enslaved servants. Ely et al., *History of the First Congregational Church*, 310.

41 *captured at age two* After her capture in 1676, Jane was sold in Stonington at age six, then passed to an owner named Cooper with an agreement that she would be freed after nine years. Barbara W. Brown and James M. Rose, *Black Roots in Southeastern Connecticut* (New London, CT, 2001), 396. For the distribution of Indian war captives and the servitude of Indian children see Warren, *New England Bound*, 92ff., 104.

41 *first deacon* Joseph Peck Sr.'s older brother Jeremiah Peck (1623–1699) served as Saybrook's minister in 1666 when Moses Noyes began preaching in the town's east quarter. Joseph Peck Sr. held multiple town offices, serving as Lyme's schoolmaster for more than a decade. Also active in trade, he exported barrel staves produced by his sawmill on the Eight Mile River and sold "cider by retail during the want of an ordinary." He passed his position as Lyme's ordinary keeper in 1702 to his son-in-law Thomas Anderson (1672–1746), who, the town agreed, "shall have liberty to sell about one hundred gallons of rum out of jars by the gallon or quart." See Ira B. Peck, *A Genealogical History of the Descendants of Joseph Peck* (1868), 390; EPP, box 2; *LR*, 40–41 (February 1, 1680/1), 44 (April 17, 1683), 83 (January 25, 1696/7), 93 (April 6, 1702), 122 (March 4, 1708/9).

41 *account book* Account Book of Joseph Peck Jr., CSLMC. In a will recorded in 1716 and witnessed by Moses Noyes Jr., Joseph Peck Sr. bequeathed to his son his house, barn, warehouse, and tracts of meadow. Photocopy, EPP, box 7.

41 *Jack man servant* Ely et al., 307.

43 *a certain molato* LLR, 4:170 (January 13, 1725/6).

43 *in consideration* LLR, 4:79 (May 9, 1729). Benjamin Reed's father John Reed (1679–1732) had assisted Joseph Peck Sr. in the transport of twenty thousand barrel staves out of Lyme. *LR*, 122 (March 4, 1708/9).

43 *baptized Oxford* Ely et al., 241, 242, 310, 243.

43 *all sound* Cited in Salisbury and Salisbury, 1:293–94.

44 *four older children* Below Temperance's deed of sale, the town book lists the births of three children to Oxford and Temperance, servants of Mr. Richard Lord Jr.: "Zachary their son was born the

23 day of October 1726"; "Luke was born the 14th day of May 1728"; "Jordan their son was born the 30 day of October 1732." LLR, 4:170.

44 *consequential families* Martha J. Lamb claimed in "Lyme: A Chapter in American Genealogy," *Harper's New Monthly Magazine* (1876), 7:318, that before the Revolution "all the consequential families in Lyme owned negro slaves."

44 *deacon* Both Captain Renold Marvin (1669–1737) and his son Deacon Renold Marvin (1698–1761) served as church deacons and successively inherited the large estate of Lieutenant Renold Marvin (1632–1676), but likely John Bradick sold Caesar to the younger Renold Marvin. See George Franklin Marvin and William T. R. Marvin, *Descendants of Reinold and Matthew Marvin of Hartford, Ct.* (Boston, 1904), 48, 56.

44 *Caesar* LLR, 5:8 (March 25, 1731); Brown and Rose, 471.

44 *Chloe* *VR*, 19; Brown and Rose, 479.

44 *Cato* Ely et al., 305.

44 *Phillis* Ely et al., 246.

44 *Lucy* Ely et al., 246, 311.

44 *in preaching* ESR, 24 (April 30, 1734).

45 *great wealth* Salisbury and Salisbury, 2:47; Noyes and Noyes, 181; Jackson Turner Main, "The Economic and Social Structure of Early Lyme," in Willauer, *Lyme Miscellany*, 36. For the local influence of John Griswold, who was elected to the legislature twenty-eight times between 1721 and 1757, see Stark, *Lyme, Connecticut*, 47.

45 *sold and delivered* Salisbury and Salisbury, 2:48.

45 *bill of sale* CSLMC. See also Daniel Lathrop Coit, *A Memoir of Daniel Lathrop Coit of Norwich, Connecticut, 1754–1833* (Norwich, CT, 1907), 3–5. For the trading of enslaved people in New London see Christopher Paul Sawula, "'The Hidden Spring of Prejudice and Oppression': Slavery and Abolitionism in Connecticut" (unpublished thesis, Boston College, 2008), 20–21. For a record of New London ships that carried enslaved people from Africa in 1757 see Anne Farrow, *The Logbooks: Connecticut's Slave Ships and Human Memory* (Middletown, CT, 2014).

45 *Bristo* Brown and Rose, 469.

45 *bye and secret place* Cited in Cornelia Hughes Dayton, *Women before the Bar: Gender, Law, and Society in Connecticut*, 1639–1789 (Chapel Hill, NC, 1995), 256–58.

45 *London* *Connecticut Gazette*, September 5, 1777. Cited in Brown and Rose, 528.

45 *Lyme's ministers* Neighboring ministers also owned enslaved servants, and Rev. William Hart (1713–1784) in Saybrook purchased a "Negro boy" in 1749 from Jabez Huntington (1719–1786), a wealthy Norwich merchant engaged in the West Indies trade. See Frances Manwaring Caulkins, *History of Norwich, Connecticut* (Hartford, 1866), 328; D. Hamilton Hurd, *History of New London County, Connecticut* (Philadelphia, 1882), 313.

45 *native captives* For the treatment and sale of native captives see Michael L. Fickes, "'They Could Not Endure That Yoke': The Captivity of Pequot Women and Children after the War of 1637," *New England Quarterly* 73, no. 1 (March 2000): 58–81; Christine M. Delucia, *Memory Lands: King Philip's War and the Place of Violence in the Northeast* (New Haven, CT, 2018), 295–97; Warren, 91–99.

45 *considerable expense* James Noyes to John Allyn, October 1676, photocopy, Yale Indian Papers Project, Yale University. Cited in Warren, 99–100.

45 *sold in Barbados* Not only captured Narragansetts but those who surrendered were sold in Barbados, where they endured harsh labor on sugar plantations that created wealth for English investors. A pamphlet published in London detailed the severe consequences of a rumored slave revolt in June 1675, a year before James Noyes described Narragansett men trying to escape being sold as slaves. See *Great Newes from the Barbadoes. Or, A True and Faithful Account of the Grand Conspiracy of The Negroes against the English, and The Happy Discovery of the same. With the number of those that were burned alive, Beheaded, and otherwise Executed for their Horrid Crimes* (London, 1676); Dunn, *Sugar and Slaves*, 257–58; Warren, 91–95.

A Dark House

47 *I must now offer* Rev. Azariah Mather, *A Discourse Concerning the Death of the Righteous* (New London, CT, 1731). Photocopy, FCCOL.

47 *printed version* The sermon, "Printed & sold by T. Green" in New London, does not state when the eulogy was delivered.

48 *dissenting beliefs* For the threat posed to the "Standing Order" by the gathering of Baptist churches in Waterford, Lyme, and Stonington see William Buell Sprague, *Annals of the American Pulpit: Baptist* (New York, 1859), 26ff.; Caulkins, *History of New London*, 439.

48 *their Errors* Moses Noyes attended with Azariah Mather a meeting in Lyme in 1727 about the growing strength of "those sectaries." The formal debate that followed between Rev. John Bulkley from Colchester and Elder Valentine Wightman (1681–1747) from Groton filled Lyme's meetinghouse. Mather stood at the door at "about Ten of the Clock, the hour agreed upon," together with Rev. George Griswold from the east parish and Rev. John Hart (1682–1756) from Guilford, to await Elder Wightman's arrival. Contending views of religious discipline, baptism by immersion, and public taxation unfolded in the meetinghouse for seven hours before Mather closed the debate with prayer. See John Bulkley, *An Impartial Account of a Late Debate at Lyme in the Colony of Connecticut* (New London, 1729). A confusion of names apparently resulted in the later claim, which became fixed in local lore, that Cotton Mather visited Moses Noyes in Lyme. In his *Memorial Discourse* Rev. William B. Cary stated in 1876: "At what time the Baptists were here first in any strength, it is difficult to determine, but about the year 1727 Mr. Noyes was much troubled by the preaching of their peculiar tenets here, and conferred with Cotton Mather of Boston who came to Lyme at that time, in regard to it, and they jointly held some discussion with the Baptists, who, however, continued to increase." Cotton Mather, Azariah Mather's kinsman, was by then elderly, and his diary does not mention a visit to Lyme. He died in Boston later that same year. See Cary, *Memorial Discourse*, 16; Chris Beneke, *Beyond Toleration: The Religious Origins of American Pluralism* (Oxford, 2006), 29.

48 *studying theology* Rev. Jonathan Greenleaf (1785–1865), "Memoir of the Reverend Jonathan Parsons," *American Quarterly Register* 14 (1841): 110. Parsons's daughter Lydia Parsons Greenleaf (1755–1854), Jonathan Greenleaf's mother, was born in Newbury a decade after her father removed from Lyme.

48 *as a probationer* Parsons, "An Account of the Revival," *CH*, 67:120 (June 9, 1744).

48 *continue Mr. Parsons* ESR, 11 (April 2, 1730).

48 *In that day* *CH*, 68:123 (June 16, 1744). See also Greenleaf, 110; Dexter, *Biographical Sketches of the Graduates*, 389, Douglas I. Winiarski, *Darkness Falls on the Land of Light: Experiencing Religious Awakening in Eighteenth-Century New England* (Chapel Hill, NC, 2017), 434–36.

48 *wheat at seven shillings* ESR, 12 (May 29, 1730).

49 *unanimously confirmed* ESR, 13 (August 14, 1730).

49 *courtship letter* For Parsons's two "flowery" courtship letters in January 1729/30 and July 1730 see Winiarski, 336. Hannah Edwards did not marry until 1745/6 when she wed Judge Seth Wetmore (1700–1788), a prominent lawyer and wealthy merchant who built for his bride an elegant Georgian-style mansion on his thousand-acre estate in Middletown. See Kenneth P. Minkema, "Hannah and Her Sisters: Sisterhood, Courtship, and Marriage in the Edwards Family in the Early Eighteenth Century," in *New England Historical and Genealogical Register* 146 (January 1992): 47. For Judge Wetmore's wealth and influence, including a description of his slaves, see James Carnahan Wetmore, *The Wetmore Family of America, and Its Collateral Branches* (Albany, 1861), 282–86. See also Susan P. Schoelwer, "Hannah Edwards Wetmore's Shoes," in *Connecticut Needlework: Women, Art, and Family, 1740–1840* (Hartford, 2010), 38–39. The parlor of the Wetmore house was installed in 1986 in the Wadsworth Atheneum in Hartford. See Diana Ross McCain, "Parlor of a 'River God' at Atheneum," *Hartford Courant*, April 15, 1998.

49 *went to the ordination* Hempstead, *Diary*, 232; FCR, 13 (March 17, 1731).

49 *refused to take* Because of "some Scruples then upon my Mind about the Validity of our Ordinations," Parsons later wrote, he "refus'd to take the Oversight of the Church, until the 17th of the following March." *CH*, 68:121 (June 16, 1744). See also Dexter, 389. In *Religion and the American Mind: From the Great Awakening to the Revolution* (Cambridge, MA, 1966), Alan Heimart describes (29) the perplexity about theological currents that led Parsons to visit prominent British theologian George Berkeley (1685–1753) in Rhode Island, although Parsons "quickly decided against Episcopal ordination." For the early history of the Episcopal Church in Connecticut see A. B. Chapin, *A Sermon Delivered in Christ Church, West Haven, on the Hundredth Anniversary of Laying the Foundation of the Church* (New Haven, CT, 1839), 6–8.

49 *"Presbyterian" ordination* For "Presbyterians" as the name given to Congregationalists see Blake, *Early History of the First Church*, 2:150.

49 *the general platform* "Immediately before I took the Oversight of the Flock," Parsons wrote, "I did, before the Council and the Brethren of the Church, expressly renounce the Articles for Church Discipline drawn up at Saybrook, and took the general Platform of the Gospel for my rule." *CH*, 67:121 (June 16, 1744). See also *A Letter from a Gentleman in the Country, to his friend in Boston, respecting some late observations upon the conduct, of the Rev. Mr. Jonathan Parsons, while he was minister at Lyme in Connecticut* (Boston, 1757), 3–4; Joseph Tracy, *The Great Awakening: A History of the Revival of Religion in the Time of Edwards and Whitefield* (Boston, 1842), 133.

49 *ordination sermon* Azariah Mather, *A Gospel Star, or Faithful Minister: A discourse had at the ordination of Reverend Mr. George Beckwith in the North Society of Lyme, January 22, 1729/30* (New London, CT, 1730). Participating in Parsons's ordination were Rev. William Worthington (1695–1756) from Saybrook's west parish, Rev. Eliphalet Adams (1677–1753) from New London, and Rev. Jared Elliot (1685–1763) from Killingworth. For Elliot's doubts about the validity of Presbyterian ordination see Sprague, 270.

Confessions

51 *April 4th* FCR, (April 4, 1731).

51 *notebook* *Record of Baptisms, Marriages and Persons who owned the Covenant, 1737–1761*, CCHS.

51 *a marriage* Rev. Moses Noyes likely did not perform the marriage of James Smith and Elizabeth Way, entered in the handwritten notebook and also in the land records. LLR, 2:175 (December 16, 1724).

51 *twenty shillings* ESR, 24 (April 30, 1734).

51 *lascivious carriage* See Nancy Hathaway Steenberg, *Children and the Criminal Law in Connecticut: Changing Perceptions of Childhood* (New York, 2005), 163–66. Steenberg's examination of the case of *Rex vs. David Deming* cites New London County Court documents, box 175, June 1736, case 370.

52 *stroked her belly* Cited in Steenberg, 164.

52 *pleaded not guilty* Cited in Steenburg, 166.

52 *My conduct* FCR, 16–17 (January 1, 1735/6). The date has been written over in the record book.

53 *restored* FCR, 17 (n.d., 1737).

53 *General Court had resolved* *PR*, 8:12–13 (October 8, 1735), 8:95 (May 12, 1737).

53 *only Baptists* Connecticut's General Court in 1729 discharged "the people called Baptists" from "the payment of taxes for the support of the Gospel ministry in this government and for building meeting houses." ESR, 44 (April 17, 1738); *PR*, 8:257 (October 9, 1729).

53 *frame the meeting house* ESR, 40 (September 29, 1737), 44 (April 17, 1738). The third meetinghouse measured forty by sixty feet, with twenty-four feet between the sill and the plate. Ely et al., *History of the First Congregational Church*, 52.

55 *use of his dwelling* ESR, 48 (September 13, 1739).

55 *proceed not further* ESR, 52 (January 28, 1739/40).

55 *greedy ministers* FCR, 18–19 (December 6, 1739).

55 *ill conduct* ESR, 48 (April 12, 1739).

55 *desire of the pastor* FCR, 20 (January 19, 1739/40).

55 *As confessions continued* When Rev. William B. Cary reviewed the records of Parsons's ministry, he remarked that "a singular mania possessed the people of Lyme under his preaching to publicly profess their sins." Cary, *Memorial Discourse*, 11.

55 *his wife Catherine* FCR, 17–18 (April 1739). Connecticut's General Court ruled in 1727 that when "any married persons shall be accused . . . for committing fornication with each other before marriage," they would suffer only "one half the penalty by law ordered against such offenders." *PR*, 7:95 (May 11, 1727).

55 *intemperance* FCR, 20 (January 1741).

55 *Lucy, the enslaved servant* FCR, 21 (May 17, 1741). Parsons baptized Lucy, together with Elizabeth Greenfield, on June 7, 1741, and a year later, on August 9, 1742, admitted Lucy to the church. Ely et al., 246, 313.

55 *fornication* FCR, 21 (May–December, 1741).

The Minister's Wife

57 *His wife was given* Lamb, "Lyme," 323.

57 *beauty and spirit* Lamb, 323.

57 *colorful anecdote* For Martha Lamb's visit to Lyme in 1874, and for early drafts of the manuscript, see "Lyme, Conn." (October 1874), Martha J. Lamb Papers, New-York Historical Society. Evelyn McCurdy Salisbury and her father Charles J. McCurdy (1797–1891) edited and comment-

ed on one early draft. "If you can't read father's handwriting," Mrs. Salisbury wrote in the margin, "send it to me for interpretation."

58 *turned their meetings* *CH*, 68:122 (June 16, 1744).

58 *severe mental struggle* Greenleaf, "Memoir," 111.

58 *Sometimes I thought* Cited in Greenleaf, 111.

59 *natural temper* Greenleaf, 115.

59 *portrait* John Singleton Copley's biographer notes that the portrait of Jonathan Parsons shows "only the head and shoulders" and observes that Parsons "wears a large white wig puffed at the sides, a black silk robe and bands, and holds a Bible in front of him." It describes the minister's features as "strong and prominent." After acquiring a copy, presumably of the Copley portrait, Rev. William Cary wrote, "I thought at first it was an enlarged photo finished in crayon, but upon closer inspection I am inclined to think it a crayon copy of the painting." Another copy hangs today in the Old South Church in Newburyport, but the location of the original portrait, and also of a pastel portrait of Mrs. Phoebe Parsons, possibly by Copley, is not known. A medallion of unknown date showing a youthful and smiling Mrs. Parsons remained in 1892 in the possession of a descendant in New York. See Frank William Bayley, *The Life and Works of John Singleton Copley* (Boston, 1915), 191; Neil Jeffares, *Dictionary of Pastellists before 1800* (Norwich, CT, 2006); William B. Cary to Charles H. Ludington, November 16, 1883, Ludington Family Collection, LHSA; Theodore Parsons Hall, *Family Records of Theodore Parsons Hall and Alexandrine Louise Godfrey of "Tonnancour," Grosse Pointe, near Detroit, Michigan* (Detroit, 1892), 15.

59 *passion for fine clothes* Lamb, "Lyme," 323.

59 *dandy of a husband* Jim Lampos and Michaelle Pearson, *Remarkable Women of Old Lyme* (Charleston, SC, 2015), 14.

59 *thirteen children* Dexter, *Biographical Sketches of the Graduates*, 391.

59 *funeral sermon* Rev. John Searle (1721–1787), *Funeral Sermon at Newburyport, Dec. 30, 1770, occasioned by the Death of Mrs. Phebe Parsons. Consort of Rev. Jonathan Parsons* (Boston, 1771). Parsons had offered the introductory prayer at Searle's ordination in Stoneham on January 17, 1758. Silas Dean, *A Brief History of the Town of Stoneham, Mass: From Its First Settlement to the Year 1843* (Stoneham, MA, 1870), 28.

Out of Darkness

61 *The humble memorial* *Memorial of George Griswold and Jonathan Parsons* (May 6, 1734), Yale University Library manuscript collection.

61 *Three hundred acres* *PR*, 7:524 (October 10, 1734). De Forest, *History of the Indians* (381), noted that the Niantics in 1672 "had no land of their own, and were then furnished with three hundred acres by Lyme, on condition of bringing in a wolf's head annually." General Court records indicate that Thomas Bull and others in 1651/2 "resigned up to the Court one hundred acres of the grounds laid out at Niantic to them . . . which said hundred acres the Court grants liberty to the Indians that formerly possessed and planted the same, to possess and plant for the future, so long as they carry on peaceably and justly towards the English." Twenty years later in 1672 the Court gave Bull liberty to exchange another hundred acres with the Niantic Indians, but in 1680, when the Niantic sachem requested that the Court assign a piece of land "for himself and people," Lyme's deputies affirmed "there is a sufficiency of land allotted to him already." In 1684 the Court ordered, after the Niantics complained that "some English have taken possession of some of their land," that they

"shall not be dispossessed of any of their lands without it be by course of law." De Forest, 381–82; *PR*, 1:228 (October 6, 1651), 1:230 (March 2, 1651/2), 2:174 (May 9, 1672), 2:189 (October 17, 1672), 3:56 (May 13, 1680), 3:144 (May 8, 1684).

61 *Court intervention* *PR*, 1:400 (May 14, 1663).

62 *inquire into the wrongs* *PR*, 7:491 (May 7, 1734), 7:524 (October 10, 1734). See also Olive Tubbs Chendali, *East Lyme: Our Town and How It Grew* (Mystic, CT, 1989), 6.

62 *said Niantic Indians* *PR*, 8:38 (May 13, 1736). At the same session the Court directed that "at the next public Thanksgiving," every ecclesiastical society or parish would provide a contribution "for the civilizing and christianizing of the Indian natives in this Colony."

62 *our school* Cited in William De Loss Love, *Samson Occom and the Christian Indians of New England* (Boston, 1899), 199. See also Chendali, 6–7.

62 *increased for a considerable time* *CH*, 67:113 (June 9, 1744). See also Linford D. Fisher, *The Indian Great Awakening: Religion and the Shaping of Native Cultures in Early America* (Oxford, 2012), 74.

62 *poor, ignorant* *CH*, 67:113 (June 9, 1744).

62 *added the names* Ely et al., *History of the First Congregational Church*, 247. By then Parsons had already preached to the Indians in Niantic "once a fortnight for some time." Greenleaf, "Memoir," 113. See also Vicki S. Welsh, *And They Were Related, Too: A Study of Eleven Generations of One American Family!* (2006), 26–29.

63 *twenty or upward* *CH*, 67:113 (June 9, 1744). De Forest (385) states that these were "the first of the tribe who forsook their ancient superstitions; and, at all events, they were the first who cordially embraced the Christian faith."

64 *the case of Ann Chesno* *Record of the church on the case of Ann Chesno, an Indian woman* (January 1744/5), CSLMC. See also a supporting opinion provided by six "Ministers and Christians," including Rev. George Beckwith and Rev. Jonathan Parsons, "that the woman was involuntary in the whole affair, and that she never did consent to take the man properly as her husband." Cited in Jane T. (Hills) Smith, *Last of the Nehantics* (1894), East Lyme Historical Society, 8.

64 *confession for the sin* FCR, 23 (July 1, 1744).

64 *had so little* *CH*, 67:113 (June 9, 1744).

64 *thirteen or fourteen* Albert Bushnell Hart, ed., *Hamilton's Itinerarium: Being a Narrative of a Journey from Annapolis, Maryland* [. . .] (St. Louis, 1907), 199. For analysis, based on Stiles's drawings, of Niantic wigwams as a southern New England house type see William C. Sturtevant, "Two 1761 Wigwams at Niantic, Connecticut," *American Antiquity* 40, no. 4 (October 1975): 437–444.

64 *steadily declined* John Pfeiffer estimates the number of Nehantic (Niantic) people living in what is now East Lyme, Lyme, and Old Saybrook at the time of contact in the early decades of the seventeenth century as over six hundred and traces a sharp decline in population in the eighteenth century. See Pfeiffer, "Post-Contact-Populations of the Nehantic Reservation of Lyme, Connecticut," *Bulletin of the Archaeological Society of Connecticut* 59 (1996): 70.

65 *seven Niantic men* De Forest, 385.

65 *10 families* *No. of Nyhantic Tribe of Indians, Taken Oct. 7, 1761*, in *Extracts from the Itineraries and Other Miscellanies of Ezra Stiles, D.D., 1755–1794*, ed. Franklin Bowditch Dexter (New Haven, CT, 1916), 130.

65 *in 1825* For the declining Niantic population between 1780 and 1865 and the reports of Indian overseers see Daniel R. Mandell, *Tribe, Race, History: Native Americans in Southern New England, 1780–1880* (Baltimore, 2008), 5; see also Love, *Samson Occom*, 200.

65 *passed a law* *The Public Statute Laws of the State of Connecticut* (Hartford, 1839), 358. The state authorized compensation in 1773 for personal property to "any individual member of the Niantic tribe." *Special Acts and Resolutions of the State of Connecticut* (Hartford, 1880), 7:511.

65 *declared the Niantics extinct* Pfeiffer, 70; Sam Libby, "Now the Nehantics Ask U.S. Recognition," *New York Times*, August 2, 1998.

65 *Mercy Ann Nonesuch* Smith, 26–29; Mandell, 143.

Great Danger

67 *The parish is small* Jonathan Parsons to Benjamin Coleman, December 16, 1741, cited in Greenleaf, "Memoir," 113.

67 *undoubted alteration* Greenleaf, 114. See also Tracy, *Great Awakening*, 134.

67 *burned the sermons* Greenleaf states (114) that Parsons "had actually burnt up the sermons he had written during the first five years of his ministry, as unworthy of preservation." A handwritten sermon, *God governs by his Providence*, dated "Lyme First Society—Feb. 22, 1736" and preserved in the Lyme Historical Society Archives, likely written by Parsons, may be one sermon of the earliest sermons the minister did not destroy (see fig. 033).

67 *news of Mr. Whitefield's* *CH*, 68:125 (June 16, 1744).

67 *land and banks* Cited in George Leon Walker, *Some Aspects of the Religious Life of New England* (New York, 1897), 91.

68 *came not by the way* *CH*, 68:125 (June 16, 1744).

69 *men and their wives* ESR, 53 (November 7, 1740).

69 *more than 140 souls* Jonathan Parsons to Benjamin Coleman, December 16, 1741, cited in Greenleaf, "Memoir," 113.

69 *more detailed* Five members of Lyme's church to whom Parsons read aloud his detailed account of the Great Awakening attached their fervent endorsement to the last installment. "Much more could have been added," they said. *CH*, 73:162 (July 21, 1744).

69 *revivalist newspaper* For the central role played by *Christian History* in the construction of the Great Awakening see Timothy E. W. Gloege, "The Trouble with *Christian History*: Thomas Prince's 'Great Awakening,'" *Church History* 82, no. 1 (March 2013): 125–65.

69 *vast falsehoods* *CH*, 67:118 (April 14, 1744). Parsons mentioned, in addition, "so many prejudices in the minds of people, against the late serious effusion of the holy spirit; and so many misrepresentations of it respecting this place in particular."

69 *some hints* *CH*, 67:119 (April 14, 1744).

69 *burned with love* *CH*, 69:135–36 (June 23, 1744).

69 *great danger* *CH*, 70:138 (June 30, 1744).

69 *errand* "Sometimes I had 30 in a day; and sometimes many more, all upon the grand affairs of their souls." *CH*, 70:141 (June 30, 1744).

69 *above one hundred and eighty* *CH*, 71:151 (July 7, 1744). Parsons also acknowledged his repeated

use of numbers to demonstrate the achievements of the revival in his parish: " 'Tis possible," he wrote, "that some may think me fond of numbers." *CH*, 71:151 (July 7, 1744).

69 *daily and in great numbers* *CH*, 70:44 (June 30, 1744).

69 *left their sports* *CH*, 70:150 (July 7, 1744).

69 *administered the sacrament* *CH*, 70:147 (June 30, 1744).

70 *feasting, music* *CH*, 69:136 (June 23, 174).

70 *some young women* *CH*, 69:136 (June 23, 174).

70 *those that could not* *CH*, 70:137 (June 30, 1744).

70 *assembly in general* *CH*, 70:139 (June 30, 1744).

70 *unhappy case* *CH*, 70:143 (June 30, 1744).

70 *had not known* *CH*, 72:153 (July 14, 1744).

70 *impassioned sermon* For Davenport's trial in Boston, his arrest in Hartford, and the accompanying newspaper coverage see Lisa Smith, *The First Great Awakening in Colonial American Newspapers: A Shifting Story* (New York, 2012), 139–43.

71 *sacrificial blaze* For the religious frenzy created in New London in 1743 when Davenport urged a "sacrificial blaze of worldly goods" see Harry S. Stout and Peter Onuf, "James Davenport and the Great Awakening in New London," *Journal of American History* 70, no. 3 (December 1983): 556–78; Caulkins, *History of New London*, 454–56.

71 *greatly loved* *CH*, 72:154 (July 14, 1744).

71 *divine impulse* Rev. George Beckwith, *Christ the Alone Pattern of Christian Obedience. Two sermons preached at Lyme North Society, August 23, 1741* (New London, CT, 1742). See also Tracy, 236.

71 *funded the printing* The published sermons list "the names of 54 persons who on hearing of the foregoing sermons, willingly contributed to their publication."

71 *with the lights* Eleazar Mather to Rev. Mr. [Mather] Byles (1706–1788), n.d., cited in Stark, *Lyme, Connecticut*, 27. For Eleazar Mather's influence in Lyme see Dexter, *Biographical Sketches of the Graduates*, 607; Stark, 50.

72 *purposes to preach* *Boston Gazette*, August 20, 1745.

72 *to Lyme East Society* Hempstead, *Diary*, 446–47.

72 *would have mentioned* Assertions that Whitefield preached in Parsons's parish may result from the account in Caulkins's *History of New London*, 459, which notes, without specifying the east parish: "from Lyme, the whole party crossed over to Long Island." Blake states in his *Early History of the First Church* (2:135): "From here Mr. Whitefield went to East Lyme, and from there to New York and Georgia."

72 *continuing criticism* For the spread of critical views of Whitefield and his avoidance of holding meetings in opposition to local wishes see Winiarski, 353–58.

72 *became inscribed* For the claim that Whitefield preached in Lyme's west parish see Edward E. Salisbury, *The Griswold Family of Connecticut* (New Haven, CT, 1884), 153. Greenleaf in 1841 ("Memoir," 115) remarks vaguely that in Newbury, as at Lyme in former years, Parsons's house was Whitefield's home but does not mention Whitefield preaching a sermon in Lyme. Cary (*Memorial Discourse*, 10), states: "tradition says Whitefield came to Lyme to visit Parsons, and preached to

the people, gathered beneath, from the great rock in the rear of the present church." Ely et al., in *History of the First Congregational Church*, 60, also acknowledges the influence of local tradition and notes that Whitefield "is said to have stood on a ledge, ever since known as The Whitefield Rock, and enthralled the multitude gathered in the garden near Mr. Parsons' home." For an imaginative description of the purported multitude and the claim that August 12, 1745, "was the dawn of the Great Awakening in Lyme" see Jim Lampos and Michaelle Pearson, *Revolution in the Lymes: From the New Lights to the Sons of Liberty* (Charleston, SC, 2016), 29–30.

Scandalous Reports

75 *Tis with regret of mind* Matthew Griswold to Council delegates, September 2, 1746, Solomon Williams Papers, LHSA.

75 *things amiss* *CH*, 70:152 (July 7, 1744).

75 *than any Indian* A yearlong gap in church records follows the report of this meeting. The next entry, in June 1744, reports Edmund Dorr's submission of a complaint against Deacon Marvin for defying a vote by church members. FCR, 22 (July 4, 1743), 22–23 (June 13, 1744); Ely et al., *History of the First Congregational Church*, 55–62.

75 *publish[ed] the same* Five Brethren, letter of complaint, August 24, 1744, Solomon Williams Papers, LHSA. In his *Christian History* report, Parsons defended such outcries, asserting that those who "cry out, faint, speak aloud in a public assembly at an improper time" were "under divine influence." *CH*, 69:132 (June 23, 1744). For a detailed examination of the breakdown of ecclesiastical order in Lyme see Winiarski, *Darkness Falls*, 335–52. Winiarski suggests (345) that Parsons "ignored, elided, or, more likely, lied about the Dorr-Marvin controversy" in his effort to construct a public persona for a published account of the revival.

76 *in the face* Edmund Dorr to Rev. Jonathan Parsons, April 4, 1744, Solomon Williams Papers, LHSA. Dorr signed his letter to the minister "your injured brother."

76 *to release* FCR, 23–24 (November 26, 1744).

76 *opinions lately discussed* Hart, *Hamilton's Itinerarium*, 199–200. For Dr. Hamilton's views of Whitefield's religious enthusiasm and the impact of the revivalist's oratorical skills on weak minds see Robert Micklus, *The Comic Genius of Dr. Alexander Hamilton* (Knoxville, TN, 1990), 108–9.

76 *demand satisfaction* FCR, 28–29 (December 25, 1744).

76 *mutually chosen* FCR, 37 (October 7, 1745).

77 *no entries* Reports of church meetings resumed in June 1746.

77 *His own account* Greenleaf, "Memoir," 114. In a funeral sermon preached in Newbury in 1770 after the death of Whitefield, Parsons stated, "My first acquaintance with Mr. Whitefield, was at New Haven, in October 1740, which was five years before I settled here, by his advice and influence." Jonathan Parsons, *To Live Is Christ, To Die Is Gain, A Funeral Sermon Preached on the Death of the Rev. Mr. George Whitefield* (Portsmouth, NH, 1771), 20.

77 *I came to visit* Cited in Greenleaf, 114.

77 *his arrival* In *Reminiscences of a Nonagenarian* (Newburyport, MA, 1897), 206–7, Sarah Smith Emery provides a timeline: the nineteen disaffected members separated on January 3, 1746; they extended an invitation to Parsons at the advice of Whitefield on January 22; and the installation took place on March 19. See also Douglas L. Winiarski, "The Newbury Prayer Bill Hoax: Devotion and Deception in New England's Era of Great Awakenings," *Massachusetts Historical Review* 14 (2012): 70–71.

77 *considerable opposition* John J. Currier, *"Ould Newbury": Historical and Biographical Sketches* (Boston, 1896), 512, states that "vigorous efforts were made to prevent the installation of Mr. Parsons." See also Currier, *History of Newbury, Mass., 1635–1902* (Boston, 1902), 382.

77 *family's minister* FCR, 49 (March 11, 1757). Edmund Dorr, born in Roxbury, where his father served as town selectman, moved to Lyme in 1716. R. H. Walworth, *Hyde Genealogy: Or, The Descendants, in the Female as Well as in the Male Lines* (Albany, 1864), 53.

77 *I take this people* Currier, "Ould Newbury" 382.

77 *Mutual Council* FCR, 40 (September 6, 1746). The consequential meeting to choose a Mutual Council convened first at Parsons's house, then adjourned to Captain Barnabus Tuttle's (1698–1773) dwelling, and adjourned again to the dwelling house of Captain Timothy Mather, where "the above said Church voted, on the same day above said, that this Church submit to the judgment of the Council."

77 *distributed blame* Ely et al., 61.

Difficulties among Ourselves

79 *To prevent present difficulties* FCR, 42 (November 15, 1746).

79 *for advice* ESR, 74 (April 3, 1746; May 21, 1746), 75 (August 29, 1846).

79 *dealt in coin* Edward E. Salisbury, *Mr. William Diodate (of New Haven from 1717 to 1751) and His Italian Ancestry* (New Haven, CT, 1875), 6, 33.

79 *ordination* FCR, 43 (December 10, 1746).

79 *new wharf* LLR, April 12, 1751. Susan Hollingsworth Ely and Margaret Wellington Parsons, *The Parsonage* (Old Lyme, 1983), 13.

79 *rebuilt the bridge* *Town Meeting Book, 1733–1876* (1752). Cited in James, *Educational History*, 83.

79 *in very bad repair* Hart, *Hamilton's Itinerarium*, 199.

79 *ferry wharf* James, 84.

79 *mile markers* Willauer, *Lyme Miscellany*, 203.

80 *census count* "The Census of 1756," *PR*, 10:617.

80 *had withdrawn* FCR, 43 (April 27, 1748).

80 *set up a worship* FCR, 48 (March 16, 1752).

80 *suddenly raised* A question about Parsons had already arisen in 1752 when the Ecclesiastical Society considered "whether it will do anything respecting the Rev. Mr. Jonathan Parsons, not returning all, or part of the settlement this Society gave him . . . when he left the work of the Gospel ministry in this Society." A committee was appointed to settle the affair "in a just & equitable manner." Ecclesiastical Society records do not mention the outcome. ESR, 99 (November 7, 1752).

80 *two versions* FCR, 48½ (August 19, 1756), 49 (March 11, 1757).

81 *chose that moment* In a series of bequests, Parsons had recently gifted a portion of his substantial property in Lyme to his eldest son, Marshfield Parsons, who married there in 1755. His third son, Samuel Holden Parsons (1737–1789), had also returned to Lyme and studied law with his uncle Matthew Griswold. The return from Newbury of the minister's sons, both actively involved in meetinghouse affairs, may have prompted the renewed defense of Parsons. See LLR, 9:174 (October 30, 1752); Charles S. Hall, *Life and Letters of Samuel Holden Parsons* (New York, 1968), 13.

81 *unsigned letter* *Letter from a Gentleman in the Country* (Boston, 1757).

82 *engaged in adultery* ESR, 118–20 (February 2, 1759). See also Stark, *Lyme, Connecticut*, 40–41.

82 *blacken, ruin, & defame* New London County Court Files, June 1758, photocopy, EPP, box 5, LHSA. Cited in Stark, 40.

82 *summoned for testimony* New London County Court Files, March 4, 1759, photocopy, EPP, box 5, LHSA.

82 *upheld the verdict* New London County Court Files, May 29, 1758; October 3, 1759, photocopy, EPP, box 5, LHSA. See also Ely et al., *History of the First Congregational Church*, 44.

82 *then excluded* *PR*, 11:244 (May 10, 1759).

82 *unhappy difficulties* ESR, 119–20 (February 2, 1759).

82 *agree on terms* ESR, 124 (January 28, 1760).

83 *proper Ecclesiastical Council* ESR, 124 (January 29, 1760). See also James, *Educational History*, 90.

83 *accomplished widow* Mary, the eldest daughter of John Gardiner, fifth proprietor of Gardiners Island, had eloped in 1760 with Rev. Elijah Blague (1730–1762), her father's domestic chaplain. She was said to have acquired as a young woman "many accomplishments at school in Boston," and Elijah Blague, who graduated from Yale in 1750, was deemed beneath her station. Blague died in Saybrook in April 1762 at age thirty-two, and eight months later his widow married Rev. Stephen Johnson. See Curtiss Crane Gardiner, ed., *Lion Gardiner, and His Descendants* (St. Louis, 1890), 117; Jeannette Edwards Rattray, *East Hampton History* (East Hampton, NY, 1953), 341; Dexter, *Biographical Sketches of the Graduates*, 229.

83 *vexed and grieved* William Gordon, *The History of the Rise, Progress, and Establishment of the Independence of the United States* (New York, 1801), 117. Cited in Minor Myers Jr., "Letters, Learning, and Politics in Lyme: 1760–1800," in Willauer, *Lyme Miscellany*, 59.

Slavery or Independence

85 *The calamities which impend* Stephen Johnson, *Some Important Observations, occasioned by, and Adapted to, the Public Fast, Ordered by Authority, December 18th A.D. 1765 On Account of the Peculiar circumstance of the Present Day, Now humbly offered to the Publick* (Newport, RI, 1766). Transcript, LHSA.

85 *preached a sermon* The printed sermon filled "61 rather large octavo pages, which would make about 75 pages of ordinary quarto manuscript." J. H. Trumbull to Edward E. Salisbury, April 16, 1878, in Anson Phelps Stokes, *Memorials of Eminent Yale Men* (New Haven, CT, 1914), 1:349. For discussion of the fast-day sermon see Bernard Bailyn, "The Reverend Stephen Johnson and the Stamp Act in Lyme: Religious and Political Thought in the Origins of the Revolution," in Willauer, *Lyme Miscellany*, 89–92.

85 *strong opposition* Stark, *Lyme, Connecticut*, 56–57.

85 *widely circulated letter* Alice M. Baldwin, *The New England Clergy and the Revolution* (Durham, NC, 1928), 99–102.

85 *likely encouraged* John McCurdy had assembled a substantial library, and Myers concludes that "Johnson's publications offer tacit evidence of the many hours he had spent with McCurdy's law books." William Gordon states that Stephen Johnson consulted Mr. McCurdy, "who undertook to convey the pieces he might pen to the New-London printer, so secretly as to prevent the author's being discovered." See Myers, "Letters, Learning, and Politics," 58; Gordon, *History of the Rise*, 117; Stark, 47–48, 59. For discussion of the published letters see Bailyn, 82–88.

85 *My dear friends* Cited in Willauer, 207–11.

86 *Do not those* Cited in Salisbury and Salisbury, *Family Histories*, 330.

87 *mock trial* Cited in Willauer, 205–7. See also Stark, 57–58.

88 *God-given gift* For the rhetorical opposition of liberty and slavery see Peter A. Dorsey, *Common Bondage: Slavery as Metaphor in Revolutionary America* (Knoxville, TN, 2009), 14–15, 21–22, 32–36.

88 *delivered a sermon* Bailyn, 81–82, 92, describes Johnson's fast-day sermon in 1765 as a "brilliant performance" but considers his Election Day sermon in 1770 "an ordinary performance that follows the formulas of the genre loosely and without flair."

88 *reduced to abject slavery* Stephen Johnson, *Integrity and Piety the best principles of a good administration of government* (New London, CT, 1770), 13.

88 *deputy governor* For the role played by Samuel Holden Parsons in the surprise election in 1769 of his uncle Matthew Griswold see Stark, 48, 65–66.

88 *Is there not* Johnson, *Integrity*, 36.

88 *eyes of the public* Gordon, 117.

88 *human bondage* For antislavery arguments after the Stamp Act see Mary Stoughton Locke, *Anti-slavery in America from the Introduction of African Slaves to the Prohibition of the Slave Trade* (Boston, 1901), 40, 50–62. See also Samuel Hopkins, *Works: With a Memoir of His Life and Character* (Boston, 1854), 1:116, 160; William Patten, *Reminiscences of the Late Rev. Samuel Hopkins, D.D. of Newport, R.I.* (Providence, 1843), 80–87; David S. Lovejoy, "Samuel Hopkins: Religion, Slavery, and the Revolution," *New England Quarterly* 40, no. 2 (June 1967): 227–43. For Rev. Nathaniel Niles's *Discourse on Liberty* (June 5, 1774) see Coffin, *History of Newbury*, 340; Dorsey, 32–36.

88 *remained silent* No evidence that Stephen Johnson owned slaves has been found, but two of his children had marriage ties to slave-owning families. His daughter Sarah Johnson (1748–1802) married in 1772 Matthew Griswold's eldest son, John Griswold (1752–1812), and his son Captain Stephen Johnson (1753–1791) married in 1774 Richard Lord's granddaughter Ann Lord Johnson (1754–1838). The federal census shows that Ann Johnson's father, Enoch Lord (1725–1814), still owned five slaves in 1990 when Captain Stephen Johnson advertised in the *Connecticut Gazette* for the return of a runaway named Sawn, age about twenty-two. Cited in Brown and Rose, *Black Roots*, 572.

88 *in New London County* See Levi Hart, *Liberty Described and Recommended, preached to the Corporation of Freemen in Farmington, and published at their desire* (September 20, 1774), 20. See also Dexter, *Biographical Sketches of the Graduates*, 656–59; Dorsey, 42. For Hart's friendship with Hopkins see Hopkins, *Works*, 1:121. For letter to *Norwich Packet* see Caulkins, *History of Norwich*, 329; Hurd, *History of New London County*, 313. See also Herbert Baker Adams, ed., *Labor, Slavery, and Self-Government* (Baltimore, 1893), 392.

89 *anonymous writer* The writer was widely assumed to be Aaron Cleveland Jr. (1744–1815), a minister's son, Norwich manufacturer, and outspoken opponent of slavery. For slavery in Norwich see Adams, 129.

89 *illegally held* Matthew Griswold to Joseph Wanton, June 19, 1773, cited in Caroline Hazard, *Thomas Hazard son of Robert, called College Tom: A Study of Life in Narragansett in the XVIIIth Century* (Boston, 1893), 252. For Matthew Griswold's 1795 argument supporting slavery, intended for publication, see Sophia Fidelia Hall Coe, *Memoranda Relating to the Ancestry and Family of Sophia Fidelia Hall* (Meriden, CT, 1902), 154.

89 *strowling vagrants* For views of enslaved blacks as "innately libidinous, immoderate, and prone to crime" see Bradley, *Slavery*, 7–8; John Wood Sweet, *Bodies Politic: Negotiating Race in the American North, 1730–1830* (Baltimore, 2003), 239.

89 *made provision that year* New London County Court Probate Records, 1773, #1930, cited in Brown and Rose, 586.

89 *national synod* *Records of the Presbyterian Church* (Philadelphia, 1841), 453, 457, 459; Junius Rodrigus, ed., *Encyclopedia of Emancipation and Abolition in the Transatlantic World* (New York, 2007), 300.

89 *his friend* Johnson had notified Ezra Stiles in 1766 about his letters in "five several papers in Sept. and Oct. past." Stephen Johnson to Ezra Stiles, March 3, 1766, cited in Salisbury and Salisbury, 2:323.

89 *census count* *PR*, 14:487 (January 1, 1774).

89 *led the legislature to ban* *PR*, 14:329 (October 13, 1774). For the nonimportation law as an effort to prevent more black people from coming to Connecticut see Griffin R. Watson, "The Land of Steady Habits: Anti-abolition and the Preservation of Slavery in Connecticut" (unpublished conference paper, 2016), 8, 15.

Revolutionary Chaplain

91 *At the same meeting* ESR, 155 (May 2, 1775).

91 *news of fighting* Willauer, *Lyme Miscellany*, 243.

91 *Lexington alarm* Henry P. Johnston, ed., *The Record of Connecticut Men in the Military and Naval Service during the Revolution, 1775–1783* (Hartford, 1889), 16; Stark, *Lyme, Connecticut*, 74. For Lyme's politically active role on the eve of war see James, *Educational History*, 97–99.

91 *included the appointment* *PR*, 14:417, 430 (April 26, 1775). Hall, *Life and Letters*, 28; Stark, 77.

91 *granted its minister* ESR, 155 (May 2, 1775).

91 *foot soldiers* Johnston, 72–73; Stark, 77.

91 *Dispatched from New London* Hall, 29.

91 *the next day* John Ely, pension application (1832), cited in Willauer, 268–69. See also *History of the Ely Reunion*, 54.

92 *out of danger* S. H. Parsons to his wife, June 21, 1775, cited in Hall, 31–32.

92 *unsigned sermon* Sermon No. 373, *A Discourse for a Fast*, was preached in Milford, Connecticut, on July 20, 1775, then again in Wallingford "before the Association" in May 1776 and in Derby, Connecticut, on April 22, 1778. By the latter two dates, Johnson had completed his service as chaplain.

93 *in camp* Stephen Johnson to Matthew Griswold, October 6, 1775, cited in Salisbury and Salisbury, *Family Histories*, 2:322.

93 *more healthy* Infectious diseases had spread rapidly among soldiers defending Boston until a smallpox hospital helped control contagion. See Louis C. Duncan, *Medical Men in the American Revolution* (Pennsylvania, 1931), 53.

94 *military discharge* Johnston, 72.

94 *passed through Lyme* Local tradition places General Washington overnight at the home of John

McCurdy on April 10, 1776, but financial records and an itinerary suggest that he spent that night instead in Guilford and arrived in New Haven in the early morning of April 11. Evelyn McCurdy Salisbury referred to the bedroom behind her living room as the "Washington room" but acknowledged she reached that conclusion since Washington was known to have passed through Lyme on a certain date on his way to New Haven, and he would "naturally choose Lyme as the stopping point—what town could compare for charm?" See "Expenses of Journey to New York, 4–13 April 1776," in *George Washington*, Revolutionary War Series, ed. Philander D. Chase (Charlottesville, VA, 1991), 4:40–42; Katharine Ludington, *Old Lyme—and Our Family* (Lyme, CT, 1923), 101.

94 *effect of the application* Stephen Johnson to Abigail Leverett, April 16, 1776, cited in Salisbury and Salisbury, 2:318.

94 *Ecclesiastical Society meeting* Ecclesiastical Society records do not mention the meeting or its outcome.

95 *I have received* Stephen Johnson to Abigail Leverett, May 8, 1776, cited in Salisbury and Salisbury, 2:319.

95 *famous in Lyme* Ely et al., *History of the First Congregational Church*, 66.

95 *reception among* John Eddy to Madame Johnson, June 18, 1776, cited in Salisbury and Salisbury, 2:321.

95 *marital happiness* John Eddy to Madame Johnson, July 17, 1776, cited in Salisbury and Salisbury, 2:322.

95 *impassioned letter* Colonel Samuel Selden to Captain Joshua Huntington, July 6, 1776, cited in Willauer, 253–54. See also Stark, 82–83; Sophie Selden Rogers et al., *Selden Ancestry: A Family History* (Oil City, PA, 1931), 83–93.

96 *died in the attempt* Johnston, 101; Stark, 83–84.

96 *British attack* Hall, 41–49.

96 *after a long* Greenleaf, "Memoir," 115.

96 *funeral sermon* John Searle, *The Character and Reward of a Good and Faithful Servant, A Funeral Sermon Occasioned by the Death of Rev. Jonathan Parsons* (Newburyport, MA, 1779), liv. See also Dexter, *Biographical Sketches of the Graduates*, 53–55. Searle, who noted that he had heard Jonathan Parsons preach at Lyme, described the deceased minister's elocution as "either solemn and grave, majestic and commanding, terrifying and alarming, soft and persuasive, gentle and melting, insinuating and alluring, as occasion required." Some, Searle remarked, "have not scrupled to call him one of the greatest preachers of the present age."

96 *right to occupy* LLR, 12:108 (November 9, 1768).

96 *remaining property* LLR, 13:99 (October 19, 1771).

96 *within a year* Dexter, 391; Greenleaf, 115.

96 *in the vault* Before illness prevented Whitefield's return to London, he had intended to be buried beside his wife, Elizabeth James Whitefield (1704–1768), in the vault of the chapel built for him in 1756 on Tottenham Court Road, known as the Whitfield Tabernacle. Parsons's funeral sermon for his friend and mentor in 1770 stated that the touring minister had "died by a fit of the asthma, at six o'clock this morning, in my chamber." Whitefield's funeral was attended "by about six thousand people within the walls of the church, while many thousands were on the outside, not being able to find admittance," and, for a graveside service, "at one o'clock all the bells in town were tolled for half an hour, and all the ships and other vessels in the harbor gave their proper signals of mourn-

ing." See Parsons, *To Live Is Christ*; John Gillies, ed., *Memoirs of the Late Reverend George Whitefield* (London, 1812), ii.

96 *Devoted followers* Visitors carried away remnants of Whitefield's burial garments, and sometime before the remodeling of Newbury's meetinghouse in 1829, "the large bone of Mr. Whitefield's right arm mysteriously disappeared." John J. Currier, *History of Newburyport, Mass., 1764–1905* (Newburyport, MA, 1906), 266; Currier, *"Ould Newbury,"* 521. See also Jessica M. Parr, *Inventing George Whitefield: Race, Revivalism, and the Making of a Religious Icon* (Jackson, MS, 2015), 114–30, 131–32; "Buried Treasure," *Boston Globe*, July 19, 2009.

96 *fervent admirer* Rev. Joseph Prince, a grandnephew of Rev. Thomas Prince, was known as "the Blind Evangelist." John B. Prince, *The Prince Family of Hull and Boston* (New Brunswick, NJ, 1976), 78–80.

96 *church record book* Minutes of only one church meeting appear in the record book between 1770 and 1780, but Johnson continued to receive his annual salary.

96 *remained vulnerable* Matthew Griswold to Governor Trumbull, September 2, 1775. Cited in Willauer, 248–49.

96 *town meetings* Lyme inhabitants appointed a committee in October 1777 "to supply (in their absence) the families of such as shall volunteer by enlistment into said service, with all necessaries which they may need for their support" and also voted "to procure immediately one shirt, either linen or flannel, one hunting shirt—or frock, one pair of woolen overalls, one or two pairs of woolen stockings, and one pair of good shoes for each man, commissioned officer, or soldier in the Continental Army belonging to the said Town of Lyme." Cited in Willauer, 256.

96 *calamities of the times* Cited in Amelia Leavitt Hill, "The New President of Yale College in 1778," *Connecticut Magazine* (Hartford, 1899), 5:420.

96 *with all convenient* ESR, 163 (November 27, 1780), 167 (September 5, 1782), 173 (November 22, 1784).

96 *ordination sermon* In September 1783 Rev. Frederick W. Hotchkiss (1762–1844) succeeded his father-in-law Rev. William Hart as Saybrook's minister. See Frederick Fosdick, *The First Church of Christ (Congregational), Old Saybrook, Conn.* (Middletown, CT, 1896), 46; Edward M. Chapman, ed., *The First Church of Christ in Saybrook, 1646–1946* (New Haven, CT, 1947), 151.

96 *personal reminiscence* "Old Lyme, Connecticut," *New York Observer*, n.d., scrapbook, 31, LHSA. See also David Brainard Hall, *The Halls of New England: Genealogical and Biographical* (Albany, 1883), 629–30.

96 *theological discourse* Stephen Johnson, *The Everlasting Punishment of the Ungodly, Illustrated and evinced to be a Scripture Doctrine: and the Salvation of all Men, As taught in several late Publications, confuted* (New London, CT, 1786), FCCOL.

97 *distributing his* property Will of Stephen Johnson, photocopy, FCCOL.

97 *estate inventory* Photocopy, FCCOL; cited in Ely et al., 66.

97 *nursed the flame* George Bancroft, *History of the United States of America* (Boston, 1876), 3:499, 520.

97 *fuller portrait* A family history states that little is known about the life of "Parson Johnson." Salisbury and Salisbury, 2:345. Bailyn, in *Reverend Stephen Johnson* (92), notes that except for his political writing in the fall of 1765, "little otherwise is known" about Johnson.

Invitations

99 *Voted that the Society Committee* ESR, 176 (November 27, 1786).

99 *raised in Newport* In Newport Mr. Channing had been "for a time under the ministry of Rev. Samuel Hopkins." Dexter, *Biographical Sketches of the Graduates*, 2:183; Blake, *Early History of the First Church*, 2:207–12. See also Caulkins, *History of New London*, 589.

99 *would marry* Channing may have become familiar with Lyme through William Noyes Jr. (1760–1834), his schoolmate at Yale, where both were members of the Linonian Society. After his marriage in 1787, he made frequent visits to Lyme and two years later preached a funeral sermon for his wife's elder sister Anna McCurdy Strong (1760–1789). Blake, 2:212; Salisbury and Salisbury, *Family Histories*, 2:83–84; Dexter, 2:183–86. See also *A Catalogue of the Linonian Society of Yale College* (1841), 17; Kathy M. Umbricht Straka, "The Linonian Society Library of Yale College: The Formative Years, 1768–1790," in the *Yale University Library Gazette*, April 1980, 183–84.

99 *indefatiguable in his attention* Steenberg, *Children and the Criminal Law*, 68–71, provides a detailed examination of court documents and newspaper coverage of the murder case. See also Steenberg, "Murder and Minors: Changing Standards in the Criminal Law of Connecticut, 1650–1853," in *Murder on Trial, 1620–2002*, ed. Robert Asher et al. (Albany, 2005), 113–34; Caulkins, *History of New London*, 576–77; Julie Stagis, "A Girl, 12, Is Hanged in Connecticut for Murder in 1786," *Hartford Courant*, April 1, 2014.

100 *execution sermon* Henry Channing, *God Admonishing His People of Their Duty, as Parents and Masters. A sermon, preached at New-London, December 20th, 1786. Occasioned by the execution of Hannah Ocuish, a mulatto girl, aged 12 years and 9 months. For the murder of Eunice Bolles, aged 6 years and 6 months* (New London, CT, 1786). See Caulkins, 577.

100 *ordination sermon* Ezra Stiles, *A Sermon Delivered at the Ordination of the Reverend Henry Channing* (New London, CT, 1787). Rev. Levi Hart offered the prayer of ordination. Blake, 2:211; Caulkins, 588.

100 *ordination elsewhere* Lemuel Tyler served as minister in Preston from 1789 to 1810; David Hale served in Lisbon from 1790 to 1803; Stanley Griswold served in New Milford from 1790 to 1802. FCR, 51 (July 3, 1787), 55 (July 14, 1788), 55 (May 7, 1789). See Henry F. Bishop, *Historical Sketch of Lisbon, Conn. from 1786 to 1900* (New York, 1903); Samuel Orcutt, *History of the Towns of New Milford and Bridgewater, Connecticut, 1703–1882* (Hartford, 1882), 257.

100 *accepted an invitation* ESR, 188 (October 19, 1789); FCR, 55 (November 21, 1789).

100 *went to farming* Stiles, 412.

100 *two hundred pounds* ESR, 189 (October 19, 1789). James, *Educational History*, notes (105) that "the goods of the farm and the goods of trade share proportionately with money in the fulfillment of the contract."

101 *that the pews* ESR, 193 (December 26, 1791).

101 *wealthiest inhabitants* For John McCurdy's wealth and Lyme's increasing prosperity see Main, "Economic and Social Structure of Early Lyme," 44–45.

101 *younger merchants* Stevens, 7–9; Ely and Parsons, *Parsonage*, 13–15; Stark, *Lyme, Connecticut*, 50–51; James, 104. The Ecclesiastical Society granted liberty to Captain Thomas Griswold Wait (1765–1850) in 1793 to build a wharf on land owned by the Society near the town bridge and to extend eastward so far only as not to obstruct the passage. ESR, 197 (April 25, 1793).

101 *coastal vessels* Stevens, 14–16; Ely and Parsons, 13–15.

101 *sloop named* Peggy Stevens, 14.

101 *he owned* See *Heads of Families at the First Census* (Baltimore, 1972), 123.

102 *inventory* Cited in Ely and Parsons, 63–66.

102 *merchant prince* For the mercantile career of Samuel Mather Jr. see Ely and Parsons, 13–17.

102 *for the future* Town Meeting Book (1792), 281. Cited in James, 103.

102 *faded notebook* *Lyme, Connecticut, Justice Court Records of William Noyes*, CSLMC.

103 *submitted a letter* FCR, 60 (August 8, 1792).

103 *maturely deliberated* FCR, 61–62 (September 19, 1792).

103 *again fell ill* Joseph Anderson, ed., *The Town and City of Waterbury, Connecticut* (New Haven, CT, 1896), 3:618–19.

103 *clock manufacturing* Henry Bronson, *The History of Waterbury, Connecticut* (Waterbury, CT, 1858), 437.

103 *shrewd Waterbury retailers* David R. Meyer, *The Roots of American Industrialization* (Baltimore, 2003), 84.

103 *excommunication* Dexter, 504.

Silver Tankard

105 *Voted that the sum* ESR, 75 (January 6, 1804).

105 *invited* ESR, 197 (October 10, 1793); FCR, 67 (October 30, 1793).

105 *held and finished* William Noyes to Lathrop Rockwell, October 7, 1793, FCCOL Papers, LHSA.

105 *in the parlor* FCR, 69 (January 14, 1794).

105 *funeral sermon* Lathrop Rockwell, *A Sermon Delivered at the Funeral of Matthew Griswold, Late Governor of the State of Connecticut* (New London, CT, 1802).

105 *In our opinion* ESR, 219 (December 24, 1800).

105 *to dissolve* ESR, 222 (February 25, 1801).

105 *such measures* ESR, 221 (January 8, 1801).

105 *did not judge* Rev. Lathrop Rockwell to First Ecclesiastical Society Committee, December 24, 1800, FCCOL Papers, LHSA.

106 *needed repair* ESR, 223 (December 27, 1802).

107 *cupola* ESR, 242–43 (August 20, 1805).

107 *kept in the meeting house* FCR, 78 (March 31, 1808).

107 *shipping flour* Richard Cornelius McKay, *South Street: A Maritime History of New York* (New York, 1971), 92–95; Walter Barrett, *The Old Merchants of New York* (New York, 1885), 158.

107 *owned and chartered* Stevens, *Old Lyme* (18) notes that ships built in Connecticut River yards increased New York's shipping some 15 percent a year. See also James, *Educational History*, 123.

107 *three hundred ships* Peter Eisenstadt, ed., *The Encyclopedia of New York State* (Syracuse, NY, 2005), 501. See also Chauncey M. Depew, *1795–1895: One Hundred Years of American Commerce* (New York, 1895), 2:596–97.

107 *new governor* The election in 1811 was closely watched in Lyme, and after votes had been returned from 104 towns, New Haven lawyer George Hoadly (1781–1857) informed Rev. Matthew Noyes that "it is now ascertained that Mr. Griswold is elected Governor for the ensuing year . . . [with] a 715 majority." The letter also noted that "in Lyme the votes were for Mr. T[readwell] 18, Mr. G 165." George Hoadly to Rev. Matthew Noyes, April 15, 1811, Rev. Matthew Noyes Papers, LHSA.

108 *proclamation* *By His Excellency Roger Griswold, Esq., Governor and Commander in Chief in and over the State of Connecticut*, August 1812.

108 *chaplain* See *The Connecticut Registrar, 1812* (New London, CT, 1812), 111.

108 *rowed upriver* For primary accounts of the raid on Essex see Jerry Roberts, *The British Raid on Essex: The Forgotten Battle of the War of 1812* (Middletown, CT, 2014), 148–51.

108 *I was at* Charles Griswold to Ebenezer Lane, April 18, 1814, William Griswold Lane Memorial Collection, Yale University Library.

109 *east gallery* ESR, 207 (December 21, 1795).

109 *slavery declined* For a detailed examination of Connecticut's protracted steps toward abolition, including the act passed in 1784 that approved gradual emancipation and allowed eventual freedom at age twenty-five to the future born children of those enslaved, see David Menschel, "Abolition without Deliverance: The Law of Connecticut Slavery, 1784–1848," *Yale Law Journal* 111, no. 1 (September 2001), 186ff.

109 *white persons* ESR, 262 (December 29, 1814).

Architecture and Adornment

111 *To perform the work* Contract with Samuel Belcher (December 23, 1815), photocopy, Congregational Church Papers, LHSA. The original contract with Samuel Belcher has not been discovered, but a typescript of unknown origin survives. See also Aymar Embury, *Early American Churches* (New York, 1914), 115–18.

111 *sell such effects* ESR, 263 (July 11, 1815).

111 *said to be saved* Ely et al., *History of the First Congregational Church*, 77.

111 *district schoolhouses* ESR, 263 (July 11, 1815).

111 *approved a request* Cited in Ely et al., 82.

111 *bleak and solitary* Timothy Dwight, *Travels in New-England and New-York* (New Haven, CT, 1821), 521: "The church stands in a bleak and solitary spot, on the acclivity of the hill which is nearest the river."

111 *field adjoining* The three-quarter-acre parcel "on the corner next adjoining north of the Inn kept by Mrs. Lois Parsons" was bounded "on the north by the Turnpike road leading to the Ferry, on the east by the highway in front of Richard McCurdy's dwelling house," and was sold to the Ecclesiastical Society "for the sole and exclusive purpose of erecting and maintaining a Meeting house or houses thereon." LLR, 28:70 (February 7, 1815).

111 *help defray* Appeal to the governor, FCCOL, cited in Ely et al., 82.

111 *thrift and practicality* See Jerrold T. Jones, "Meeting House to Church: The Effect of Puritanism on 19th Century New England Church Architecture," unpublished manuscript, Congregational Foundation for Theological Studies, October 30, 1992, 6–7.

112 *At a dedication* Brockway preached from Genesis 28:17: "This is none other than the house of God, and this is the gate of heaven." The minister fell from the cupola during construction of the meetinghouse, and his serious injuries required that he deliver the dedication sermon while seated. Ordained in Ellington in 1799, Brockway was raised in Lebanon, where his father, Rev. Thomas Brockway (1748–1807), born in Lyme, served as minister during Lathrop Rockwell's youth. Rev. Thomas Brockway died in 1807 at his sister's home in Lyme. See Diodate Brockway, *A Sermon, Delivered in Ellington, June 25th, 1806: At the Dedication of the New Meetinghouse, in That Place* (Hartford, 1807); Alice K. Pinney, "Ellington," *Connecticut Quarterly* 3 (1897): 192–93; Gretchen Buggelin, "New England Orthodoxy and the Language of the Sacred," in *American Sanctuary: Understanding Sacred Spaces*, ed. Louis P. Nelson (Bloomington, IN, 2006), 27; *Connecticut Courant*, July 8, 1807.

112 *hand-stitched notebook* *Book of Architectural and Mechanical Drawings*, CCHS. Nine pages in a notebook of unsigned drawings show details of Lyme's fourth meetinghouse. Whether they were made as practice drawings, practical working drawings, or a record of the building after completion is not known. See David W. Dangremond, "The Enigmatic Samuel Belcher: A Preliminary Report," unpublished manuscript (n.d.), LHSA, 7–8. See also Kirk Shivell, *The Steeples of Old New England: How the Yankees Reached for Heaven* (Annapolis, MD, 1998), 239–40.

112 *religious ceremonies* Cornerstone inscription, June 10, 1816.

112 *procession* "Outline of ceremony at laying of cornerstone," June 10, 1816, Congregational Church Papers, LHSA. See also Ely et al., 83–84.

114 *be one of the finest* *Middlesex Gazette*, June 19, 1816.

114 *House of God* For the metamorphosis of the New England meetinghouse from a "neutral, functional space set aside for but not restricted to the purposes of congregational assembly for worship" to a sacralized "House of God" see Paul W. Williams, "Metamorphosis of the Meetinghouse," in *Seeing Beyond the Word*, ed. Paul Corby Finney (Grand Rapids, MI, 1999), 481–82.

114 *an eighth* Salisbury and Salisbury, *Family Histories*, 1:100.

115 *to devise* FCR, 83 (July 5, 1817), 44 (October 1818), 85 (April 1819).

115 *Society do accept* ESR, 269 (August 19, 1817).

115 *no town meeting* ESR, 272 (September 30, 1817). See also Ely et al., 87: "The erection of this classic building brought to a close the era of religious services and town meetings held under the same roof."

115 *preamble* Cited in Richard Buel Jr. and George J. Willauer, eds., *Original Discontents: Commentaries on the Creation of Connecticut's Constitution of 1818* (Middletown, CT, 2007), 187.

116 *religious instruction* James, *Educational History*, 62ff., 125, traces the Ecclesiastical Society's control of Lyme's schools after 1712 and notes that until 1818 "primary schools opened with prayer and the reading of scripture and Saturday afternoon was devoted to teaching the Congregational catechism."

116 *negro girl* *Manual of the First Congregational Church in Lyme* (1880), 9, FCCOL.

116 *also designed* Susan H. Ely and Catherine W. Randall, "The John Lee Sill House Built in 1817," unpublished manuscript (August 1985), FCCOL.

116 *carpenters* Stevens, *Old Lyme*, 14–15; *Landmarks of Old Lyme, Connecticut* (Old Lyme, CT, 1968), 19.

117 *largest schooner* Stevens, 15.

117 *mercantile success* By 1812 George Griswold served as director of both the Columbia Insurance Company and the Bank of America. Charles C. Griswold (1787–1869) moved in 1818 to the port of Savannah to oversee growing profits in the southern trade. *Portrait Gallery of the Chamber of Commerce of the City of New York* (1890), 133; Stevens, 19. For the Griswold family's success in the China trade after 1820 see McKay, *South Street*, 94–95. For the rapid rise of cotton planting along the southern coast and the increase in profits from what came to be called "white gold" see Sven Beckert, *Empire of Cotton: A Global History* (New York, 2005), 102–3.

117 *whipping post* Cary, *Memorial Discourse*, 8: "In one corner of the church yard stood that old relic of primitive times, the whipping post. . . . The stocks were erected on the opposite side of the main street."

117 *enslaved servant* Lewis Lewia, baptized in 1795, married Governor Matthew Griswold's enslaved servant Margaret Crosley (1766–1845), whom Rev. Stephen Johnson had baptized as an infant in 1767. Brown and Rose, *Black Roots*, 97, 229. For Lewis Lewia's epigraph describing him as "honest and pious" see R. Warren Conant, "Saybrook-by-the-Sea," The *International*, September 1899, 7:186.

Women Gathering

119 *The first quarterly meeting* Female Reading Society notebook, LHSA.

119 *benevolent groups* For the missionary movement in Connecticut see Williston Walker, *A History of the Congregational Churches in the United States* (New York, 1898), 311–14. For a list of contributions to foreign missions in 1807 from five Female Societies in Connecticut (Litchfield, Hampton, Woodbury, Windham, Willington) see the *Connecticut Evangelical Magazine: and Religious Intelligencer*, February 1809, 56.

119 *to Christianize* Cited in Fisher, *Indian Great Awakening*, 200.

119 *by 1810* A Female Foreign Mission Society in Lyme contributed $30 to missionary endeavors in 1819, with Lois Matson (1772–1825), the unmarried sister of deacon Nathaniel Matson (1765–1861), serving as treasurer of a newly convened Female Foreign Mission Society. That group apparently formed when Rockwell hosted at his home that year the Connecticut Missionary Society's annual meeting. The Missionary Society conveyed specific thanks "to the choir of singers, for their attendance and performance on the present occasion." The *Missionary Herald* (Boston, 1819), 258; *Proceedings of the General Association of Connecticut* (Hartford, 1819), 168.

119 *auxiliary groups* Charles Roy Keller, *The Second Great Awakening in Connecticut* (New Haven, CT, 1942), 125. For women's organizations in the context of America's early voluntary associations see Keith Melder, "Ladies Bountiful: Organized Women's Benevolence in Early 19th-Century America," *New York History* 48, no. 3 (July 1967): 231–32. See also Lisa Joy Pruitt, *A Looking Glass for Ladies: American Protestant Women and the Orient in the Nineteenth Century* (Macon, GA, 2005), 12–21; R. Pierce Beaver, *All Loves Excelling: American Protestant Women in World Mission* (Eugene, OR, 1968), 22.

119 *Charitable Female Association* Oliver Wendell Esbree, *The Rise of the Missionary Spirit in America, 1790–1815* (Eugene, OR, 2013), 58.

119 *devotional and educational* For women's prayer groups and the feminization of Protestantism see Nancy Cott, *The Bonds of Womanhood: Woman's Sphere in New England, 1760–1835* (New Haven, CT, 1977), 132–36. For women's reading circles see Mary Kelley, *Learning to Stand and Speak: Women, Education, and Public Life in America's Republic* (Durham, NC, 2006), 134–36.

119 *prayer of a brother* Female Reading Society notebook, LHSA.

120 *art of embroidery* Mrs. Griffin, whose father Edmund Dorr had vigorously opposed the revivalism of Rev. Jonathan Parsons, studied embroidery in Boston. Noyes and Noyes, *Noyes-Gilman Ancestry*, 165–66.

121 *I am happy* George Griffin to Phoebe Lord, July 27, 1813, Ludington Family Collection, LHSA.

121 *live with her brother* George Griffin to Phoebe Lord, April 23, 1813; July 27, 1813; August 25, 1814, Ludington Family Collection, LHSA.

121 *allowed women* Mary Way, age forty-two, had recently advertised in 1811 in a New York newspaper: "Mary Way, portrait and miniature painter from New-London, Connecticut. Takes likenesses upon ivory or glass in colors or gold landscapes or views of country seats, &c &c. Paintings not approved may be returned without charge at her painting room, No. 95 Greenwich-Street." Way charged $20 for a miniature painted on ivory. See Ramsay MacMullen, *Women of the Brush: Their Family, Art, Life and Letters, 1797–1833* (New Haven, CT, 1997), 20–23.

121 *rent her farm* *Connecticut Gazette*, February 23, 1814.

121 *prepared young men* Rev. Samuel Griswold (1795–1875), a great-grandson of Rev. George Griswold, was among those who prepared for Yale in Lyme's parsonage. Rev. Matthew Noyes Papers, LHSA; *Congregational Quarterly*, 1876, 18:427.

122 *sometimes boarded* Phoebe Lord to Julia Ann Lord, January 23, 1827, Ludington Family Collection, LHSA.

122 *inventory* Inventory of John L. Sill (1820), EPP, box 6, LHSA.

122 *any other book* Myers, 50.

Revivals

125 *Mr. Colton is unremitting* Harriet Lord to Julia Ann Lord, September 4, 1831, Ludington Family Collection, LHSA.

125 *ornamental trees* ESR, 310 (July 25, 1828).

125 *spirit of social reform* For the convergence of progressive ideas about theology with growing support for mission societies, Sunday schools, temperance organizations, and abolition see Timothy L. Smith, *Revivalism and Social Reform: American Protestantism on the Eve of the Civil War* (New York, 1957), 60ff.

125 *seasoned pastor* Dexter, *Biographical Sketches of the Graduates*, 642; William Cogswell, ed., *The New Hampshire Repository*, vol. 1 (1846), 103; Robert F. Lawrence, *The New Hampshire Churches* (1866), 21.

125 *diligently and seriously* FCR, 89 (January 10, 1829).

125 *Even the Bible* Phoebe Lord to Julia Ann Lord, December 8, 1826, Ludington Family Collection, LHSA.

126 *Many thousands* Harriet Lord to Julia Ann Lord, August 26, 1827, Ludington Family Collection, LHSA. See also *The Diary of Josiah Burnham, 1818–1857*, which notes that some four thousand people gathered in September 1827 at Ayres Point in Saybrook for three days of singing and preaching. Cited in James, *Educational History*, 128. For anecdotes about revival meetings in Lyme's north parish led by Rev. David Huntington (1743–1812) see James E. Harding, *Lyme Yesterdays: How Our Forefathers Made a Living on the Connecticut Shore* (Stonington, CT, 1967), 47–48.

127 *paid to Samuel Miner* *Account book, 1830–1941*, Congregational Church Papers, LHSA.

127 *younger brother* For Rev. Edward Dorr Griffin's career and influence see John Woodbridge, "Review of Dr. Griffin's Sermons," *Literary and Theological Review*, June 1839, 224–27. For discussion of Griffin's call for emotional restraint see Mark Rogers, "Edward Dorr Griffin and the Edwardsian Second Great Awakening" (PhD diss., Trinity Evangelical Divinity School, 2012), 108: "Griffin and his fellow Edwardsians deradicalized the First Great Awakening . . . in order to promote another Awakening, this time more pure and, hopefully, longer lasting." For Griffin's evangelism and his commitment to the cause of missions see David W. Kling, "Edwards in the Second Great Awakening: The New Divinity Contributions of Edward Dorr Griffin and Asahel Nettleton," in *After Jonathan Edwards: The Courses of the New England Theology*, ed. Oliver D. Crisp and Douglas A. Sweeney (Oxford 2012), 133–37.

127 *giv[ing] themselves* Daniel Rogers Noyes to Catherine Lord, June 10, 1831, Ludington Family Collection, LHSA.

129 *long-serving minister* Vail, ordained in 1780 and Hadlyme's minister for fifty years, had prepared Edward Dorr Griffin for the ministry. Griffin preached his first sermon in Vail's Hadlyme pulpit in 1792. See Woodbridge, 223; *Manual History, Congregational Church, Hadlyme, Conn.* (Hartford, 1914), 32–36.

129 *progress of the revival* Harriet Lord to Julia Ann Lord, September 4, 1831, Ludington Family Collection, LHSA.

129 *few men* For the predominant role of women in the Second Great Awakening see Susan Hill Lindley, *You Have Stepped Out of Your Place: A History of Women and Religion in America* (Louisville, KY, 1996), 59–61; Cott, *Bonds of Womanhood*, 132.

129 *affectionate letter* Edward Dorr Griffin to Julia Ann Lord, January 19, 1837, cited in William Buell Sprague, *Memoir of the Rev. Edward D. Griffin, Compiled Chiefly from His Own Writings* (Albany, 1838), 212.

Entire Abstinence

131 *Resolved: That it is the peculiar and solemn duty* FCR, 91–92 (January 1, 1830).

131 *unite their exertions* *Constitution of the Lyme Auxiliary Society for the Promotion of Temperance* (December 12, 1828), Temperance Society notebook, LHSA.

132 *generally acknowledged* *Temperance Address. Delivered at a meeting in the Neck Road School House in Lyme Friday evening February 26, 1830. And also at the Meeting House in Lyme on Sunday evening.* LHSA.

132 *compensation for services* New London County probate records, September 15, 1819, photocopy, EPP, box b, LHSA.

132 *intemperance and mismanagement* Appointment of Overseer, April 6, 1829, Lyme Public Hall Archives.

133 *Prince has been* Daniel R. Noyes to Rev. M. Noyes, February 1, 1826, Matthew Noyes Papers, LHSA.

133 *Negro man Pomp* *Connecticut Gazette*, December 15, 1816; cited in Brown and Rose, *Black Roots*, 272.

134 *died in Northford* "Slaves of William Noyes," scrapbook, Noyes Papers, Lyme Historical Society Archives, LHSA.

134 *surviving receipt* Matthew Noyes Papers, box 2, #39, LHSA.

134 *town records* *VR*, 69; Brown and Rose, 144.

134 *posted a notice* *Connecticut Gazette*, December 31, 1817, cited in Brown and Rose, 144.

135 *woman of color* FCR, 92–93 (May 5, 1830).

135 *I call upon you* Chester Colton, *Admonition of Nancy*, FCCOL Papers, LHSA.

135 *she be cut off* FCR, 97 (December 29, 1830).

135 *similar judgments* FCR, 97–98 (February 20, 1831), 99 (February 14, 1831), 100–101 (March 24, 1831), 101–2 (April 10, 1836), 103 (May 5, 1836).

135 *wicked person* FCR, 97 (December 29, 1830).

135 *An assessment* *Report of the Executive Committee of the Connecticut Temperance Society* (Hartford, 1834), 6.

Erasing the Records

137 *Whereas the report* ESR, 347 (June 29, 1840).

137 *difficulties now existing* ESR, 360 (December 24, 1839).

137 *this Society by reason* ESR, 361 (January 1, 1840).

137 *committee's claim* Ely et al., *History of the First Congregational Church* (91), notes that the difficulties existing in the Society in 1839 are nowhere given in detail and remarks that the alleged lack of funds in the treasury may have been "a reflection on the relations between pastor and congregation."

137 *account book* The Ecclesiastical Society's account book shows cash on hand in 1838 of $256.46, in 1839 of $321.95, and in 1840 of $310.59. FCCOL Papers, LHSA.

137 *subscription covered* ESR, 363 (January 7, 1840).

137 *I presume* Chester Colton to Gentlemen, June 17, 1840, FCCOL Papers, LHSA.

137 *in relation to* Letter to Council members, June 30, 1840. Below the text of the Society's letter, "Chester Colton, Pastor," wrote: "I consent to the calling of a Council to act in reference to my dismission." FCCOL Papers, LHSA.

138 *no ambiguity* Dutton "resigned his charge on the 8th of June, 1842, chiefly on account of some difference of opinion between him and his people, particularly on the subject of Slavery. He was an earnest and vigorous friend to the cause of emancipation." *Annals of the American Pulpit* (New York, 1856), 489. See also Kelsea Jeon, "Abolition and Religion: A Moral Question with a Political Answer" (Yale University seminar paper, spring 2017), 7–9.

138 *contrary to the principles* *Constitution of the New-England Anti-Slavery Society: With an Address to the Public* (Boston, 1832), 8.

138 *did not belong* For the fracturing of Connecticut churches over the slavery question see Jeon, 5–6. Also see Hugh Davis, "Leonard Bacon, the Congregational Church, and Slavery, 1845–1861," in *Religion and the Antebellum Debate over Slavery*, ed. John R. McKivigan and Mitchell Snay (Athens, GA, 1998), 222.

139 *gagging pulpit* Charles H. Levermore, "Two Centuries and a Half in Guilford, 1639–1889," *New England Magazine*, December 1889, 1:424. For opposition to abolition in Guilford see also Bernard C. Steiner, *History of Slavery in Connecticut* (Baltimore, 1893), 76–77.

139 *refused to allow* See Donald E. Williams Jr., *Prudence Crandall's Legacy: The Fight for Equality in the 1830s* (Middletown, CT, 2014), 104–7.

139 *outspoken supporter* Samuel J. May, "Miss Prudence Crandall and the Canterbury School," in *Some Recollections of Our Antislavery Conflict* (Boston, 1869), 39–72.

139 *delivered the sermon* *Proceedings of the General Association of Connecticut*, June 1833, 4, 8.

140 *paid dues* Ralph Randolph Gurley, ed., *The African Repository and Colonial Journal* (Washington, DC, 1833), 8:351.

140 *by the colored citizens* *Proceedings of the New England Slavery Society at Its First Meeting, Boston, January 9, 1833*, 39. For the colonization debate see Alice Dana Adams, *The Neglected Period of Antislavery in America, 1808–1831* (Radcliffe College, 1908), 66; William Lloyd Garrison, *Thoughts on African Colonization* (Boston, 1832), 49; Louis R. Mehlinger, "The Attitude of the Free Negro toward African Colonization," *Journal of Negro History* 1, no. 3 (June 1916): 286; James M. Rose and Barbara W. Brown, *Tapestry: A Living History of the Black Family in Southeastern Connecticut* (New London, CT, 1979), 41.

141 *praying [for]* *Journal of the Senate, January 25, 1838* (Washington, DC, 1838), 192–93.

141 *Our Abolitionists* John Wilson to Charles Griswold, August 1838, Old Lyme Historical Society archives. For the speech in Philadelphia Hall by abolition leader Angelina Grimké Weld (1805–1879), after which she linked arms with supporters and walked through the streets, see Ira V. V. Brown, "Racism and Sexism: The Burning of Pennsylvania Hall" (1976), *Phylon* 37:130–31.

141 *Widespread publicity* For the sensation provoked by the African captives' arrival in New London and New Haven see Manisha Sinha, *The Slave's Cause: A History of Abolition* (New Haven, CT, 2016), 407; Howard Jones, *Mutiny on the* Amistad*: The Saga of a Slave Revolt and Its Impact on American Abolition, Law, and Diplomacy* (New York, 1987), 197; Joseph Kifala, *Free Slaves, Freetown, and the Sierra Leonean Civil War* (New York, 2017), 135; Marcus Rediker, *The* Amistad *Rebellion: An Atlantic Odyssey of Slavery and Freedom* (New York, 2012), 127.

141 *promoted education* Bacon joined the Religious Education Committee that urged intellectual and religious instruction for *Amistad* captives. Kifala, 135. For his early colonization advocacy and belief that repatriation would hasten the end of slavery see Leonard Woolsey Bacon, *The Services of Leonard Bacon to African Colonization* (Washington, DC, 1900); Davis, 222–23.

141 *That the system* *Minutes of the General Association of Connecticut at Their Meeting in New Haven, June 1840* (Hartford, 1840), 8.

141 *in notes* Martha Brainerd Farwell, manuscript notes on church history, n.d., FCCOL Papers, LHSA; Ely et al., 91–92.

Separations

143 *Amanda Robbins has* FCR, 113 (July 1, 1842).

143 *first parish chose* FCR, 108 (April 27, 1841); ESR, 352 (April 12, 1841); Hurd, *History of New London County*, 560.

143 *packet ship* Wellington "Visit of the Duke of Wellington to the St. Katharine Docks," *Times* (London), July 29, 1837.

144 *cotton and turpentine* Daniel Chadwick to Nancy Chadwick, January 4, 1832, Chadwick Papers, LHSA.

144 *immigrants* For conditions in steerage on the packet ship *Corinthian* commanded by Captain Daniel Chadwick in 1828 see Thomas Augustus Trollope, *What I Remember* (New York, 1887), 110–14.

144 *changed its name* ESR, 369 (December 29, 1842).

144 *had pledged* FCR, 114–15 (July 1, 1842).

144 *connected himself* FCR, 118 (March 1, 1843).

144 *case of Mrs. Mary Outel* FCR, 117 (October 29, 1842).

144 *small group* Hurd, 205.

144 *ten families* Edmund Delaney, *St. Joseph's Parish, More Than a Century of Faith* (Chester, CT, 1991). For the history of Catholicism in Connecticut see "The Formation and Consolidation of the Multi-Ethnic Diocese in Hartford," in *European Immigrants and the Catholic Church in Connecticut, 1870–1920*, Center for Migration Studies, vol. 5 (September 1987), 24ff.

144 *separatist church* Hurd, 540; Stiles, *Sermon Delivered*, 266. See also Stark, *Lyme, Connecticut*, 34–35; Bruce P. Stark, *Address on the 250th Anniversary of the Founding of the Grassy Hill Congregational Church* (November 24, 1966). Pledge statements and other records of the Grassy Hill Church are preserved in the Lyme Public Hall archives.

144 *began preaching* Grassy Hill Cemetery records list Rev. Seth Lee as "Pastor of the Strict Congregation Church." See also William H. Hill, ed., *Genealogical Table of the Lee Family* (Albany, 1851), 16.

145 *We are breaking* Stiles, 474. Some seventeen Baptist families had left Lyme by 1768 to settle the new town of Marlowe, New Hampshire, where a tract of hilly, uninhabited land had been granted seven years earlier to a group of prominent First Society members, among them William Noyes and Marshfield Parsons. Baptist meetings in Marlowe were then held in log homes built by Nathan Huntley (1726–1798) and other Lyme natives. Hamilton Child, *Gazetteer of Cheshire County, N.H., 1736–1885* (Syracuse, NY, 1885), 313–14, 317; *Genealogies of Connecticut Families: From the New England Historical and Genealogical Register* (Baltimore, 1998), 1:242.

145 *destitute of a place* Hurd, 559.

145 *power of God* Methodist Church papers, LHSA; *Deep River (CT) New Era*, July 30, 1926.

147 *applied in 1848 for dismissal* FCR, 123 (September 1848).

147 *unanimously regard[ed]* FCR, 124 (January 4, 1850).

147 *amid some strong* D. S. Brainerd, *Sermon Preached in Old Lyme on the Twenty-Fifth Anniversary of His Pastorate* (July 1, 1866), 8–9, FCCOL.

Improvements

149 *The history of this church* D. S. Brainerd, *Sermon Preached*, 7.

149 *strip of land* LLR, 36:311 (August 7, 1845), 36:325, 36:326 (August 11, 1845).

149 *for the comfort* Ely et al., *History of the First Congregational Church*, 97; LLR, 35:305 (January 30, 1846).

149 *for such other* LLR, 35:356 (February 17, 1848).

149 *wealth and influence* Walter Barrett, *The Old Merchants of New York City* (New York, 1864), 261; McKay, *South Street*, 89–96.

149 *handsome fortune* Allyn, *Black Hall,* 64; *Landmarks of Old Lyme,* 23.

150 *The improvements* Helen Powers Griswold to Captain Robert H. Griswold, February 23, 1848, Griswold Family Letters, LHSA.

150 *much more elegant* Helen Powers Griswold to Captain Robert H. Griswold, August 18, 1841, and August 27, 1841, Griswold Family Letters, LHSA.

151 *in Canton* Dexter, *Biographical Sketches of the Graduates,* 199. A fire in the N. L. & G. countinghouse destroyed its shipping records, and the date of its entry into trade with China cannot be established. John Cleve Green (1800–1875), who worked for the firm as a youth and became its agent in Canton after 1823, later married Richard Griswold's sister. Robert Greenhalgh Albion, *The Rise of New York Port, 1815–1860* (New York, 1939), 431; Jacques M. Downs, *The Golden Ghetto: The American Commercial Community at Canton and the Shaping of American China Policy, 1784–1844* (New York, 1997), 168.

151 *like the* Panama The sturdy wooden tea boxes with the N. L. & G. label that shipped on four successive vessels named *Panama* made the term "Panama tea" familiar in American households. William F. Griswold (1804–1851), Captain Robert Griswold's older brother, served as master on several of the *Panama*'s Pacific crossings.

151 *Fitzhugh-patterned* For Fitzhugh porcelain see Craig Clunas, ed., *Chinese Export Art and Design* (London, 1987), 60; Jean McClure Mudge, *Chinese Porcelain for the Export Trade* (Wilmington, DE, 1981), 115–16; Herbert Schiffer, Peter Schiffer, and Nancy Schiffer, *Chinese Export Porcelain: Standard Patterns and Forms, 1780–1880* (Exton, PA, 1975), 11–12. The Griswold family's collection of Fitzhugh china was given to the Florence Griswold Museum in 1985.

151 *cottage design* A. J. Downing, *Cottage Residences: A Series of Designs for Rural Cottages and Cottage-Villas, and Their Gardens and Grounds* (New York, 1842), 34.

152 *Dr. Cutcheon* Evelyn McCurdy, *Diary,* March 20, 1848, and April 9, 1848, Evelyn McCurdy Salisbury Papers, Old Lyme Historical Society.

153 *Sabbath worship moved* FCR, 124 (October, n.d., 1851).

153 *plan for altering* ESR, 384 (December 31, 1849).

153 *carpenters to remove* Martha Gillette Pond documented the meetinghouse changes in her ballad *A Simple Story Now Told in Rhyme, Concerning a Darkened Window in Lyme* (1895), FCCOL.

153 *preached again* FCR, 124 (Otober, n.d., 1851).

153 *organ was set up* FCR, 125 (October, n.d., 1851).

153 *train ferry* Reuben Champion Jr. to sister [Susan Champion Avery], June 16, 1852, Champion Papers, LHSA.

153 *From the twenty-second* *Report of the Board of Directors of the New Haven and New London Railroad Co.* (New Haven, CT, 1853), 3, Coult Papers, LHSA.

153 *infrastructure improvements* Until rail service began, regularly scheduled steamboat service connected New York and Lyme. See W. DeLoss Love, "The Navigation of the Connecticut River," in *Proceedings of the American Antiquarian Society* (Worcester, MA, 1904), 416–20.

154 *approved his petition* *Resolutions and Private Acts Passed by the General Assembly of the State of Connecticut* (New Haven, CT, 1854), 247–49. Division of the town had been discussed at least since 1851 when Stephen L. Peck submitted a petition for the creation of "a new Town by the name of North Lyme." Town Meeting Reports, vol. 3 (May 3, 1851). See also Harding, *Lyme Yesterdays,* 62.

154 *to disturb* See Ely et al., 96–97: "Lyme somehow seemed untouched" during the period of national stress and political conflict before the Civil War.

154 *atrocious abomination* Cited in Davis, "Leonard Bacon," 223.

154 *lifetime member* *The African Repository and Colonial Journal* (Washington, DC, 1853), 223.

154 *his sermons* See, for example, sermons preached by Brainerd on February 5, 1854, and July 8, 1864, LHSA. For the deliberate avoidance of the topic of slavery in Connecticut churches see Jeon, "Abolition and Religion," 15.

154 *church meetings* James Burnett's "obstinate persistence" in unchristian conduct resulted in his excommunication in 1853, and then "case of the Smith family," who refused to participate in the ordinances because of an unspecified dispute with the minister, brought a sequence of rebukes and disciplinary actions that spread over a decade. See FCR, 125 (March 4, 1853), 126 (April 29, 1853), 128 (February 12, 1856), 129–33 (September 5, 1856), 133–34 (February 10, 1857).

154 *given to the work* Cary, *Memorial Discourse*, 12.

155 *outspoken Democrat* For James A. Bill as "a red hot Democrat" in a solidly Republican district see Harding, 63.

155 *supported the right* For James Buchanan's views on slavery see Donald V. Weatherman, "James Buchanan on Slavery and Secession," *Presidential Studies Quarterly* 15, no. 4 (Fall 1985): 798ff.

155 *all-absorbing subject* Cited in Ludington, *Old Lyme*, 42–43.

This Dreadful Rebellion

157 *God only knows* Daniel R. Noyes to Josephine Noyes Ludington, January 16, 1861, Ludington Family Collection, LHSA.

157 *115 men* *List of the Soldiers and Sailors from the Town of Old Lyme, Connecticut, Who Served in the Civil War* (1921), LHSA. Another list, compiled in 2011, identifies 129 who served in the Civil War. See Norm Stitham, "Old Lyme Civil War Volunteers, 1861–1865," unpublished booklet (July 2011), Old Lyme Phoebe Griffin Noyes Library.

157 *to preserve the Union* See the detailed analysis of Connecticut's Civil War controversies in Matthew Warshauer, *Connecticut in the American Civil War: Slavery, Sacrifice, and Survival* (Middletown, CT, 2011), 93–100.

157 *financial incentives* Old Lyme Town Meeting Book, 3:34 (July 26, 1862), 35 (August 14, 1862), 43 (August 8, 1863). For Old Lyme's payment of "$16,913 for bounties, premiums, commutation, and support of families" see W. A. Crofut and John M. Moeris, *The Military and Civil History of Connecticut during the War of 1861–65* (New York, 1868), 847.

157 *Gravely wounded* Dione Longley and Buck Zaidel, *Heroes for All Time: Connecticut Civil War Soldiers Tell Their Stories* (Middletown, CT, 2015), 71–73; Wick Griswold, *Griswold Point: History from the Mouth of the Connecticut River* (Charleston, SC, 2014), 77–80.

158 *Our father and mine* Kate E. Peckham to Robert B. Peckham, February 4, 1863, cited in Stitham, n.p.

158 *died there of typhoid* For the death of Private Ebenezer J. Clark on January 20, 1863, see *Catalogue of Connecticut Volunteer Organizations, to July 1, 1864* (Hartford, 1864), 756–57.

159 *We are having* Charles Noyes Chadwick to Enoch Noyes, April 13, 1863, photocopy, Noyes Papers, LHSA.

159 *You must have had* Enoch Noyes to Ellen Noyes Chadwick, April 26, 1863, photocopy, Noyes Papers, LHSA.

159 *We are well blessed* Enoch Noyes to Ellen Noyes Chadwick, April 26, 1863, photocopy, Noyes Papers, LHSA.

160 *rifle pit* Enoch Noyes diary, June 10, 1863, photocopy, Noyes Papers, LHSA.

160 *I am thankful* Enoch Noyes to Laura Banning Noyes, June 13, 1863, photocopy, Noyes Papers, LHSA.

160 *sharp opposition* See Warshauer, 98, 108–10; Joanna D. Cowden, "The Politics of Dissent: Civil War Democrats in Connecticut," *New England Quarterly* 56 (December 1989): 538–54; Longley and Zaidel, 29–31.

160 *Democrats alias Copperheads* Charles Noyes Chadwick to Enoch Noyes, April 13, 1863, photocopy, Noyes Papers, LHSA.

160 *election reports* Phoebe Griffin Noyes to Josephine Noyes Ludington, April 6, 1863, Ludington Family Collection, LHSA.

160 *most "hateful"* Antipathy to local Copperheads among Brainerd's parishioners continued as the war ended. Daniel Noyes worried in 1865 about the influence that James A. Bill might have on the "good copperheads" in Old Lyme. "Bill is now trying hard to get power & control down here," he wrote to his son. Two months later Evelyn McCurdy complained that funding for Old Lyme's schools was "under the control of our lowest class of men, mostly copperheads, who will not yield it up because it gives them power." Daniel R. Noyes to Charles Phelps Noyes, January 28, 1865, Ludington Family Collection, LHSA; Evelyn McCurdy to Charles H. Ludington, March 1, 1865, Ludington Family Collection, LHSA.

161 *I do not like* Phoebe Griffin Noyes to Charles Phelps Noyes, July 6, 1863, Ludington Family Collection, LHSA.

161 *church fair* Phoebe Griffin Noyes to her children, February 22, 1864, Ludington Family Collection, LHSA.

163 *newspaper comments* Cited in "Paint the Church Yellow," *Old Lyme Gazette*, July 18, 1974.

163 *great trouble* Phoebe Griffin Noyes to Charles Phelps Noyes, October 6, 1867, Charles Phelps Noyes Papers, LHSA.

163 *men prevailed* ESR, 407 (September 10, 1867). The Ecclesiastical Society resolved on September 10 that "this meeting prefer that the outside of the church be painted white, and that the committee be instructed to confer with the Sister's Society and endeavor to come to some agreement with them."

163 *in Hartford* See Carole Nichols, *Votes and More for Women: Suffrage and After in Connecticut* (New York, 2013), 6–7.

163 *a motion* FCR, 141 (March 5, 1869).

A Wealth of History

165 *And here let me urge* Cary, *Memorial Discourse*, 15.

165 *men of culture* Evelyn McCurdy Salisbury to Charles H. Ludington, January 9, 1875, Ludington Family Collection, LHSA. Evelyn McCurdy had married as his second wife Yale professor Edward E. Salisbury (1814–1901), nine years her senior, in 1872.

165 *in a* Memorial Discourse Church members voted in May to publish three hundred copies of Cary's address. FCR, 149 (May 15, 1876).

165 *celebration* James, *Educational History*, 183.

166 *earliest records* E. N. Chadwick, "Solicitation for the Centennial in Old Lyme," read in church (August 1876), Miscellaneous, box 2, #39, LHSA.

166 *beautiful and quiet* *Hartford Courant*, September 13, 1876.

166 *Church members invited* FCR, 149 (September 1, 1876).

166 *claim of descent* William Cary was the great-grandson of John Ely, who served with Colonel Parsons's regiment at Bunker Hill in 1775. Margaret Elizabeth Dunbar Stuart, *History of the Ely Reunion, Held at Lyme, Conn., July 10th, 1878* (New York, 1879), 51.

166 *a stranger* Cary, 3.

166 *ordination* FCR, 151 (November 22, 1876).

166 *imbibed a dislike* William B. Cary, "1860," unpublished memoir (1917), 40, photocopy, FCCOL.

166 *Wilderness campaign* For a description of Captain Cary during the Wilderness campaign as "a resolute man, as you can readily see looking into his steady dark eyes," see Vincent L. Burns, *The Fifth New York Cavalry in the Civil War* (Jefferson, NC, 2014), 179. For an account of Cary "embroiled in a sharp little brawl" with a Confederate infantry corps and "stubbornly resisting the enemy's advance" see Gary W. Gallagher, *The Wilderness Campaign* (Durham, NC, 1997), 118.

167 *somewhat war-wise* William B. Cary, "Lincoln," unpublished memoir (1917), 123, photocopy, FCCOL.

167 *great soul* Cary, "Lincoln," 128.

167 *frontier towns* The General Assembly of the Presbyterian Church listed William B. Cary in its Kansas synod in May 1873. *New York Evangelist*, May 29, 1873, 6. Cary preached the sermon at a newly organized church in Ashton, Kansas, twenty miles south of Abilene, on June 7, 1874. See *New York Observer and Chronicle*, June 18, 1874, 195.

167 *providentially directed* ESR, 422 (September 23, 1876).

167 *railroad bridge* Ian Hubbard, *Crossings: Three Centuries from Ferry Boats to the New Baldwin Bridge* (Greenwich, CT, 1993), 19.

167 *rises and falls* "America: November and December, 1867," in John Forster, *The Works of Charles Dickens* (1899), 35:403.

167 *Artists are beginning* Ellen Noyes Chadwick to Martha J. Lamb [Coleman], November 5, 1874, Martha J. Lamb Papers, New-York Historical Society.

167 *this ancient* Lamb, "Lyme," 313.

168 *strikingly ornate* Lamb, 318.

168 *loveliest nooks* Lamb, 328.

168 *Mrs. Lamb's article* *New-York Commercial Advertiser* (n.d.), Clipping File, Ludington Family Collection, Clipping File, LHSA.

168 *steeplechase* *New York Evening Mail*, September 10, 1877, Clipping File, Ludington Family Collection, LHSA.

168 *archery shoot* Grace Allen to unknown, August 30, 1880, Ludington Family Collection, LHSA.

169 *former estate* Salisbury and Salisbury, *Family Histories*, 1:316; *Genealogical and Biographical Record of New London County* (Chicago, 1905), 703.

169 *Mrs. Robert H. Griswold* *New York Herald-Tribune*, August 26, 1878, 6.

169 *moving account* William B. Cary, "A Meeting," unpublished manuscript, photocopy, FCCOL.

169 *war stories* Ely et al., *History of the First Congregational Church*, 105.

169 *profusely & beautifully* Harriet Lord to Charles Phelps Noyes and Lily Gilman Noyes, January 1877, Ludington Family Collection, LHSA.

169 *emotional burdens* W. B. Cary, "Why Farmers' Wives Become Insane," *New York Observer and Chronicle*, August 21, 1879, 272.

169 *availability of pistols* William B. Cary, "Carrying Pistols," *Independent*, August 18, 1881, 3.

169 *cheap alcohol* Wm. B. Cary, "The Little Red House and Its Victims," *Independent*, June 21, 1883, 5. For an earlier account of the winter fire on Neck Road see Phoebe Griffin Noyes to Charles Phelps Noyes, March 5, 1875, Ludington Family Collection, LHSA.

170 *detailed account* W. B. Cary, "Revival Experiences during the Great Awakening in 1741–44 in New London County, Conn.," *New Englander and Yale Review*, November 1883, 731–39.

170 *he arranged* The portrait of Jonathan Parsons was given to the church by Henry E. Parsons, a descendant living in Ohio. Cary went to the depot to pick up the picture, unpacked it, then "left it standing in the Conference Room, where I suppose it will be best to hang it." W. B. Cary to Charles H. Ludington, November 10, 1883, Ludington Family Collection, LHSA.

170 *already secured* FCR, 160 (March 2, 1883).

170 *most unexpected* FCR, 161 (April 19, 1884).

171 *Perhaps another* FCR, 161 (April 19, 1884).

171 *seek another* Salisbury and Salisbury, 1:xix.

171 *this separation* FCR (April 29, 1884), 164.

171 *accepted a call* Cyrus Henry Brown, "Days and Recollections of North Stonington," paper read before the Westerly, Rhode Island, Historical Society, November 9, 1916.

171 *ventured into politics* Cary offered the opening prayer at the General Assembly on April 11, 1899. *Journal of the Senate of the State of Connecticut* (Hartford, 1899), 698.

172 *drafted legislation* *Hartford Courant*, February 4, 1899, 4.

172 *Some sincere* "Report of Protestant Chaplain," *Report of the Directors of the Connecticut State Prison* (Hartford, 1916), 47–48.

172 *Fighting Parson* "Rev. William Cary, Prison Chaplain, and Veteran Dies," *Hartford Courant*, October 8, 1923.

172 *lessons of the past* Cary, *Memorial Discourse*, 15.

172 *Shall we not* Cary, *Memorial Discourse*, 19.

A Story Told in Rhyme

175 *Forty years pass away* Pond, *Simple Story.*

175 *exceeding beauty* *New York Tribune* (n.d., 1887), Clipping File, Ludington Family Collection, LHSA; *New Haven Register*, August 27, 1887, cited in Ely et al., *History of the First Congregational Church*, 109.

175 *later serve* For Marshall's architectural achievements, including churches in Brooklyn and Colorado Springs, the Tarrant Building in Manhattan, and a house for Rudyard Kipling in Vermont, see National Register of Historic Places Report, First Congregational Church, Colorado Springs (2002), 13. For his design for a "Crossway" to connect the Pennsylvania Railroad Station with the new Grand Central Station see "'The Crossway': Civic Improvements for New York City" (November 1912), in *The Origins of Modern Architecture: Selected Essays from "Architectural Record,"* ed. Eric Uhlfelder (New York, 1998), 235.

176 *built by her uncle* Sarah Sill Wells, *Old Silltown: Something of Its History and Ancestry* (Evanston, IL, 1912), 56. After Mr. Sill, listed in earlier New York City directories as a grocer at 85 South Street, died in 1874, Martha Pond moved from Milford to Old Lyme to live with her widowed aunt Mary Pond Sill. The Sills named their only child, who drowned at age ten in the Connecticut River, Richard Griswold Sill.

177 *received by the town* Salisbury and Salisbury, *Family Histories*, 1:xix.

177 *singular beauty* "Beginning His Work," *New London Telegram*, July 16, 1884, FCCOL.

177 *elegant collation* "Ordained on Historic Ground: The New Pastor of Lyme's Ancient Church," *New York Tribune*, June 22, 1884. Congregational Church Papers, LHSA.

177 *early meetinghouses* Leonard Bacon, *The Church in Its Locality, to Which Is Appended Some Account of the Early Meetinghouses of the First Church* (Hartford, 1879).

178 *enlarging and heightening* James Griswold to Charles H. Ludington, December 3, 1885, Ludington Family Collection, LHSA.

179 *inspirational sermon* B. W. Bacon, *Beautifying the House of the Lord* (September 12, 1886), 3, 6, FCCOL.

179 *untiring efforts* Clipping, n.d. Clipping File, Ludington Family Collection, LHSA.

179 *wider field* Salisbury and Salisbury, 1:xix.

179 *letter of resignation* Benjamin W. Bacon, "To the First Church of Christ in Old Lyme," *Hartford Courant*, December 14, 1888.

179 *something not* Benjamin Wisner Bacon, *The Genesis of Genesis* (Hartford, 1892), xix.

179 *finest Biblical scholars* *Outlook*, March 28, 1896, 580.

179 *early termination* ESR, 178 (December 28, 1888).

179 *secur[e] the services* Chas. G. Bartlett to Charles H. Ludington, December 31, 188, Ludington Family Collection, LHSA.

179 *large, commodious* *Christian Union*, 1889, n.p., LHSA.

180 *vote on matters* ESR, 170 (February 26, 1885).

Progress and Philanthropy

183 *There is a natural and proper satisfaction* Shirley, *Discourse*, 3.

183 *His sermon* Katharine Ludington to Helen Gilman Brown, October 28, 1889, Brown-Gilman Papers, New York Public Library.

183 *address was given* FCR, 186 (August 31, 1893).

184 *elucidate some points* Shirley noted that "the history of this Old Lyme Congregational Church has already been given to us in outline" and that William Cary had already provided "the essential items concerning this edifice." But his own address relied on works of "contemporaneous history," like "the narratives of John Mason . . . and the testimony of other contemporaneous witnesses." Shirley, 3–4.

184 *in the midst* Cary, *Memorial Discourse*, 4.

184 *intercourse of the first settlers* Shirley, 7.

184 *full tide of church-life* Shirley, 11.

184 *so-called 'nigger pews'* Shirley, 17.

184 *used their dues* Ladies Benevolent Society notebook, FCCOL.

184 *prohibitory amendment* *Sound Breeze*, October 22, 1889. See also "The Prohibition Defeat in Connecticut," *Public Opinion: A Comprehensive Summary of the Press throughout the World on All Important Current Topics* (Washington, DC, 1890), 8:12.

185 *Gospel meetings* *Sound Breeze*, April 10, 1894.

185 *recently spoken* *New Haven Daily Morning Journal and Courier*, January 23, 1894.

185 *Old Lyme Temperance Union* FCR, 188 (January 3, 1895).

186 *broad avenue* *Sound Breeze*, September 19, 1893.

186 *no one would go* Josephine Ludington to Charles Phelps Ludington, September 9, 1897, Noyes-Gilman Papers, New York Public Library.

186 *withdrew all support* Evelyn McCurdy Salisbury to Miss Elizabeth Griswold, *Sound Breeze*, September 22, 1896. See Alma Merry Tatum, *For the Love of Books: The Story of the Public Libraries of Old Lyme* (Old Lyme, CT, 1997), 16–23.

186 *of promoting* FCR, 194 (January 31, 1897).

186 *heartily regret* FCR, 195 (April 22, 1897).

186 *deep regret* FCR, 196 (April 27, 1897).

186 *directly felt* FCR, 190 (January 2, 1896).

187 *Probably no one* Farwell, manuscript notes on church history, n.d., n.p., FCCOL Papers, LHSA.

187 *Guests arriving* R. S. Griswold to Charles Phelps Noyes, June 23, 1898, Ludington Family Collection, LHSA.

187 *opened the dedication* *Proceedings at the Opening of the Phoebe Griffin Noyes Library, Old Lyme, Connecticut* (June 23, 1898), 9, Ludington Family Collection, LHSA.

Nostalgia amid the Elms

189 *It is seldom* *Ladies' Home Journal*, November 16, 1906.

189 *historic charm* See also Carolyn Wakeman, *The Charm of the Place: Old Lyme in the 1920s* (Old Lyme Historical Society, 2011).

189 *Edinburgh* John William Siddall, ed., *Men of Hawaii: Being a Biographical Reference Library, Complete and Authentic, of the Men of Note and Substantial Achievement in the Hawaiian Islands* (Honolulu, 1917), 264.

189 *put up a large tent* *Sound Breeze*, April 30, 1897. For the origins of the Holiness movement see William Kostlevy, *Holy Jumpers: Evangelicals and Radicals in Progressive Era America* (New York, 2010), 17–36.

189 *Since the days* "'Holy Ghosters': Doings of Religion Crazed Fanatics in Connecticut," *Sacramento Daily Union*, December 16, 1897.

194 *recently nearly knocked* *Freethinker*, November 28, 1897, 17:759. See also *Plainville News*, October 28, 1897; *Meriden Morning Record*, October 30, 1897.

194 *left town* "Lyme's 'Holiness Band': 'Professor' Anderson Will Go to Jerusalem," *Meriden Morning Record*, April 27, 1898.

194 *There was an exciting* "The Lyme Holiness Band: Wilbur F. Anderson, the Former Leader, Reappears with New Doctrine," *New York Times*, November 20, 1898.

195 *Lyme is particularly* *The New-York Daily Tribune*, August, n.d., 1902, Clipping File Ludington Family Collection, LHSA.

195 *its portrait* *New York Times*, September 2, 1906.

196 *was looking* Margaret Axson Elliott to Jessie Wilson Sayre, July 5, 1906, photocopy, LHSA.

196 *sunny old-time Sabbath* *Ladies' Home Journal*, November 16, 1906. See also Earl M. Page, "Arthur Ignatius Keller," in *Art of Illustration: Selected Works by Arthur Ignatius Keller*, Meadowbrook Art Gallery, Oakland University (Rochester, MI, 1994).

196 *recent photograph* John Baynes's interest in Old Lyme followed the marriage of his sister Lillian Baynes (1871–1916) to Hartford artist Walter Griffin (1861–1935), an Old Lyme art colony member. Other photographs by John Baynes of the town's scenic locations appear in Katharine Abbott, *Old Paths and Legends of New England* (New York, 1908).

196 *mail-order copy* "For ten cents we will send a copy to any address, carefully packed in a strong tube, and with all the postage paid, as long as the limited supply lasts," *Ladies' Home Journal*, November 1906. Louisa Griswold's jigsaw puzzle was later given to the Florence Griswold Museum.

196 *for the quickening* FCR, 209 (n.d.).

196 *pressed home* FCR, 211 (August 5, 1906).

196 *harmonious relations* Katharine Ludington, undated manuscript, Congregational Church Papers, LHSA.

196 *most interesting sermon* *Honolulu Star-Bulletin*, November 24, 1917, 37.

Flames at Midnight

199 *Perhaps we loved* Katharine Ludington to Helen Gilman Brown, July 14, 1907, Brown-Gilman Papers, New York Public Library.

199 *Soon after twelve* Rev. Edward M. Chapman, *Diary*, photocopy, LHSA.

199 *December 1906* FCR, 218 (December 3, 1906).

200 *It was but* *Deep River New Era*, July 5, 1907.

200 *Church could not* Katharine Ludington to Arthur Ludington, July 4, 1907, Ludington Family Collection, LHSA.

200 *the old spire* Ludington, *Old Lyme*, 133.

200 *burned suspiciously* *Deep River New Era*, June 21, 1907; *New London Day*, July 3, 1907.

200 *If such a thing* *Deep River New Era*, July 19, 1907.

201 *Who is the devil* Childe Hassam to Florence Griswold, July 30, 1907, Florence Griswold Papers, box 1, LHSA.

201 *It was not* *Deep River New Era*, July 12, 1907. See also George Dudley Seymour, "Some Account of Col. Samuel Belcher," in *Researches of an Antiquary: Five Essays on Early American Architects* (New Haven, CT, 1928), 26: "As long as it stood, the fabric was the pride of Lyme, and its praise was in the mouths of the citizens and the art-colony thereof."

202 *voiced the sorrow* Katharine Ludington to Arthur Ludington, July 10, 1907, Ludington Family Collection, LHSA.

202 *whole town* Katharine Ludington to Helen Gilman Brown, July 14, 1907, Brown-Gilman Collection, New York Public Library.

202 *The matter* *Deep River New Era*, July 19, 1907.

202 *told him* *New London Day*, January 31, 1907.

202 *High Heaven* *Deep River New Era*, September 10, 1909.

Restoring the Country Church

205 *There was a time* Woodrow Wilson, "The Country Church: Address at Dedication of First Congregational Church, Lyme, Connecticut," June 19, 2010, photocopy, FCCOL.

206 *church was filled* *Deep River New Era*, June 20, 1910.

206 *time was long* E. M. Chapman, *The Stone of Help*, November 8, 1908, 4, FCCOL.

206 *must be as nearly* *New Haven Register* (n.d.), cited in *Deep River New Era*, July 12, 1907.

208 *Unless sentiment* "Letters from the People," *Deep River New Era*, July 4, 1907. For Ernest Chadwick's earlier account of the architectural history of the meetinghouse see "The Evolution of Aestheticism: Idea of Structural Beauty as Embodied at the Church at Lyme," *Connecticut Magazine*, 1902, 8:201–4.

208 *up-to-date* Building Committee minutes, FCCOL.

208 *No doubt* Evelyn McCurdy Salisbury to Walter C. Noyes, July 12, 1907, FCCOL.

208 *fireproof brick building* Katharine Ludington to William Adams Brown, July 15, 1907, Brown-Gilman Papers, New York Public Library.

208 *There is talk* "Letters to the People," *Deep River New Era*, July 26, 1907.

208 *animated discussion* Building committee minutes, FCCOL.

210 *this winter* Chapman, *Stone of Help*, 11, FCCOL.

210 *unusually large* *Deep River New Era*, September 10, 1909.

210 *keen struggle* *Deep River New Era*, June 24, 1910.

210 *unique in the annals* Ernest Greene, "First Congregational Church at Old Lyme," clipping (n.d.), FCCOL.

210 *original pillars* *Deep River New Era*, June 24, 1910.

210 *backward look* Chapman, *Stone of Help*, 4.

210 *The burning* Ludington, *Lyme*, 134.

Illustration Credits

2 *Exact Map of New England and New York*. New York Public Library Digital Collections.

3 Map of Saybrook and Lyme. Stiles Papers, Beinecke Rare Book and Manuscript Library, Yale University.

4 *View of the Great Meadows*. Privately printed from Moses S. Beach and Rev. William Ely, *The Ely Ancestry* (New York, 1902), facing p. 33. Noyes-Ely box 6, #9. Noyes-Ely Family Collection. Lyme Historical Society Archives at the Florence Griswold Museum.

5 *The Old Noyes House at Newbury, Mass*. Photograph. Charles Phelps Noyes and Emily H. (Gilman) Noyes, Noyes-Gilman Ancestry (St. Paul, MN, 1907), facing p. 12. Florence Griswold Museum Library.

6 Page 000: Henry Ward Ranger (1858–1916), *Meetinghouse Hill*. Oil on canvas. Old Lyme–Phoebe Griffin Lord Library.

10 Edward F. Rook (1870–1960), *Bradbury's Mill Dam*, ca. 1905. Oil on canvas. Florence Griswold Museum, gift of the Hartford Steam Boiler Inspection and Insurance Company.

11 *Meetinghouse Hill Cemetery*. Photograph. Amber Pero, 2018.

13 *Meetinghouse Hill Mile Marker*. Photographs: Lyme Street: Black Hall to Sill Lane, #160. Lyme Historical Society Archives at the Florence Griswold Museum.

15 *he Road to Eden*. Photograph. Noyes-Ely Family Collection, box 7, #1. Lyme Historical Society Archives at the Florence Griswold Museum.

16 *Sunday Afternoon Tradition*. Photograph. Ludington Album. Lyme Historical Society Archives at the Florence Griswold Museum.

18 Ellen Noyes Chadwick (1824–1900), *House of Rev. Moses Noyes*. Pencil on paper. Noyes Papers, #3. Lyme Historical Society Archives at the Florence Griswold Museum.

19 Ruth Noyes gravestone. Photograph, Ely-Plimpton Papers, box 6, #5. Lyme Historical Society Archives at the Florence Griswold Museum.

21 *Governor Gurdon Saltonstall*. Oil on canvas. Yale University Art Gallery, gift of Roswell Saltonstall.

22 *Wonders of the Invisible World: Being an Account of the Trials of Several Witches, Lately Executed in New-England*. Library of Congress, Geography and Map Division.

23 *A Modest Enquiry into the Nature of Witchcraft*, 1697, by John Hale. Courtesy of Historic Beverly.

25 Collegiate School Charter. General Collection, Beinecke Rare Book and Manuscript Library, Yale University.

26 John Hart diploma. General Collection, Beinecke Rare Book and Manuscript Library, Yale University.

30 *Cottonus Matheris* (Cotton Mather). Engraved, painted, and published in Boston by Peter Pelham, 1728. Mezzotint. Metropolitan Museum of Art, New York, bequest of Charles Allen Munn, 1924.

31 William Chadwick (1879–1962), *Bathers at Griswold Beach*, ca. 1915. Oil on board. Florence Griswold Museum, gift of the artist.

33 Cottonus Matheris (Cotton Mather), Diary, 1681–1724. Courtesy of the American Antiquarian Society.

36 John Smibert (1688–1751), *Judge Samuel Sewall*, 1729. Oil on canvas. Photograph ca. 2019, Museum of Fine Arts, Boston.

38 *Grave of Samuel Pierpont*. Postcard. First Congregational Church of Old Saybrook Archives.

39 Thomas W. Nason (1889–1971), *Congregational Church, Hamburg, Connecticut*, n.d. Wood engraving on paper. Florence Griswold Museum, gift of Janet Eltinge.

42 Lyme Land Records 4:170 (January 21, 1725/6).

43 Lyme Land Records 4:79 (May 9, 1729).

44 Map of the "Yland of Barbados." British Library Board.

47 Moses Noyes gravestone. Photograph. Ely-Plimpton Papers, box 6, #5. Lyme Historical Society Archives at the Florence Griswold Museum.

48 *A Discourse Concerning the Death of the Righteous*. General Collection, Beinecke Rare Book and Manuscript Library, Yale University.

49 *Diary of Joshua Hempstead of New London, Connecticut, Covering a Period of Forty-Seven Years, from September, 1711, to November, 1758.* New London County Historical Society, New London, CT.

52 *Daniel R. Noyes House*. Photograph. Phoebe Griffin Noyes Album. Ludington Family Collection. Lyme Historical Society Archives at the Florence Griswold Museum.

53 "God governs by His providence," 1736. Attributed to Rev. Jonathan Parsons. Manuscripts, box 2, #45. Lyme Historical Society Archives at the Florence Griswold Museum.

54 William Coult, floor plan of 1739 meetinghouse, 1876. FCCOL.

58 *Martha J. Lamb*. Photographs: Miscellaneous Portraits. Lyme Historical Society Archives at the Florence Griswold Museum.

58 *Jonathan Parsons*. Photograph of artwork (after John Singleton Copley), artist unknown. Ludington Album. Lyme Historical Society Archives at the Florence Griswold Museum.

59 *A Funeral Sermon Occasioned by the Death of Mrs. Phebe Parsons*. Monographs P–Z, #Se. Lyme Historical Society Archives at the Florence Griswold Museum.

62 Ezra Stiles, Map of Connecticut—southern shoreline. Beinecke Rare Book and Manuscript Library, Yale University.

63 Plan of Eliza and Phoebe Moheage's Wigwam. Beinecke Rare Book and Manuscript Library, Yale University.

64 *Mercy Ann Nonsuch Matthews*. Photograph. East Lyme Historical Society Archives.

65 Charles de Wolfe Brownell (1822–1909), *Joshua's Seat, August 22, 1858*. Watercolor on paper. Florence Griswold Museum, purchase.

68 *Whitefield, the celebrated Preacher*. Engraving. Whitefield album. First Congregational Church Collection. On deposit, Lyme Historical Society Archives at the Florence Griswold Museum.

69 *The Christian History, Containing Accounts of the Revival and Propagation of Religion in Great-Britain, America &c. For the Year 1744*. Beinecke Rare Book and Manuscript Library, Yale University.

70 Jonathan Parsons, *Wisdom justified of her Children*, First Congregational Church of Old Lyme Archives, gift of Everett Fisher.

71 *Front of the Old Johnson House, between the Rivers District*. Photographs 8001–8013. Miscellaneous Photos: Houses. Lyme Historical Society Archives at the Florence Griswold Museum.

71 *Old Mather House*, detail. Photograph. Noyes-Ely Family Collection, box 7, #1. Lyme Historical Society Archives at the Florence Griswold Museum.

71 Small gold case displaying George Whitefield's thumb. Photograph. Used with permission from the Methodist Collection of Drew University, Madison, NJ.

73 *Charles Ludington, Whitefield Rock*. Photograph. Ludington Album. Lyme Historical Society Archives at the Florence Griswold Museum.

76 J. Parsons note. Woodward Papers, Solomon Williams Papers #10. Lyme Historical Society Archives at the Florence Griswold Museum.

80 *Scene on Lieutenant River, Lyme, Conn*. Postcard. Noyes-Ely Family Collection, box 7, #1. Lyme Historical Society Archives at the Florence Griswold Museum.

82 Corner chair, formerly owned by Rev. Stephen Johnson. Photograph, First Congregational Church of Old Lyme Archives.

86 Map of Lyme parishes. Stiles Papers. Beinecke Rare Book and Manuscript Library, Yale University.

87 Line engraving by Paul Revere, adapted from an English print. 14.9 cm x 19.7 cm. Boston, P. Revere, 1765. Collection of the Massachusetts Historical Society.

88 Samuel King (1749–1819), *Ezra Stiles*. Oil on canvas. Yale University Art Gallery, bequest of Dr. Charles Jenkins Foote.

92 *A Plan of the Town and Harbour of Boston*. Library of Congress, Geography and Map Division.

93 "A Discourse for a Fast," Sermon No. 373. Matthew Noyes Papers, box 2, #44. Lyme Historical Society Archives at the Florence Griswold Museum.

94 *John McCurdy House*. Photographs: Lyme St. to Library Lane, #103. Lyme Historical Society Archives at the Florence Griswold Museum.

95 Powder horn scribed by Samuel Selden, ivory, 1776. Selden, Samuel, 1723–1776. 37 cm x 13.3 cm. Collection of the Massachusetts Historical Society.

97 Stephen Johnson, *The Everlasting Punishment of the Ungodly*, 1786. FCCOL.

99 Ralph Earl, *Mrs. Henry Channing and Her Son*, 1793. Oil on canvas. © 1991 Christie's Images Limited.

100 *God admonishing his People of their Duty, as Parents and Masters*. Fenimore Art Museum Library, Cooperstown, NY. Coll: McDade #720; Evans 19547.

101 Ellen Noyes Chadwick (1824–1900), *View of Ferry Point.* Oil on canvas. Florence Griswold Museum, gift of Mr. and Mrs. Robert Krieble.

102 James Martin, *Portrait of Judge William Noyes*, ca. 1798. Pastel on paper over wood panel. Florence Griswold Museum purchase with contributions from Geoffrey Paul, David Dangremond, John and Werneth Noyes, and Gay Myers.

106 *A Correct Map of Connecticut from actual Survey*. Engraved by A. Doolittle. New Haven, 1797. Published for Dr. Trumbull's History of Connecticut. Library of Congress, Geography and Map Division.

107 *Samuel Mather, Jr., House, ca. 1883*. Photographs: Lyme St., Cong. Church, Salisbury House, #101A. Lyme Historical Society Archives at the Florence Griswold Museum

108 *Old Waite House, Rowland's Store, Gen. Perkins House, Lyme St., 1880*. Noyes-Ely Family Collection, box 7, #1. Lyme Historical Society Archives at the Florence Griswold Museum.

109 John Frazee (1790–1852), *Bust of George Griswold III*, ca. 1842. Marble. Florence Griswold Museum, gift of the Honorable Mr. John Davis Lodge.

109 Town of Old Lyme [detail showing breastwork of 1812]. F. W. Beers, 1868. Lyme Historical Society Archives at the Florence Griswold Museum.

112 *Western View of the Central Part of Ellington*. J. W. Barber, preliminary drawing for Connecticut Historical Collections, 1836. Connecticut Historical Society.

113 Order of the ceremony to be used at the laying of the cornerstone of the Meeting House of the first Society of Lyme. Old Lyme Church Papers, box 1, #3. Lyme Historical Society Archives at the Florence Griswold Museum.

114 Communion service of silver. Photograph, Lyman Allyn Museum, New London, First Congregational Church of Old Lyme Archives.

115 *Capt. Robert H. Griswold House*. Photographs: Lyme St. to FG house, 106–108, #108. Lyme Historical Society Archives at the Florence Griswold Museum.

116 Volute, Florence Griswold House porch. Photograph, Amy Kurtz Lansing, 2017.

120 Phoebe Griffin Noyes (1797–1875), *Portrait of Phoebe Griffin Lord*, ca. 1820. Watercolor and gouache on paper. Florence Griswold Museum, Gift of Jane & Townsend Ludington.

121 *Old Lord House*. Photographs: Lyme St. to Library, #106. Lyme Historical Society Archives at the Florence Griswold Museum.

122 James Martin, *Portrait of Abigail Noyes*, ca. 1798. Pastel on paper over wood panel. Florence Griswold Museum purchase with contributions from Geoffrey Paul, David Dangremond, John and Werneth Noyes, and Gay Myers.

123 Eunice Noyes (1791–1870), Mourning scene, 1810. Silk embroidery. Paul Foundation, Essex, CT (Photograph: Jody Dole).

126 *West View of Lyme, Conn*. J. W. Barber, preliminary drawing for Connecticut Historical Collections, 1836. Connecticut Historical Society.

127 Samuel Waldo and William Jewett (American, 1783–1874), *Edward Dorr Griffin* (1770–1837), third president of Williams College 1821–36, professor 1808–22, c. 1821. Oil on panel. $32\frac{11}{16}$ x 25½ in. (83 x 64.7 cm). Williams College Museum of Art, Williamstown, MA, museum purchase, with funds provided by an anonymous donor (86.25.1).

128 *Harriet Lord*. Photograph. Phoebe Griffin Noyes Album. Ludington Family Collection. Lyme Historical Society Archives at the Florence Griswold Museum.

132 *he Drunkard's Progress, or the Direct Road to Poverty, Wretchedness & Ruin*, designed and published by J. W. Barber, New Haven, CT. Library of Congress, Popular Graphic Arts, LC-USZC4-3263.

133 *Dr. Richard Noyes*. Photograph. Phoebe Griffin Noyes Album. Ludington Family Collection. Lyme Historical Society Archives at the Florence Griswold Museum.

134 James Martin, *Portrait of Mary Ann Noyes*, ca. 1798. Pastel on paper over wood panel. Paul Foundation, Essex, CT (Photograph: Jody Dole).

138 *Congregational Meetinghouse*. Photographs: Lyme St, Cong. Church, Salisbury House, #102. Lyme Historical Society Archives at the Florence Griswold Museum.

139 *Abolitionist Church, Third Congregation Church, Christian Science Church, 49 Park Street*. Photograph by Henry S. Davis, from Photography by Henry S. Davis, selected and reprinted from the albums of Shelton W. Dudley Sr., 2001. Edith B. Nettleton Historical Room, Guilford Free Library.

140 *Rev. William B. Cary's Parsonage Study*. Photograph, First Congregational Church of Old Lyme.

143 *Rev. Davis S. Brainerd House*. Photographs: Kendall Banning Collection. Lyme Historical Society Archives at the Florence Griswold Museum.

145 *Grassy Hill Church, Lyme, Connecticut*. Photograph, ©Steve Rosenthal, 2012.

146 *Academy and Baptist Church*. Photographs: Lyme St Boxwood to Library, #105. Lyme Historical Society Archives at the Florence Griswold Museum.

146 *Methodist Church, July 1988*. Methodist Church Old Lyme, Organizations, box 1, #20. Lyme Historical Society Archives at the Florence Griswold Museum.

150 *Congregational Church*. Photographs: Lyme St, Cong. Church, Salisbury House, #102. Lyme Historical Society Archives at the Florence Griswold Museum.

151 *Conference House*. Photograph, First Congregational Church of Old Lyme.

152 *Richard S. Griswold House, Later Called Boxwood*. Stereograph card. Photographs: Lyme St., Boxwood to Library Lane, #104. Lyme Historical Society Archives at the Florence Griswold Museum.

152 Unidentified maker, N.L.G.G. tea box used on the ship *Cohota*, ca. 1844. Wood, paper. Florence Griswold Museum, gift of Mr. and Mrs. David J. Powell.

153 Fitzhugh porcelain, Florence Griswold Museum dining room. Florence Griswold Museum, gift of Mr. and Mrs. Griswold Terry Atkins. Photograph, Tammi Flynn, 2015.

154 Congregational Church interior, ca. 1880. Photograph, First Congregational Church of Old Lyme.

155 *Phoebe Griffin Noyes*, ca. 1865. Photograph. Noyes-Ely Family Collection, box 6, #10. Lyme Historical Society Archives at the Florence Griswold Museum.

158 *Rev. Davis S. Brainerd*. Photograph, First Congregational Church of Old Lyme.

158 *Capt. John Griswold*. Photograph. Phoebe Griffin Noyes Album. Ludington Family Archive. Lyme Historical Society Archives at the Florence Griswold Museum.

159 *Capt. Enoch Noyes*. Photograph. Noyes-Ely Family Collection, box 7, #5. Lyme Historical Society Archives at the Florence Griswold Museum.

160 *The Copperhead Party—in Favor of a Vigorous Prosecution of Peace!* Library of Congress, Prints and Photographs Division, LC-USZ62-132749.

161 *Assault of the Second Louisiana (Colored Regiment on the Rebel Works at Port Hudson), June 27, 1863.* Library of Congress, Prints and Photographs Division, LC-USZ62-133081.

162 George Bump hymnal. Manuscripts. Lyme Historical Society Archives at the Florence Griswold Museum.

166 *Rev. William B. Cary.* Photograph, First Congregational Church of Old Lyme.

167 *Ellen Noyes Chadwick.* Photograph. Noyes-Ely Family Collection, box 7, #5. Lyme Historical Society Archives at the Florence Griswold Museum.

168 *Pierpont House Hotel.* Photographs: Black Hall to Sill Lane, #50. Lyme Historical Society Archives at the Florence Griswold Museum.

169 Fidelia Bridges (1834–1923), *Wild Roses among Rye*, 1874. Watercolor and gouache over pencil. Florence Griswold Museum, Gift of the Hartford Steam Boiler Inspection and Insurance Company.

170 *View of Lyme.* Martha Lamb, "Lyme: A Chapter of American Genealogy," *Harper's Magazine*, February 1876. Monographs G–Lu, #L. Lyme Historical Society Archives at the Florence Griswold Museum.

171 *Congregational Church.* Martha Lamb, "Lyme: A Chapter of American Genealogy," *Harper's Magazine*, February 1876. Monographs G–Lu, #L. Lyme Historical Society Archives at the Florence Griswold Museum.

172 Florence Griswold (1850–1937), *Harp*. Autograph Album, 1876. Ink on paper. Florence Griswold Museum Purchase with funds provided by Mr. and Mrs. David W. Dangremond.

173 *Scenes of Old Lyme.* Autograph Album, 1876. Ink on paper. Florence Griswold Museum purchase with funds provided by Mr. and Mrs. David W. Dangremond.

176 Abraham L. Laiblin (1872–1916), *Martha G. Pond*, ca. 1904. Oil on canvas. Private collection.

176 "A Simple Story Now Told in Rhyme concerning a Darkened Window in Lyme," 1895. Old Lyme Church Papers, box 1, #10. Lyme Historical Society Archives at the Florence Griswold Museum.

177 *Rev. Benjamin Wisner Bacon.* Photograph, First Congregational Church of Old Lyme.

178 *Meetinghouse Interior*, ca. 1887. Photograph, First Congregational Church of Old Lyme.

180 *Old Lyme Concert Band*, ca. 1886. Photograph, First Congregational Church of Old Lyme.

184 Centennial address invitation, 1893, First Congregational Church of Old Lyme.

185 "Boxwood" class—Feb. 27, 1902. Photograph. Lyme St. Boxwood to Library, #104.1–104.12. Lyme Historical Society Archives at the Florence Griswold Museum.

186 *Evelyn McCurdy Salisbury.* Photograph. Noyes-Ely Family Collection, box 8, #9. Lyme Historical Society Archives at the Florence Griswold Museum.

187 *Phoebe Griffin Noyes Library.* Photograph. Noyes-Ely Family Collection, box 6, #10. Lyme Historical Society Archives at the Florence Griswold Museum.

190 Childe Hassam (American, 1859–1935), *Church at Old Lyme, Connecticut*, 1905. Oil on canvas, support: 36¼ x 32¼ inches (92.07 x 81.91 cm); framed: 47 x 43 x 3½ inches (119.38 x 109.22 x 8.89 cm). Collection Albright-Knox Art Gallery, Buffalo, NY; Albert H. Tracy Fund, 1909 (1909.6). Image courtesy of the Albright-Knox Art Gallery.

191 *Old Lyme Meetinghouse*, ca. 1905. Photograph, First Congregational Church of Old Lyme.

192 *Old Lyme Congregational Church*. Photograph. Ludington Album. Lyme Historical Society Archi ves at the Florence Griswold Museum.

193 Arthur I. Keller (1866–1925), *Ladies' Home Journal* cover, November 1906. Oversized box 10. Lyme Historical Society Archives at the Florence Griswold Museum.

194 *Sunday School Teachers and Students*, ca. 1905. Photograph, First Congregational Church of Old Lyme.

195 *Communion Table, Autumn*, ca. 1888. Photographs: Lyme St. Cong. Church to Salisbury House, #102. Lyme Historical Society Archives at the Florence Griswold Museum.

197 *Katharine Ludington*. Photograph. Ludington Family Collection. Lyme Historical Society Archives at the Florence Griswold Museum.

200 *Rev. Edward M. Chapman*. Photograph, First Congregational Church of Old Lyme.

201 *Congregational Church with Charles Ludington House*, ca. 1905. Photograph. Ludington Album. Lyme Historical Society Archives at the Florence Griswold Museum.

202 Public meeting announcement, 1907, First Congregational Church of Old Lyme.

205 Samuel J. Woolf (1880–1949), *Woodrow Wilson*, ca. 1920. Lithograph. Florence Griswold Museum, gift of Mrs. and Mrs. Stuart P. Feld.

206 *Laying the Cornerstone,* 1908. Photographs: Lyme St., Cong. Church, Salisbury House, #102A. Lyme Historical Society Archives at the Florence Griswold Museum.

207 *Old Lyme Meetinghouse with Staging*, 1909. Ludington Family Collection. Lyme Historical Society Archives at the Florence Griswold Museum.

209 *Church at Old Lyme*. Photograph, ©Steve Rosenthal, 2011.

Index

Page numbers in *italics* indicate illustrations; page numbers with "n" indicate notes.

Garnet Books

Titles with asterisks (*) are also in the Driftless Connecticut Series

Garnet Poems: An Anthology of Connecticut Poetry Since 1776*
Dennis Barone, editor

The Connecticut Prison Association and the Search for Reformative Justice*
Gordon Bates

Food for the Dead: On the Trail of New England's Vampires
Michael E. Bell

The Long Journeys Home: The Repatriations of Henry 'Ōpūkaha'ia and Albert Afraid of Hawk*
Nick Bellantoni

Sol LeWitt: A Life of Ideas*
Lary Bloom

The Case of the Piglet's Paternity: Trials from the New Haven Colony, 1639–1663*
Jon C. Blue

Early Connecticut Silver, 1700–1840
Peter Bohan and Philip Hammerslough

The Connecticut River: A Photographic Journey through the Heart of New England
Al Braden

Tempest-Tossed: The Spirit of Isabella Beecher Hooker
Susan Campbell

Connecticut's Fife & Drum Tradition*
James Clark

Sunken Garden Poetry, 1992–2011
Brad Davis, editor

Rare Light: J. Alden Weir in Windham, Connecticut, 1882–1919*
Anne E. Dawson, editor

The Old Leather Man: Historical Accounts of a Connecticut and New York Legend
Dan W. DeLuca, editor

Post Roads & Iron Horses: Transportation in Connecticut from Colonial Times to the Age of Steam*
Richard DeLuca

The Log Books: Connecticut's Slave Trade and Human Memory*
Anne Farrow

Birding in Connecticut*
Frank Gallo

Dr. Mel's Connecticut Climate Book
Dr. Mel Goldstein

Forever Seeing New Beauties: The Forgotten Impressionist Mary Rogers Williams*
Eve M. Kahn

Hidden in Plain Sight: A Deep Traveler Explores Connecticut
David K. Leff

Maple Sugaring: Keeping It Real in New England
David K. Leff

Becoming Tom Thumb: Charles Stratton, P. T. Barnum, and the Dawn of American Celebrity*
Eric D. Lehman

Homegrown Terror: Benedict Arnold and the Burning of New London*
Eric D. Lehman

The Traprock Landscapes of New England*
Peter M. LeTourneau and Robert Pagini

Westover School: Giving Girls a Place of Their Own
Laurie Lisle

Heroes for All Time: Connecticut's Civil War Soldiers Tell Their Stories*
Dione Longley and Buck Zaidel

The Listeners: U-boat Hunters During the Great War
Roy R. Manstan

Along the Valley Line: A History of the Connecticut Valley Railroad*
Max R. Miller

Crowbar Governor: The Life and Times of Morgan Gardner Bulkeley*
Kevin Murphy

Fly Fishing in Connecticut: A Guide for Beginners
Kevin Murphy

Water for Hartford: The Story of the Hartford Water Works and the Metropolitan District Commission
Kevin Murphy

African American Connecticut Explored
Elizabeth J. Normen, editor

Henry Austin: In Every Variety of Architectural Style
James F. O'Gorman

Breakfast at O'Rourke's: New Cuisine from a Classic American Diner
Brian O'Rourke

Ella Grasso: Connecticut's Pioneering Governor*
Jon E. Purmont

The British Raid on Essex: The Forgotten Battle of the War of 1812*
Jerry Roberts

Making Freedom: The Extraordinary Life of Venture Smith
Chandler B. Saint and George Krimsky

Under the Dark Sky: Life in the Thames River Basin
Steven G. Smith

Welcome to Wesleyan: Campus Buildings
Leslie Starr

Barns of Connecticut
Markham Starr

Gervase Wheeler: A British Architect in America, 1847–1860*
Renée Tribert and James F. O'Gorman

Forgotten Voices: The Hidden History of a Connecticut Meetinghouse
Carolyn Wakeman

Connecticut in the American Civil War: Slavery, Sacrifice, and Survival*
Matthew Warshauer

Inside Connecticut and the Civil War: One State's Struggles
Matthew Warshauer, editor

Connecticut Architecture: Stories of 100 Places
Christopher Wigren, Connecticut Trust for Historic Preservation

Prudence Crandall's Legacy: The Fight for Equality in the 1830s, Dred Scott, and Brown v. Board of Education*
Donald E. Williams Jr.

Riverview Hospital for Children and Youth: A Culture of Promise*
Richard Wiseman

Stories in Stone: How Geology Influenced Connecticut History and Culture
Jelle Zeilinga de Boer

New Haven's Sentinels: The Art and Science of East Rock and West Rock*
Jelle Zeilinga de Boer and John Wareham

About the Author

Carolyn Wakeman is a former professor at the University of California at Berkeley, where she served as faculty chair of the Graduate School of Journalism. Her works on Asia and Connecticut history have appeared in numerous journals and publications, including the *Journal of Asian Studies* and *Shakespeare Quarterly.*